THE MASTER LIBRARY

DOTH NOT WISDOM CRY
AND UNDERSTANDING PUT FORTH HER VOICE
BY ME PRINCES RULE AND NOBLES
EVEN ALL THE JUDGES OF THE EARTH

The Appellate Court Building, New York

IV-Title

THE WISDOM OF THE LAW
From a painting by Henry O. Walker

THE
MASTER LIBRARY

THE
LIVING WISDOM

VOLUME FOUR

THE FOUNDATION PRESS, INC.
CLEVELAND, OHIO.   SPRINGFIELD, MASS.   KANSAS CITY, MO.

TO

THE ONCOMING GENERATION

AND TO ALL WHO WOULD HAVE A NEW

VISION OF THE BEAUTY AND

THE POWER OF THE

MESSAGE OF

LIFE

EDITORIAL BOARD

General Editor

WALTER SCOTT ATHEARN, A.M., LL.D.

Dean, Boston University School of Religious Education and Social Service
Chairman of the Committee on Education of the International Sunday School
Council of Religious Education
Author of "The Church School," "Religious Education and American Democracy,"
"A National System of Religious Education," etc., etc.

Art Editor

HENRY TURNER BAILEY

Director of the Cleveland School of Art, and of the John Huntington Polytechnic
Institute, Cleveland
Author of "The Blackboard in Sunday School," "The Flush of The Dawn,"
"Photography and Fine Art," "Twelve Great Paintings," "Symbolism
for Artists," etc., etc.

Associate Editors

CHARLES REYNOLDS BROWN, A.M., S.T.B., D.D., LL.D., Dean, The
Divinity School, Yale University, New Haven, Connecticut.

FREDERICK CARL EISELEN, A.M., B.D., Ph.D., D.D., Dean, Garrett
Biblical Institute and Professor of Old Testament History
and Literature, Evanston, Illinois.

JOHN RICHARD SAMPEY, D.D., LL.D., Professor of Old Testament History and Literature, Southern Baptist Theological Seminary,
Louisville, Kentucky.

WILBUR FISK TILLETT, A.M., D.D., LL.D., S.T.D., Dean, Vanderbilt
University, Nashville, Tennessee.

IRA MAURICE PRICE, A.M., B.D., Ph.D., LL.D., Professor of Semitic
Languages and Literature, University of Chicago, Chicago,
Illinois.

ALBERT EDWARD BAILEY, A.M., Professor of Religious Art and Archæol-
ogy, Boston University, Boston, Massachusetts.

JAMES ISAAC VANCE, A.M., D.D., LL.D., Pastor, First Presbyterian
Church, Nashville, Tennessee.

GEORGE LIVINGSTONE ROBINSON, A.M., Ph.D., D.D., LL.D., Professor
of Old Testament History and Literature, McCormick Theological Seminary, Chicago, Illinois.

ELSON IRVING REXFORD, M.A., D.D., LL.D., D.C.L., Principal, Diocesan
Theological College, Montreal, Canada.

ix

PREFACE

NO nation ever loved its land more deeply than did Israel. That love has been undying. Even today aged Jews gather each week beside the foundations of the walls of the Temple, bewail its ruin and pray for its rebuilding. The powerful movement called Zionism is working all the time to make it possible for the Jews of the world to regain their national home. There were many patriotic poets in the olden days who sang their love of country. They pictured its beauty and sacredness; they lamented its sorrows and foresaw doom to its enemies; they looked forward to its future glory and to its world-wide influence. The conditions they beheld in their land have been repeated in other lands; the tendencies they noted and deplored exist today in our own country; and the lessons they learned as to what constitutes a nation's real glory and prosperity are lessons that we need to learn.

Some of these patriotic poets were also prophets. The prophets were not so much men who foretold the future as men divinely guided who interpreted their own age. They had great and wise social ideals. We do well to study those ideals, and to realize how each one of them was first a man for his own time, and then a man who in his own time had a message for all time.

Another type of man lived in old Judea, known as "the wise man," or the sage. These were sometimes the town officials; oftener perhaps the elders of the city. They gathered in the market place and by the city gate, and exchanged wisdom; and there people collected to listen to them. They had no formal philosophy, and they probably were seldom writers. But they were close observers and shrewd thinkers, and they had developed that art, which is so dear to the Oriental, of condensing their thoughts into pithy sayings, memorable because of their brevity and their acute contrasts and similitudes. The prophets saw life in its large relations and its far-reaching significance; the sages had practical advice for the present.

What both prophets and sages have to teach us is so sound and so inspiring that we may well call this volume THE LIVING WISDOM.

THE VOICES

Heard are the voices,
Heard are the Sages,
The Worlds and the Ages:
"Choose well, your choice is
Brief and yet endless.
Here eyes do regard you
In Eternity's stillness;
Here is all fulness,
Ye brave, to reward you:
Work, and despair not."

—*Goethe*

CONTENTS

THE HOLY LIGHT

Thou sacred flame, so mellow and subdued,
    Burning with tremulous, flickering beam
    In the holy place, before the All-Supreme,
As though the very fire were all imbued

With that almighty prophet's humble soul,
    With Moses' sense of deep humility,
Whose height of feeling knew no humble goal,
    Whose aims bore naught of man's futility;

Thou, holy fire, whose light shall ever guide
The steps of wandering Israel, to the shrine
Of Him who was, who is, and ne'er will cease
To be; whose luminous fire gleams down the tide
Of centuries, both of greatness and of woe,
When Israel's greatness bore a trace divine,
When Israel's fortune sank, far, far below
Even the lot of those poor Nubian slaves,
Who served our fathers in the promised land:
To thee, O ancient light! whose very name
Is a memorial of God's earliest Word,
We look to thee, and hail the conquering hand
Of Wisdom's day, o'er spiritual night,
And breathe with God the prayer: "Let there be
    Light."   —*George Jay Holland*

THE GREAT MESSAGES OF THE PROPHETS

THE PROPHETS

Those Who Spoke to the People on Behalf of God

THE books of the prophets occupy more than one-fourth of the Old Testament. They were, and are, of the greatest importance. Yet most of us know little about them. So much has been discovered during our own generation of the meaning of these messages that a real privilege awaits us in the study of them. They do not always yield their treasures to the careless reader, but examination soon shows how each prophet had an important message for his time; a message, often, that with a little thought may be applied to conditions of our own day.

However interesting a prophet's predictions, his principal task was not to foretell but to "forth-tell," to speak in behalf of God. Today we should probably call such a man a reformer. The Hebrews had two words for "prophesy"; one meant "to see," the other "to pour forth." To them a prophet was a man of vision, and one who poured forth what he had seen.

Wherever the writings of a prophet have to do directly with the reign of a particular king, we have, in Volume Two, included them with the history of his reign. But to do justice to these great reformers and leaders we must do more than that. In the following pages each seer's purpose and message is clearly outlined, and his characteristic prophecies are so arranged as to illustrate that message most clearly.

In the section devoted to "Social Ideals of the Hebrews," other portions are included, showing how all these precepts make a consistent whole.

The prophets are here arranged, so far as known, in the order in which their books were written.

There are differences of opinion as to just what names make up the roll of the prophets. Elijah and Elisha should certainly be included among the prophets, although, so far as we know, they wrote nothing. The stories about Daniel, who was perhaps a sage rather than a prophet, are to be found among the patriotic narratives in Volume Three. The Book of Jonah, being the story rather than the sayings of a prophet, is included in that same section.

AMOS

PROPHET OF DIVINE RIGHTEOUSNESS AND SOCIAL JUSTICE

WHEN Rudyard Kipling wrote his *Recessional*, he looked the greatest empire on earth in the face when she was at the height of her power and pride. Scorning her arrogance and boasting, he called her to penitence and prayer; and he did it through the power of a deep-toned poem. So Amos faced Israel in the zenith of her power and prosperity. He denounced her iniquities, blasted her false hopes, and called her to social justice and rectitude in the name of a God who hated empty ceremonials, but who demanded that "justice roll down like waters, and righteousness as a perennial stream."

A striking figure among the prophets is Amos! A herdsman and dresser of the sycomores in the village of Tekoa, his very occupation gave him leisure for observation and thought, made him alert and fearless, quickened his imagination and widened his outlook. During his visits to the northern cities he was able to observe conditions, and he found them most disheartening. We gather from his writings that wealth and extravagance flaunted itself on every hand. There were stone palaces with ivory panels, extravagantly furnished summer-houses and winter-houses, the use of the chief oils, the choicest meats, the finest music; and all accompanied by shameless revelries and immoralities.

Religiously, all was empty ceremonial and show, though the sanctuaries were well filled and well supported. The people were made to feel that they were being highly favored by God, for did he not choose them among all the peoples of the earth? The Day of Jehovah was near at hand, a day of great light for Israel and darkness for her enemies. Politically, there were competing parties working against each other, while outwardly all seemed serene. In the meanwhile, Assyria lay along the horizon like an ominous and rising cloud. Worse still, violence and oppression prevailed everywhere, and the nobles led in vice and crime. Wealth was secured by violence, by the enslavement of the poor, by dishonesty in trade, by presents and bribes, and by the corruption of the courts.

As he brooded over these conditions, the word of the Lord came to him and compelled him to turn prophet. Where and how he got his education we have no means of knowing, but he is a standing wonder and delight among the prophets.

Again and again he appeared at the sanctuaries, denouncing, condemning, pleading, till one day he was driven from the royal sanctuary of Bethel by Amaziah the priest, to preach no more in Israel. Hereafter he wrote down his messages, thus becoming the first of the literary prophets.

TEKOA, THE HOME OF AMOS

This is a place of visions. The horizons are far away, the monotonous landscape furnishes no object for the attention, except as the temporary tents of the Bedouins may lead one to think of the problems of life. Beyond the horizon to the east and the south is the waiting desert, whence come the prostrating winds of Jehovah's judgment. In the deep chasm to the east is the Plain of Jordan, haunted by the sinister memories of Sodom and Gomorrah. Among the silences of this watchtower the prophet heard the voice of Jehovah announcing doom on recreant Israel.

AMOS

A CRY FOR TRUTH AND RIGHT

The Call of Amos

THEN answered Amos, and said to Amaziah, "I was no prophet,[1] neither was I a prophet's son; but I was a herdsman, and a gatherer of sycomore fruit: and the Lord took me as I followed the flock, and the Lord said to me, 'Go, prophesy to my people Israel.'"

The Prophet's Message

Yet destroyed I the Amorite before them, whose height was like the height of the cedars, and he was strong as the oaks; yet I destroyed his fruit from above, and his roots from beneath.

Also I brought you up from the land of Egypt, and led you forty years through the wilderness, to possess the land of the Amorite. And I raised up of your sons for prophets, and of your young men for Nazirites. Is it not even thus, O ye children of Israel? saith the Lord. But ye gave the Nazirites wine to drink; and commanded the prophets saying, "Prophesy not."

> Therefore the flight shall perish from the swift,
> And the strong shall not strengthen his force,
> Neither shall the mighty deliver himself:
> Neither shall he stand that handleth the bow;
> And he that is swift of foot shall not deliver himself:
> Neither shall he that rideth the horse deliver him-
>   self.
> And he that is courageous among the mighty
> Shall flee away naked in that day, saith the Lord.

AMOS

From a fresco by Sargent

The Prophet a Revealer of Divine Secrets

Can two walk together, except they be agreed? Will a lion roar in the forest, when he hath no prey? will a young lion cry out of his den, if he have taken nothing? Can a bird fall in a snare upon the earth, where no gin is for him? shall one take up a snare from the earth, and have taken nothing at all? Shall a trumpet be blown in the city, and the people not be afraid? shall there be evil in a city, and the Lord hath not done it?

Surely the Lord God will do nothing, but he revealeth his secret to his servants the prophets. The lion hath roared: who will not fear? The Lord God hath spoken: who can but prophesy?

For I know your manifold transgressions and your mighty sins, ye that afflict the just, that take a bribe, and that turn aside the poor in the gate from their right. There-

AMOS

From a fresco by Sargent

Amos holds the emblems of his trade, a long shepherd's crook and the sling made of braided palm fiber with which he disciplines his sheep and scares away their enemies. The face is the face of a determined man who also knows suffering. It was the fate of Amos, though a humble man, to declare the word of Jehovah before princes, to have his message rejected and himself to suffer violence for the truth's sake.

fore the prudent shall keep silence in that time; for it is an evil time.

> The virgin of Israel is fallen;
> She shall no more rise!
> She is forsaken upon her land;
> There is none to raise her up.

For they know not to do right, saith the Lord, who store up violence and robbery in their palaces. Therefore thus saith the Lord God, An adversary there shall be even round about the land; and he shall bring down thy strength from thee, and thy palaces shall be spoiled. Thus saith the Lord, As the shepherd taketh out of the mouth of the lion two legs, or a piece of an ear; so shall the children of Israel be taken out that dwell in Samaria.

Hear ye, and testify in the house of Jacob, saith the Lord God, the God of hosts, That, in the day that I shall visit the transgressions of Israel upon him, I will also visit the altars of Beth-el[2]: and the horns of the altar shall be cut off, and fall to the ground.

And I will smite the winter-house with the summer-house; and the houses of ivory shall perish, and the great houses shall have an end, saith the Lord.

Woe unto you that desire the day of the Lord! to what end is it for you? the day of the Lord is darkness, and not light: as if a man did flee from a lion, and a bear met him; or went into the house, and leaned his hand on the wall, and a serpent bit him.

RIGHTEOUSNESS IS THE ACCEPTABLE OFFERING

Thus saith the Lord to the house of Israel:

> Seek ye me, and ye shall live:
> But seek not Beth-el,
> Nor enter into Gilgal.

Seek the Lord, and ye shall live;
Seek him that maketh the Pleiades and Orion,
And turneth the shadow of death into morning,
And maketh the day dark with night;
That calleth for the waters of the sea,
And poureth them out upon the face of the earth;
The Lord is his name!

I hate, I despise your feasts,
I will take no delight in your solemn assemblies.

©*Keystone View Co.*

THE SYCOMORE FIG

Amos, beside being a shepherd, was a dresser of sycomore trees. In Amos' day these trees were abundant, and their fruit was one of the staple foods of the peasant. Today, however, sycomores are comparatively scarce, though still found in the plains about Jericho and along the seacoast. These sycomores of the Bible are not to be confused with the American sycamore, but are fig-bearing trees which often attain great size.

Though ye offer me your burnt offerings, and meal
    offerings,
I will not accept them;
Neither will I regard the peace offerings of your fat
    beasts.
Take thou away from me the noise of thy songs,
For I will not hear the melody of thy viols.
But let justice run down like waters,
And righteousness as a mighty stream.

Seek good, and not evil, that ye may live: and so the
Lord, the God of hosts, shall be with you, as ye have spoken.

The Glad Day to Come

In that day will I raise up the tabernacle of David that is
fallen, and close up the breaches thereof; I will raise up his
ruins, and I will build it as in the days of old: that they may
possess the remnant of Edom, and of all the heathen, which
are called by my name, saith the Lord that doeth this.

Behold, the days come, saith the Lord, that the plowman
shall overtake the reaper, and the treader of grapes him that
soweth seed; and the mountains shall drop sweet wine, and
all the hills shall melt. And I will bring again the captivity
of my people Israel, and they shall build the waste cities, and
inhabit them; and they shall plant vineyards, and drink the
wine thereof; they shall also make gardens, and eat the fruit
of them.

And I will plant them upon their land, and they shall no
more be pulled up out of their land which I have given them,
saith the Lord thy God.

©*Curtis & Cameron*

HOSEA

From a fresco by John S. Sargent

This figure of the prophet is one of the most attractive in Sargent's celebrated frieze. It is the face of a young man of unusual beauty, a face that expresses intellectual and spiritual riches. The voluminous garment that envelops the form and the deep shadows in the eyes suggest a desire on the prophet's part to conceal the painful experiences through which he was compelled to pass, and which he revealed to his fellow-men only because they were a symbol of God's dealings with faithless Israel. He taught that the only cure for social corruption is love—not a sentiment, but a principle of action.

HOSEA

Greatest Prophet of Redemptive Love

THE men who have given the world her truest messages of consolation, of illumination, of redemption, have been "men of sorrows and acquainted with grief." "O Love that wilt not let me go," sobbed George Matheson, as he turned from a love that did relinquish him, a light that was even then failing him, a pain that was harrowing him, a cross that was slaying him, to a Love that never lets go, a Light that never fails, a Joy that triumphs through all pain, a Cross that lifts to endless life, and so gave us one of earth's sweetest songs. But seven hundred and fifty years before Christ came to earth as the living emblem of God's eternal love, Hosea, the prophet of Israel, by experiences far sadder than Matheson's, learned, not through contrast but through analogy, of a love that would not be denied, that would not let a faithless loved one go.

How cruel was the sorrow of his life! To take to one's heart and home a pure and beautiful maiden, only to find her slowly turn profligate; to plead and woo in vain, when one might justly scorn and reject; to be openly abandoned for the sake of unworthy rivals; to call for her returning, again and again, and receive no answer; to find her reduced at last to the lowest depths of shame, and offered in public sale; then in anguish of heart to buy her at the price of a common slave, take her home again, hold her till she begins at last to trust the love she has so woefully violated, and thus to restore her to the wifehood she need never have sullied; all this constituted the victory of Hosea over the tragedy of violated love.

And this victory became doubly victorious, when it raised him to a point whence he could see the infinitely more patient, longsuffering, redeeming love of Jehovah. So sublimely sad did this vision of the enduring love of God for Israel appear, that it overshadowed and subordinated all that he himself had endured. With beautiful self-effacement, despising his own shame and sorrow in the light of the greater sadness and sorrow of a forsaken God, he carried his pitiful tragedy before the people and compelled them to gaze upon it as but the symbol of their greatest infidelity to the God who had bound Israel unto himself in an eternal wedlock of love.

No wonder, then, that Hosea is the first prophet to demand a single standard of morality. His cry, "How shall I give thee up, Ephraim?" gives us the classic expression of God's forgiving love, "broader than the measure of man's mind." He became the first prophet of repentance, anticipating the Prodigal Son in his appeal to the Prodigal Nation. No wonder Hosea stands as the greatest Old Testament exponent of the redeeming love of God! Gethsemane and Calvary must ever precede our resurrection unto eternal life and love.

13

HOSEA

ISRAEL'S RETURN

ISRAEL

WE will not any more say to the
work of our hands,
"Ye are our gods";
For in thee the fatherless findeth mercy.

JEHOVAH

I will heal their backsliding,
I will love them freely:
For mine anger is turned away from them.
I will be as the dew to Israel;
He shall grow as the lily,
And cast forth his roots as Lebanon;
His branches shall spread,
And his beauty shall be as the olive tree,
And his fragrance like Lebanon.
They that dwell under his shadow shall
     return;
They shall revive as the grain,
And grow like the vine;
And the fragrance thereof shall be as
     the wine of Lebanon.

ISRAEL

What have I to do any more with idols?

JEHOVAH

I have spoken for him, and I will take
care of him.

14

ISRAEL

I am like an evergreen fir—

JEHOVAH

From me is thy fruit found.[3]

AN UNGRATEFUL NATION

When Israel was a child, then I loved him,
And called my son out of Egypt.

I taught Ephraim also to walk,
Taking them by their arms;
But they knew not that I healed them.

How shall I give thee up, Ephraim?
How shall I cast thee off, Israel?
My heart is stirred within me;
My sympathies are kindled together.

Ephraim feedeth on wind,
And followeth after the east wind.
He daily increaseth lies and desolation;
And they make a covenant with Assyria,
And oil is carried into Egypt.

The Lord hath also a controversy with
    Judah,
And will punish Jacob according to his
    ways:
According to his doings will he recom-
    pense him.
He took his brother by the heel,
And by his strength he had power with God:

Yea, he had power over the angel, and
     prevailed:
He wept, and made supplication to him:
He found him at Beth-el,
And there he spoke with us,
Even the Lord God of hosts;
Jehovah is his memorial name.
Therefore turn thou to thy God:
Keep mercy and judgment,
And wait on thy God continually.

He is a trafficker;
The balances of deceit are in his hand:
He loveth to oppress.
Is there iniquity in Gilead?
Surely they are vanity:
They sacrifice bullocks in Gilgal;
Yea, their altars are as heaps in the
     furrows of the field.

And Jacob fled into the field of Aram,
And Israel served for a wife,
And for a wife he kept sheep.
And by a prophet the Lord brought
     Israel out of Egypt,
And by a prophet was he preserved.
Ephraim provoked him to anger most
     bitterly:
Therefore shall his blood be left upon
     him,
And his reproach shall his Lord return
     to him.

When Ephraim spoke, there was trem-
     bling;

He exalted himself in Israel;
But when he offended in Baal, he died.
Yet I am the Lord thy God from the
    land of Egypt,
And thou shalt know no God but me:
For there is no savior beside me.

REDEEMING LOVE

Behold, I will woo her,
And I will speak to her heart.
And I will give her vineyards from thence,
And the valley of Achor for a door of hope:
And she shall sing there as in the days of her youth,
And as in the day when she came up out of the land of
    Egypt.

She shall call me "my husband";
And I will betroth thee to me forever;
Yea, I will betroth thee to me in righteousness,
And in judgment, and in lovingkindness, and in mercies.
I will even betroth thee to me in faithfulness;
And thou shalt know the Lord.

ISAIAH

"The Uncrowned King Among the Prophets"

WHETHER we study him for the completeness and balance of his personal endowments or for the wonder and fulness of his call to prophecy, whether for his patriotism and statesmanship or for the loftiness and range of his prophetic vision, whether for his contribution to the life of his day or for his influence upon the mind of Christ,—from whatever angle, Isaiah holds easily the place of preëminence among the prophets of Israel and Judah.

We know little of his family, but that little is significant. He is the son of Amoz, a citizen of Jerusalem, whom Jewish tradition regards as the brother of King Amaziah. If that tradition be true, Isaiah was first cousin to Hezekiah. But whether he was thus related to the royalty of his day or not, it is very certain that he occupied a position of high respect and standing in Jerusalem and enjoyed a rare freedom of intercourse with kings and courtiers, who turned to him again and again for counsel and direction.

Moreover, he was the peer of all his contemporaries in personality and powers. The other prophets of Israel are notable for some distinguishing personal quality or achievement: Elijah for his flaming zeal, Elisha for his benevolent disposition, Amos for his passion for justice, Hosea for the tenderness of his affection, Jeremiah for his psychological insight; and so on. Isaiah is distinguished not so much by some single quality as by the perfection and harmonious blending of many and various qualities in a high-minded, symmetrical and well-poised personality. "In him," says Ewald, "are combined the profoundest prophetic emotion and purest feeling, the most unwearied, successful, and consistent activity amid all the confusions and changes of life, and, lastly, true poetic ease and beauty of style, combined with force and irresistible power." From the point of view of pure enjoyment, to read the Book of Isaiah is to ramble through a literary landscape of unalloyed loveliness and charm.

When a man as nobly privileged and as richly gifted as this one is called of God to be a prophet, we expect his call to be one of unusual force and richness. And in Isaiah's case we are not disappointed. With wonderful spiritual insight and in language sublimely beautiful, Isaiah has described his call in one of the noblest chapters in our Bible. It happened in the year that the good King Uzziah died, and while Isaiah was in the sanctuary praying over the perilous situation of his beloved country and people. Then it was that he "saw the Lord."

The vision fittingly clothed itself in the symbolism of the Holy of Holies. The mercy seat became a mighty throne, "high and lifted up,"

ISAIAH

From a fresco by John S. Sargent

Prophecy has now turned from the sinful present and from the future over-shadowed by judgment, and for the first time has caught the vision of that more distant "Day of Jehovah" when Zion shall be redeemed and the ransomed of the Lord shall return with everlasting joy upon their heads. This assurance alone is ample reward for Isaiah's lifelong labors for his people.

upon which in unbearable majesty sat the God of Israel, with his train filling the temple. The two little figures of beaten gold that usually over-arched the mercy seat transformed themselves into living seraphim stand-ing above and on either side of the throne of God. Each one had six wings: with twain they covered their feet in token of reverence; with twain they covered their faces as unable to look upon his glory; and the remaining two they held in outstretched readiness, to fly in instantaneous obedience to his every command. And while they stood about the throne, they kept singing to each other in antiphonal strains, and the burden of their song was the sovereign holiness of God, whose glory filled the whole earth. "The posts of the door moved at the voice of him that cried"; and the house was filled with the smoke of the incense of living praise.

In other words, Isaiah, in his hour of darkness and perplexity, sensed as he never had before, through the familiar symbols of the sanctuary, the reality, the holiness, the sovereign sway of Israel's God; and in that vision he found living faith, and life mission, and power. It has ever been so. In time of soul trouble and world trouble men have found their true sal-vation in heightened vision of God and in truer grasp of his eternal meaning for the life of man.

In the white light of that vision Isaiah lived and labored and prophe-sied. Over against the holiness of God he ranged the arrogance, the cor-ruptions, the vices of Israel, and denounced them with blasting force. An unrighteous nation could have no fellowship with a holy God, and, persist-ing in her sins, would go down to inevitable disaster and destruction. Only a faithful remnant would survive to become the nucleus of a new Israel. To the sovereign God of all the earth he pointed as the true salvation of Israel. Faith in him was the supreme necessity. "In quietness and con-fidence" in him would Israel find her strength; not in foreign alliances which were but indications of faithlessness and distrust. The apostasy of Ahaz served but to enhance his own faith in God, and he broke into those glowing Emmanuel prophecies predicting the sure establishment and eter-nal increase of God's government and peace on earth, despite the faithless-ness of Israel and her king, for "the zeal of the Lord" himself would perform it. In the midst of turmoil and warfare he announced the only sure basis of world peace, namely the knowledge of the will of God, understood and made the basis of all national and international life. And no prophet ever exceeded him in the fulness and splendor of his Messianic outlook.

It is no wonder that Jesus drank deeply of the springs of Isaianic thought and vision, as he traveled the road of Messianic fulfilment that led to the eternal wonder of the Cross.

IV-21

ISAIAH

From a fresco by Michelangelo

ISAIAH

THE CALL OF ISAIAH

IN the year that king Uzziah died I saw the Lord sitting upon a throne, high and lifted up, and his train filled the temple. Above it stood the seraphim: each one had six wings; with twain he covered his face, and with twain he covered his feet, and with twain he did fly.[4]

And one cried to another, and said,
"Holy, holy, holy, is the Lord of hosts:
The whole earth is full of his glory."

And the posts of the door moved at the voice of him that cried, and the house was filled with smoke. Then said I,
"Woe is me! for I am undone;
Because I am a man of unclean lips,
And I dwell in the midst of a people of unclean lips:
For mine eyes have seen the King, the Lord of
hosts."

Then flew one of the seraphim to me, having a live coal[5] in his hand, which he had taken with the tongs from off the altar: and he laid it upon my mouth, and said,
"Lo, this hath touched thy lips;
And thine iniquity is taken away, and thy sin
purged."

Also I heard the voice of the Lord, saying, "Whom shall I send, and who will go for us?"

Then I said, "Here am I: send me."

THE SONG PARABLE OF THE VINEYARD

Now will I sing to my well-beloved
A song of my beloved touching his vineyard!

A VINEYARD ON A FRUITFUL HILL

The rich valleys pictured here, though not Oriental, illustrate the beauty and joy of the vineyard of the prophet's vision, "My well-beloved hath a vineyard in a very fruitful hill: and he digged it, and gathered out the stones thereof, and planted it with the choicest vines." The vineyard was such an important factor in the life of Orientals that it figures largely in their speech and literature.

My well-beloved hath a vineyard
In a very fruitful hill:
And he digged it, and gathered out the
    stones thereof,
And planted it with the choicest vines.
He built a tower in the midst of it
And also made a winepress therein;
And he looked that it should bring forth
    grapes,
But it brought forth wild grapes.

And now, O inhabitants of Jerusalem
    and men of Judah,
Judge, I pray you, between me and my
    vineyard!
What could have been done more to
    my vineyard
That I have not done in it?
Wherefore, when I looked that it should
    bring forth grapes,
Brought it forth wild grapes?

And now I will tell you
What I will do to my vineyard:
I will take away the hedge thereof,
And it shall be eaten up;
I will break down the wall thereof,
And it shall be trodden down.
I will lay it waste;
It shall not be pruned, nor digged;
And there shall come up briers and thorns.
I will also command the clouds that
    they rain no rain upon it.

For the vineyard of the Lord of hosts
    is the house of Israel,

And the men of Judah, they are his
    pleasant plantation.
He looked for justice, but, behold!—
    oppression;
For righteousness, but, behold!— a cry.

THE KINGDOM TO COME

And it shall come to pass in the last days, that the mountain of the Lord's house shall be established in the top of the mountains, and shall be exalted above the hills; and all nations shall flow to it. And many people shall go and say, "Come ye, and let us go up to the mountain of the Lord, to the house of the God of Jacob. And he will teach us of his ways, and we will walk in his paths: for out of Zion shall go forth the law, and the word of the Lord from Jerusalem."

And he shall judge among the nations, and shall rebuke many people: and they shall beat their swords into plowshares, and their spears into pruning hooks: nation shall not lift up sword against nation, neither shall they learn war any more.

O house of Jacob, come ye, and let us walk in the light of the Lord.

THE KING OF RIGHTEOUSNESS AND PEACE

For unto us a child is born,
Unto us a son is given:
And the government shall be upon his shoulder:
And his name shall be called Wonderful, Coun-
    selor,
Mighty God, Everlasting Father, Prince of Peace.
Of the increase of his government
And of peace there shall be no end,
Upon the throne of David, and upon his kingdom,

PEACE

From a painting by William Strutt

To order it, and to establish it with judgment,
And with justice from henceforth even forever.
The zeal of the Lord of hosts will perform this.

There shall come forth a rod out of the stock of
    Jesse,
And a branch shall grow out of his roots:
And the spirit of the Lord shall rest upon him,
The spirit of wisdom and understanding,
The spirit of counsel and might,
The spirit of knowledge and of the fear of the Lord.
He shall be of quick understanding in the fear
    of the Lord;
He shall not judge after the sight of his eyes,
Neither reprove after the hearing of his ears;
But with righteousness shall he judge the poor,
And with equity decide for the meek of the earth;
He shall smite the land with the rod of his mouth,
And with the breath of his lips shall he slay the
    wicked.
Righteousness shall be the girdle of his loins,
And faithfulness the girdle of his reins.

Then the wolf also shall dwell with the lamb,
And the leopard shall lie down with the kid;
And the calf and the young lion and the fatling
    together;
And a little child shall lead them.
And the cow and the bear shall feed;
Their young ones shall lie down together;
And the lion shall eat straw like the ox;
And the nursing child shall play on the hole of
    the asp,
And the weaned child shall put his hand on the
    viper's nest.

They shall not hurt nor destroy
In all my holy mountain;
For the earth shall be full of the knowledge of
     the Lord
As the waters cover the sea.

And in that day there shall be a root of Jesse,
Who shall stand for an ensign of the people;
To him shall the Gentiles seek;
And his rest shall be glorious.

JERUSALEM DELIVERED

The poet, in his trust that God will relieve the city from its foes, pictures a processional about to enter the rebuilt gates after its deliverance.

In that day shall this song be sung in the land of Judah:

We have a strong city;
Salvation will God appoint for walls and
     bulwarks.
Open ye the gates,
That the righteous nation that keepeth the
     truth may enter in.
Thou wilt keep him in perfect peace whose
     mind is stayed on thee,
Because he trusteth in thee.
Trust ye in the Lord forever,
For in the Lord Jehovah is everlasting
     strength.

MICAH

The Peasant Prophet of Moresheth-gath

WHEN we remark that the name Micah is an abbreviation of the word Micaiah, which means "who is like Jehovah," that he lived in Moresheth, a village near the Philistine coast plain and in the westernmost section of the territory known as the Shephelah, and that his public ministry extended in all likelihood from about 735 B.C. until about 700 B.C., we have recorded about all we know with any definiteness of the personal life of the prophet Micah.

This scarcity of biographical detail is, however, compensated for by the self-revealing quality of the man's writings; for Micah writes not only with the fervor and passion of a true patriot and religionist, but also with the tenderness of a countryman in love with the soil and feeling deeply the wrongs of the humble people of the soil.

With unmistakable clearness and definiteness he charges Samaria and Jerusalem, the capitals respectively of North and South, with being the centers and generators of crime and irreligion; and in the severest terms he predicts the utter destruction of both, not callously, but with an aching heart; for Jerusalem is "the gate of my people," and over her impending doom he would "wail and howl, and go stripped and naked: wailing like the dragons and mourning as the owls."

But it is over the fate of the little country places that he grieves most. He can discern something of retributive justice in the approaching doom of Jerusalem; but no such thought lightens the sadness of his outlook upon the little villages about him. Not only were they already enduring the spoliations of the wicked and powerful rich intrenched in Jerusalem, but soon they would fall helplessly, some of them forever, before the armies who would enter Judah through those western valleys to capture and destroy. Standing by his own little home in Moresheth,[6] a thousand feet above sea level, he looks out over valleys and hillsides before him, and visualizing the swift advance of an invading host, describes their relentless onrush, naming one by one the places overrun, and playing upon their respective names in affectionate grief as he announces their capture and ruin.

In the light of all this, it is not to be wondered at that Micah should have predicted the rise of Israel's longed-for deliverer and king from among the poor. For, like his great contemporary Isaiah, Micah was no mere pessimist decrying the evils of the present. He looked beyond them to the grander future. He saw clearly that no true deliverer of Israel could arise from the tyrannous households of the nobles and rulers. Only one knowing

27

the poverty of the common people could truly deliver them and justly reign over them. From Bethlehem the humble must he arise; not from Jerusalem the oppressive. "Thou, Bethlehem Ephrathah, though thou be little among the thousands of Judah, yet out of thee shall he come forth unto me that is to be ruler in Israel, whose goings forth have been from of old, from everlasting."

And this prophet has given the world the finest statement of ethical religion:

> "He hath showed thee, O man, what is good;
> And what doth the Lord require of thee,
> But to do justly and to love mercy,
> And to walk humbly with thy God?"

And the reasonableness of these requirements he has set forth in the preceding verses, in a plea that is as tender and as persuasive as it is cogent and true.

MICAH

From a fresco by John S. Sargent

The prophet's face is hidden, his head is averted. He can look no longer at the frightful deeds which the rulers of Israel are daily committing against the humble and the poor. The whole literature of denunciation offers no parallel to the scathing eloquence of this prophet reformer. Sprung as he was from the common people, Micah was full of the violence of the revolutionist. The times were ripe for upheaval, and it was his fire that touched off the train of reform.

MICAH

"THE GREATEST SAYING OF THE OLD TESTAMENT"

THE QUESTION

WHEREWITH shall I come before the Lord,
And bow myself before the high God?
Shall I come before him with burnt offerings,
With calves of a year old?
Will the Lord be pleased with thousands of rams,
Or with ten thousands of rivers of oil?
Shall I give my first-born for my transgression,
The fruit of my body for the sin of my soul?

THE ANSWER

He hath showed thee, O man, what is good;
And what doth the Lord require of thee,
But to do justly, and to love mercy,
And to walk humbly with thy God?

THE NEED FOR MORAL REGENERATION

Hear, all ye people; hearken, O earth, and all that therein is: and let the Lord God be witness against you, the Lord from his holy temple. For, behold, the Lord cometh forth out of his place, and will come down, and tread upon the high places of the earth. And the mountains shall be molten under him, and the valleys shall be cleft, as wax before the fire, and as the waters that are poured down a steep place. For the transgression of Jacob is all this, and for the sins of the house of Israel. What is the transgression of Jacob? is it not Samaria? and what are the high places of Judah? are they not Jerusalem? Therefore I will make Samaria as a heap of the field, and as plantings of a vineyard: and I will pour down the stones thereof into the valley, and I will discover the foundations thereof. And all the graven images thereof shall be beaten to pieces, and all the hires thereof shall be burned with the fire, and all the idols thereof will I lay desolate.

FALSE AND TRUE PROPHETS

Thus saith the Lord concerning the prophets
    that make my people to err,
That bite with their teeth and cry, "Peace!"
And he that putteth not into their mouths,—
They even proclaim war against him.

Therefore it shall be night unto you, that ye
    shall not have a vision;
And it shall be dark unto you, that ye shall not
    divine;
And the sun shall go down upon the prophets,
And the day shall be black over them.

Then shall the seers be ashamed,
And the diviners confounded:
Yea, they shall all cover their lips;
For there is no answer of God.

But as for me, I am full of power by the spirit of
    the Lord,
And of judgment, and of might,
To declare to Jacob his transgression,
And to Israel his sin.

THE EXPLANATION OF GOD'S JUDGMENTS

The voice of the Lord crieth to the city,
And the man of wisdom will fear thy name:

Hear ye the rod,
And who hath appointed it.
Are there yet treasures of wickedness in the house
　　　of the wicked,
And a scant measure that is abominable?
Shall I be pure with wicked balances,
And with a bag of deceitful weights?
For the rich men thereof are full of violence,
And the inhabitants thereof have spoken lies,
And their tongue is deceitful in their mouth.
Therefore I also have smitten thee with a grievous
　　　wound;
I have made thee desolate because of thy sins.
Thou shalt eat, but not be satisfied;
And thy humiliation shall be in the midst of thee:
And thou shalt put away, but shalt not save;
And that which thou savest will I give up to the
　　　sword.

For the statutes of Omri are kept,
And all the works of the house of Ahab,
And ye walk in their counsels;
That I may make thee a desolation,
And the inhabitants thereof a hissing:
And ye shall bear the reproach of my people.

JEREMIAH

PROPHET OF THE SOUL

NO prophet's words are fuller of trembling appeals to his Lord in the face of hatred and misunderstanding than are Jeremiah's. No seer of his nation's fate was more deeply overcome at sight of the woes that it was his mission to announce. He was in truth a man of sorrows, a prophet of tears.

Jeremiah began his work by helping in the reforms of Josiah, a young prophet enthusiastically serving a young king. But after the king was killed in his foolish insurrection against Pharaoh-necho, Jeremiah lived on to see the reaction under Jehoiakim and the exile under the helpless Zedekiah. He was swept away with the captives into Egypt; and, according to tradition, was finally killed by his ungrateful countrymen.

Of all the Old Testament prophets, Jeremiah is at once the most pathetic and the most heroic. His was that rare sensitiveness of soul that could not help but suffer. And suffer he did, through a long and thankless ministry that ended in exile and martyrdom.

His bitter afflictions, instead of crushing him, only ennobled him. They brought to him, moreover, his distinctive message; for they drove him to those earnest communings with God where alone he found illumination and rest, till religion, for him, came to mean the soul's "inward fellowship with God."

That insight will stand as Jeremiah's preëminent contribution to religious life and thought. Out of it grew his doctrine of repentance and regeneration; for he believed that the hardened heart, like fallow ground, must be plowed and harrowed before the seeds of new life can take root and flourish. Out of it grew his doctrine of "the New Covenant" of life that Jehovah was some day to make with Israel, a covenant the laws of which he would write, not upon tables of stone, but upon the living tablets of human hearts. Out of it came, later, a new appreciation of the universality of the religion of Jehovah; for only as a religion becomes truly individual can it become universal.

Jeremiah was born probably in the year 650 B.C., when Manasseh, "the apostate," was still on the throne. His home was in Anathoth, a town about three and a half miles northeast of Jerusalem. His father, Hilkiah, who was a priest, doubtless early turned him toward Jehovah, despite the fact that it was from among the followers of Jehovah, chiefly, that Manasseh was "shedding much innocent blood."

When he was twenty-four years old, Jeremiah received his "call." The ecstasy of that experience he never forgot. He was poet as well as

33

prophet; and he alone, of all the prophets, associates with his call the mystic influences of nature. He tells us that it was while the almond trees were in bloom and spring breezes were laden with early fragrances that the spirit of God awakened his soul to its sense of high prophetic mission.

But, unlike Isaiah who answered readily, "Here am I; send me," Jeremiah shrank from his call in self-distrust, pleading his youthfulness and lack of experience. Something more than mystical ecstasy was needed to inflame his hesitant soul. And that something was afforded to him in a conviction, a tremendous and unshakable conviction, that God had predestined him to the work of prophecy. Add to this his further conviction that he was to be a prophet to the nations, that every message of his to Judah would involve the nations round about her, and we have, lodged in the soul of a single man, a group of driving forces altogether irresistible.

The sense of mission generated in him by these experiences was so intense that it isolated him, and turned his whole life to tragedy. It denied to him the sustaining companionship of wife and children. It pitted against him, in bitter antagonism, the very ones for whom his heart agonized, and for whom he would have gladly died; and it drove him pitilessly to the task of exhorting and condemning these scornful and rebellious people.

At the same time, this sense of being God-gripped and God-driven brought with it its own exceeding great reward. For, unable to escape God, he flung himself upon him in his hours of weariness and despair, and in converse with him found satisfaction and rest. This transformed his personal timidity into moral daring. Ofttimes when in despondency or despair he might have remained silent and proclaimed the Word of the Lord no more, he felt that Word burning in his soul as a consuming fire, till it compelled him to break his silence and proclaim it anew. It developed in him an overmastering zeal for God, and charged his soul with a power of endurance that has lifted him to a place of grandeur among the moral heroes of the world.

These personal experiences brought to Jeremiah that deeper understanding of the human heart which his messages so clearly disclose. His calls to repentance and renewed loyalty to God, Judah would not heed. How could she be so indifferent and rebellious toward God? Surely only hardness of heart could account for it! and hardness of heart was not hers by nature, as her history attested. She had acquired it through persistent disregard of God. Without loyalty of heart, the laws contained in Israel's law books were useless. If ever God restored Israel, he must change her heart. And Jeremiah felt sure that he would. He would make a new covenant with her, more potent than the old, a covenant written upon the tables of her heart. Such was Jeremiah's hope for the regeneration of Israel.

Jeremiah was himself the living ground of all he taught. Well might such a man have said from his God-stricken and God-satisfied soul: "Whom have I in heaven but thee, and there is none on earth that I desire beside thee. My heart and my flesh fail me, but God is the strength of my life and my portion forever."

JEREMIAH AT THE FALL OF JERUSALEM
From a painting by Edouard Bendemann

Here we see that awful day of destruction of which Jeremiah had so often warned his people. The Temple is in smoking ruins; the Ark is being carried off; captives are urged on under the lash; King Zedekiah himself is tied to the conqueror's chariot, while palm branches are strewn in the victor's path and troops sound the flourish of trumpets. In the midst of all this Jeremiah sits unmoved, for he knows that, as God's promised punishment was inevitable, just so surely will his redemption of Israel come to pass. He sees far into the future, and trusts God.

JEREMIAH

From a fresco by Michelangelo

The prophet has preached and labored in vain. All his tenderness, his tears, his pleadings, his threatenings, have not availed to avert the calamity which the sins of Judah and her rulers so richly deserve. The stroke has fallen; the city is laid waste; the captives have been led forth to their long exile. Only the prophet is left with his heavy memories, his unilluminated sorrow. How truly could it be said of him, "He is despised and rejected of men; a man of sorrows and acquainted with grief."

JEREMIAH

JEREMIAH'S CALL

THEN the word of the Lord came to me, saying:
  "Before I formed thee, I knew thee,
And before thou wast born, I consecrated thee."
Then said I:
  "Ah, Lord God!
    Behold, I cannot speak;
    For I am a child."
But the Lord said to me:
  "Say not, 'I am a child';
    For thou shalt go to all that I shall send thee,
    And whatsoever I command thee thou shalt speak.
    Be not afraid of their faces,
    For I am with thee to deliver thee."
Then the Lord put forth his hand and touched my mouth,
and the Lord said to me:
    "Behold, I have put words in thy mouth;
    See, I have this day set thee over the nations and king-
        doms,
    To root out, and to pull down, and to destroy,
    And to throw down, and to build, and to plant."
Moreover, the word of the Lord also came to me, saying,
"Jeremiah, what seest thou?"
  And I said, "I see a rod of an almond tree."
  Then the Lord said to me, "Thou hast seen well: for I
will hasten my word to perform it.
  "Thou therefore gird up thy loins, and rise, and speak to
them all that I command thee: be not dismayed at their faces,
lest I confound thee before them. For, behold, I have made
thee this day a defenced city, and an iron pillar, and brazen

walls against the whole land, against the kings of Judah, against the princes thereof, against the priests thereof, and against the people of the land. And they shall fight against thee; but they shall not prevail against thee; for I am with thee," saith the Lord, "to deliver thee."

©*Underwood & Underwood*

ANATHOTH, HOME OF JEREMIAH

A typical Judean village, crowning the bare summit of a little hill on the edge of the wilderness. How strange that such a little town should persist for so many centuries! And how strangely real the life of the prophet becomes as one looks upon the fields that once were his property and the misty mountains that he loved! Here, at the foot of Mount Scopus only three and a half miles from Jerusalem, the priests quietly tilled their fields, and raised figs and olives. Traces of this cultivation remain today, along with ruins of walls and foundations.

JEREMIAH'S CONFESSION

O Lord, thou knowest;
Remember me, and visit me, and avenge
       me of my persecutors;
Take me not away, in thy longsuffering:
Know that for thy sake I have suffered
       rebuke.
Thy words were found, and I did eat them;
And thy word was to me the joy and
       rejoicing of my heart:
For I am called by thy name,
O Lord God of hosts.
I sat not in the assembly of them that
       make merry, nor rejoiced;
I sat alone because of thy hand;
For thou hast filled me with indignation.
Why is my pain perpetual,
And my wound incurable, which refuseth
       to be healed?
Wilt thou indeed be to me as a deceitful
       brook,
As waters that fail?
Heal me, O Lord, and I shall be healed;
Save me, and I shall be saved:
For thou art my praise.
Behold, they say to me,
"Where is the word of the Lord? let it
       come now."
As for me, I have not hastened from
       being a shepherd to follow thee;
Neither have I desired the woeful day;
       thou knowest it:
That which came out of my lips was
       right before thee.

Be not a terror to me;
Thou art my hope in the day of evil.

JEREMIAH'S MESSAGE OF HOPE

"For, lo, the days come," saith the Lord, "that I will bring again the captivity of my people Israel and Judah," saith the Lord: "and I will cause them to return to the land that I gave to their fathers, and they shall possess it.

"Behold, I will gather them out of all countries, whither I have driven them in mine anger, and in my fury, and in great wrath; and I will bring them again to this place, and I will cause them to dwell safely: and they shall be my people, and I will be their God: and I will give them one heart, and one way, that they may fear me forever, for the good of them, and of their children after them.

"And I will make an everlasting covenant with them, that I will not turn away from them, to do them good; but I will put my fear in their hearts, that they shall not depart from me.

"I will restore health to thee, and I will heal thee of thy wounds," saith the Lord, "because they called thee an outcast, saying, 'This is Zion, whom no man seeketh after.'

"Behold, I will bring again the captivity of Jacob's tents, and have mercy on his dwelling places; and the city shall be builded upon her own heap, and the palace shall remain after the manner thereof. And out of them shall proceed thanksgiving and the voice of them that make merry: and I will multiply them, and they shall not be few; I will also glorify them, and they shall not be small. Their children also shall be as aforetime, and their congregation shall be established before me, and I will punish all that oppress them.

"And their prince shall be of themselves, and their ruler shall proceed from the midst of them; and I will cause him to draw near, and he shall approach me: for who is he that hath had boldness to approach me?" saith the Lord. "And ye shall be my people, and I will be your God.

"And it shall come to pass, when ye be multiplied and increased in the land, in those days," saith the Lord, "they shall say no more, 'The ark of the covenant of the Lord': neither shall it come to mind; neither shall they remember it; neither shall they visit it; neither shall that be done any more.

"At that time they shall call Jerusalem the throne of the Lord; and all the nations shall be gathered to it, to the name of the Lord, to Jerusalem: neither shall they walk any more after the imagination of their evil heart. In those days the house of Judah shall walk with the house of Israel, and they shall come together out of the land of the North to the land that I have given for an inheritance to your fathers.

"In those days, and at that time, will I cause the branch of righteousness to grow up unto David; and he shall execute judgment and righteousness in the land. In those days shall Judah be saved, and Jerusalem

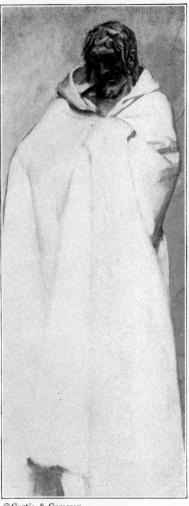

© *Curtis & Cameron*

JEREMIAH

From a fresco by Sargent

The prophet of desolation. The poise of the head and the arrangement of the locks almost suggest the poet Dante, of whom in his exile the children used to say, "See the man who has been in hell!" So, here, Jeremiah is pictured as having descended into the depths of suffering while his beloved city perished beneath the sword of Nebuchadnezzar

JEREMIAH'S GROTTO

North of Jerusalem beyond the city wall there is a hill associated with Jeremiah. Even today a large cavern is seen that has, by long tradition, been known as Jeremiah's Grotto. It is near the place where he was put in the stocks. It might have been his prison or his tomb, but it seems more likely to have been his hiding place, when it was unsafe for him to appear before the king.

shall dwell safely: and this is the name wherewith she shall be called, The Lord Our Righteousness."

JEREMIAH'S LIFE–MESSAGE

We do not know when Jeremiah spoke this oracle that follows. It was the real message of his whole life. It was probably uttered many times during the siege and captivity of Jerusalem. We may feel confident that it was the last word he left with his faithless countrymen. It is one of those great sayings that are true for all time and among all nations.

"Behold, the days come," saith the Lord,
"That I will make a new covenant with the house
of Israel,
And with the house of Judah,
Not according to the covenant that I made with
their fathers,
In the day that I took them by the hand
To bring them out of the land of Egypt:
Which covenant they broke.
But this shall be the covenant that I will make
With the house of Israel after those days:
I will put my law in their inward parts,
And write it in their hearts;
I will be their God,
And they shall be my people.
They shall teach no more every man his neighbor,
And every man his brother, saying:
'Know the Lord':
For they shall all know me,
From the least of them to the greatest of them;
For I will forgive their iniquity,
And their sin will I remember no more."[7]

NAHUM

Prophet of Retribution

"**V**ENGEANCE is mine; I will repay, saith the Lord," might well have been the text of the prophet Nahum. Nineveh, the capital of Assyria, is about to be destroyed; and as the prophet envisions the process, his soul runs over in Vesuvian streams of passionate hate and denunciation, exultation and praise.

And well he might. For Assyria had irrecoverably destroyed Israel, and ever since had been by turns a menace and a tyrant to Judah. The Assyrian empire had been built by the sword, and maintained by it. Toward those who resisted her she was merciless. She shamed their women and dashed their little ones to pieces; prisoners taken in war she ofttimes impaled upon the walls of her cities or flayed alive; captive princes and dignitaries she frequently hung up in cages, and many times had destroyed the identity of whole peoples by deportations; she taunted her victims with their inferiority and the powerlessness of their gods, and arrogantly bade them transfer their loyalties to the gods of Assyria; till her policy of terror and ruthlessness made her the most dreaded and deeply hated power in her days.

In the days of Hezekiah, Sennacherib had ridiculed Jerusalem's reliance upon Jehovah; but Isaiah championed their God, and the city was wonderfully saved from capture. But Manasseh upon succeeding to the throne had virtually dethroned Jehovah. The gods of Assyria were permitted to troop in and establish themselves in sanctuary, high place and housetop. And from the amount of blood spilled, it would seem that Manasseh took on also the Assyrian policy of ruthlessness in dealing with all who opposed him.

After much suffering and labor and waiting on the part of the faithful, a sweeping reformation was brought about in the reign of Josiah, and the gods of Assyria were, to all appearances, driven out of the land.

And now at last, Assyria, grown aged and set upon by new and vigorous enemies, has been driven within the walls of Nineveh, there to fight her final battle. This is the prospect that fires the soul of Nahum.

As Nineveh has been merciless in the past unto her foes, so will her enemies now be merciless unto her. She will be utterly destroyed,—destroyed beyond all hope of recovery. And her destruction will be but the vindication of the righteousness of God, who "is slow to anger, and great in power, and will not at all acquit the wicked."

With rare dramatic power Nahum describes the siege and destruction of the city; does it, moreover, with the fervidness of a soul on fire for God.

44

We see it all enacted before us as the grim and inevitable conclusion of a long tragedy of evil: the scarlet sheen of the besiegers, the flame-like flash of their weapons, the rumble and rattle of chariots, the clattering hoof-beats of horses, the cracking of whips, the shoutings of men, the melting fear of the doomed, the relentless surge of their foes, the shock and slash of the conflict, the vain speed of the fleeing, the wreck and loot of the city, and the dead in the midst of her ruins. And through it all he proclaims this eternal truth,—

> "Penalty for persistent wrong, though long delayed,
>   Is sure at last."

©*Curtis & Cameron*

NAHUM
From a fresco by John S. Sargent

The prophet is here astonished, but not bereft of speech. He has seen a marvel. The great city of Nineveh has fallen, she whose power reached to the four corners of the earth and whose fame ascended to heaven. She had been an instrument of vengeance in the hand of Jehovah, but now her day is come with a crash that shakes the world. Jehovah has thrown her down from her lofty seat. Thus the eye of the prophet discerns the hand of God in the history of the nations.

NAHUM

SIGNS OF GOD'S POWER

THE Lord is slow to anger, and great in power, and will not at all acquit the wicked: the Lord hath his way in the whirlwind and in the storm, and the clouds are the dust of his feet. He rebuketh the sea, and maketh it dry, and drieth up all the rivers: Bashan languisheth, and Carmel, and the flower of Lebanon languisheth. The mountains quake at him, and the hills melt, and the earth is burned in his presence, yea, the world, and all that dwell therein.

The Lord is good,
A stronghold in the day of trouble;
And he knoweth them that trust in him.

Behold upon the mountains the feet of him
That bringeth good tidings,
That publisheth peace!
O Judah, keep thy solemn feasts,
Perform thy vows;
For the wicked shall no more pass through thee:
He is utterly cut off.

THE DOOM OF NINEVEH

Woe to the bloody city!
It is all full of lies and robbery;
The prey departeth not.

All they that look upon thee shall flee from thee,
And say, "Nineveh is laid waste":
Who will bemoan her?

Whence shall I seek comforters for thee?
Art thou better than No-amon [Thebes],
That was situate among the rivers,
That had the waters round about her?

(Ashurbanipal, king of Nineveh, had taken Thebes, the proud Egyptian capital, about sixty years before, and had sacked the city with the usual Assyrian barbarity.)

Ethiopia and Egypt were her strength, and it was infinite;
Put and Lubim [Libya] were thy helpers.
Yet was she carried away, she went into captivity;
Her young children also were dashed in pieces at the head of the streets;
And they cast lots for her honorable men.

Thou also shalt be drunken; thou shalt be hid;
Thou also shalt seek a stronghold because of the enemy.
All thy fortresses shall be like fig trees with the first-ripe figs:
If they be shaken, they fall into the mouth of the eater.

Behold, the people in the midst of thee are women:
The gates of thy land shall be set wide open unto thine enemies:
The fire hath devoured thy bars.

Thy princes are as the locusts,
And thy marshals as the swarms of grasshoppers,
Which encamp in the hedges in the cold day,
But when the sun riseth they flee away,
And their place is not known where they are.

All that hear the report of thee clap their hands over thee;
For upon whom hath not thy wickedness passed continually?

ZEPHANIAH

"JEHOVAH will not do good, neither will he do evil." What a deadening opinion of God! And what a depressing commentary on the state of religion in Judah! So negative, so non-moral, so inept a conception of God consciously held by any people, could hardly result in anything better than religious sluggishness, if not a total indifference. For how could any one ever seriously count on a God who was so morally purposeless? Why should any sensible people ever fear him? Or why need they concern themselves about him at all? Such seems to have been the logical trend of affairs in Judah, for Zephaniah describes them as a people who had "thickened on their lees."

Now, this process of moral and religious thickening had been going on in Judah for a long time. The short-lived reformation of Hezekiah had been followed by a national reaction toward all manner of evils and pollutions. Manasseh, the king, had himself led the way, and in "dead earnest."

Manasseh introduced into Judah, for the first time in her history, the abominations that had polluted the sanctuaries of the North; for not only did he restore the high places which had been destroyed by his father, but he erected altars to the licentious worship of Baal and Astarte. More than that, he built in the Valley of Hinnom an altar to Molech, the cruelest of all gods, and there caused his own son to pass through the fire. He welcomed into his kingdom the Assyrian forms of stellar worship, and within the very courts of the Temple itself built altars to the "hosts of heaven." The effect of this was inevitable and widespread. The eternal impressiveness of the starry heavens captured the imagination of the people. High places and housetops everywhere became sacred places for the observation and worship of the stars.

To all these evils Manasseh added the stern Assyrian policy of the rigorous use of force. Jehovah was virtually, if not actually, deposed in favor of foreign gods; and the followers of Jehovah were mercilessly dealt with whenever they dared to raise their voices in dissent. Manasseh shed more innocent blood than had ever been shed before.

Place before all of this the fearful shock to religious faith that the destruction of Israel by pagan Assyria had brought, and add to that the fact that Judah ever since had been feeling the steady encroachment upon her own territory and life of that same dreaded power, and we have before us in brief that combination and sequence of adverse experiences that through the years had been steadily quenching Judah's faith in her God.

48

The brief reign of Amon had succeeded that of Manasseh; and now the forces of Jehovah were again in power through their control of the training of the young king Josiah, and were attempting earnestly to restore the worship of Jehovah to its former place of power in the life of the nation. But the people had become apathetic and scornful. "Jehovah will not do good," said they; "neither will he do evil."

But at this juncture, the Scythians began to make their appearance in the far North; wild and mysterious hordes, the very rumor of whose approach struck terror to the people of Judah. This shocked them out of their lethargy. And to add the terrors of conscience to the fear of the swift-moving and terrible Scythians, there arose Zephaniah, the great-great-grandson of Hezekiah, with his terrible predictions of a day of doom soon to fall upon all the world.

Zephaniah held much the same position of dignity and rank as did Isaiah. His utterances are austere and grand in their impressiveness, but lack the poetic beauty, the versatility, the religious warmth, and the sympathy of Isaiah. In his pronouncements of destruction he went further than Amos. To Amos, the "Day of the Lord" meant a day of doom for Israel only; but to Zephaniah, it was a day of cataclysmic doom for all the earth, both man and nature. In this, he stands out as the first of the apocalyptic prophets.

ZEPHANIAH

From a fresco by John S. Sargent

Sorrow and perplexity are the dominant notes of this portrait: sorrow over the sins of Judah the idolatrous—worshiper of the hosts of heaven and all the false gods of the nations round about; perplexity over the message that he must deliver, over the reforms that he must enact and the modes of speech that can best convict and persuade and inspire. Zephaniah lived in the darkest days of Israel's history, before the reforms of Josiah.

ZEPHANIAH

THE DAY OF WRATH

THE great day of the Lord is near;
It is near and hasteth greatly.
Hark! the voice of the day of the Lord;
The mighty man shall cry there bitterly.
That day is a day of wrath,
A day of trouble and distress,
A day of waste and desolation,
A day of darkness and gloominess,
A day of clouds and thick darkness,
A day of the trumpet and alarm,
Against the fenced cities,
And against the high towers.
And I will bring distress upon men,
That they shall walk like blind men,
Because they have sinned against the Lord.
For he will make even a speedy end
Of all them that dwell in the land.

Gather yourselves together; yea, gather together,
O nation not desired;
Before the decree bring forth,
Before the day pass as the chaff,
Before the fierce anger of the Lord come upon you,
Before the day of the Lord's anger come upon you.
Seek ye the Lord, all ye meek of the earth,
Who have kept his ordinances;
Seek righteousness, seek meekness:
It may be ye shall be hid
In the day of the Lord's anger.

THE HAPPIER TIME

Then will I give to the people a pure
    language,
That they may all call upon the name
    of the Lord,
To serve him with one consent.
From beyond the rivers of Ethiopia,
    my suppliants,
Even the daughter of my dispersed,
Shall bring mine offering.
In that day shalt thou not be ashamed
    for all thy doings,
Wherein thou hast transgressed against me.
For then I will take away out of the
    midst of thee
Them that exult in thy majesty,
And thou shalt no more be haughty
In my holy mountain.
I will also leave in the midst of thee
An afflicted and poor people,
And they shall trust in the name of the Lord.
The remnant of Israel shall not do iniquity,
Nor speak lies;
Neither shall a deceitful tongue be found
    in their mouth:
But they shall feed and lie down,
And no one shall make them afraid.

Sing, O daughter of Zion;
Shout, O Israel;
Be glad and exult with all the heart,
O daughter of Jerusalem.
The Lord hath taken away thy judgments,
He hath cast out thine enemy:

The King of Israel, even the Lord, is in
    the midst of thee:
Thou shalt not see evil any more.
In that day it shall be said to Jerusalem,
    "Fear thou not":
And to Zion, "Let not thy hands be slack."
The Lord thy God in the midst of thee
    is mighty,
He will save.
He will rejoice over thee with joy;
He will be silent in his love,
He will joy over thee with singing.

I will gather them that are sorrowful for the solemn
assembly, who are of thee, to whom the reproach of it was a
burden. Behold, at that time I will undo all that afflict thee:
and I will save her that halteth, and gather her that was
driven out; and I will get them praise and fame in every
land where they have been put to shame.

At that time will I bring you again, even in the time that
I gather you: for I will make you a name and a praise among
all people of the earth, when I turn back your captivity before
your eyes, saith the Lord.

HABAKKUK

QUESTIONER OF THE WAYS OF GOD,
PROPHET OF FAITHFULNESS

A FASCINATING bit of writing is this little Book of Habakkuk, and in several respects quite unique. Of the writer we know nothing save that his name, Habakkuk, means one who embraces or clings, or, as Luther has suggested, one who holds up and comforts a weeping one; that he was a contemporary of the great Jeremiah, and like him deeply sensitive under wrong.

And though the book is called prophecy, it bears very little resemblance either in form or content to the writings of the other prophets. Ordinarily a prophet is a spokesman for God unto the people, a questioner in the name of God, and a rebuker of the ways of men. Habakkuk, however, is a spokesman for the people unto God, a questioner of the ways of God with men. He holds dialogue with God and not with Israel.

He is the first to speculate on the problem of the successful prevalence of unmerited injustice and evil, and to question the adequacy of traditional teaching on the subject. He is thus, in a sense, a philosophical pioneer among the prophets.

Josiah, the good king, had enforced the law; the people had accepted it, and in obedience to it had reformed their ways. Following this grand revival had come twelve years of happiness and prosperity that stand forth as the noblest period in Judah's history. Josiah was himself the embodiment of the virtues he taught, a strong, patriotic, and high-minded ruler. And yet, Josiah had been slain in battle while fighting in an honorable cause; Israel was now enduring high-handed injustice and tyranny; and God, seemingly, was allowing it all. Right there lay the prophet's problem. Why was wrong thus allowed to prevail? Why was the law brought to naught?

The reply that the Chaldeans were being raised up to avenge the wrong only aggravated the problem; for were not the Chaldeans themselves an exceedingly wicked people? How, then, could a holy God suffer their wicked might to prevail, and use them as an avenging force? Manifestly there was something radically wrong. He could not himself solve the problem, but he could and would wait,—wait in patience upon his watchtower to see what the Lord would say to him.

And the Lord promised him a vision, and bade him wait for it. And while he waited, there flashed into his soul this bit of insight:

"Behold, his [the wicked's] soul is puffed up; it is not upright in him:
But the just shall live by his faith."

For that flash of insight we shall forever be grateful to Habakkuk. The road of unswerving faithfulness to God and duty is the road that leads through doubt to light and peace.

"The just shall live by his faith!" What a mighty statement! And what a liberating force it has been in Christian history! Paul used it to express the power of his new-found faith in Christ, and emancipated himself and early Christianity from bondage to Judaism. Luther grasped it anew and wrenched himself free from the tyranny of Rome. Wesley found it mighty unto the assuring and deepening of the soul's sense of salvation through Christ. Thoughtful Christians everywhere find it the Magna Charta of the soul.

©*Curtis & Cameron*

HABAKKUK
From a fresco by John S. Sargent

The prophet is here watching the course of world events beyond the horizon of his nation. He sees the Chaldeans, swift, bitter, terrible, who are to sweep down and overwhelm the world. The world in general deserves this inundation of punishment, and his beloved nation of Judah deserves it even more, for Judah has sinned against great light.

HABAKKUK

THE MIGHTY DELIVERER

GOD came from Teman,
And the Holy One from mount Paran.
His glory covered the heavens,
And the earth was full of his praise.
His brightness was as the light;
And he had rays coming forth from his hands;
And there was the hiding of his power.
Before him went the pestilence,
And burning bolts went forth at his feet.

He stood, and shook the earth;
He beheld, and drove asunder the nations;
And the everlasting mountains were scattered;
The perpetual hills did bow;
His ways are everlasting.

Thou didst cleave the earth with rivers;
The mountains saw thee, and they trembled;
The overflowing of water passed by;
The deep uttered its voice,
And lifted up its hands on high.
The sun and moon stood still in their habitation;
At the light of thine arrows they went,
And at the shining of thy glittering spear.

Thou wentest forth for the salvation of thy people,
Even for salvation with thine anointed.
Thou didst walk through the sea with thy horses,
Through the depth of great waters.

Although the fig tree shall not blossom,
Neither shall fruit be in the vines;
And the labor of the olive shall fail,
And the fields yield no food;
And the flock shall be cut off from the fold,
And there shall be no herd in the stalls;

Yet I will rejoice in the Lord,
I will joy in the God of my salvation.
The Lord God is my strength;
He will make my feet like hinds' feet,
He will make me to walk upon high places.

HABAKKUK'S PRAYER

Yet though the fig tree should no burden bear,
Though vines delude the promise of the year;
Yet though the olive should not yield her oil,
Nor the parched glebe reward the peasant's toil;
Though the tired ox beneath his labors fall,
And herds in millions perish from the stall;
Yet shall my grateful strings
Forever praise thy name;
Forever thee proclaim
The everlasting God, the mighty King of kings.
—*William Broome*

EZEKIEL

Prophet of the Great Transition

ELEVEN years after the first group of captives from Judah were carried into Babylonia by Nebuchadnezzar, Jerusalem was completely destroyed and her citizens exiled. The event was appalling and resulted in the dissolution of Judah as a nation. It might have resulted in the total loss of Judah's religion also; for when an ancient nation fell, the people usually threw their gods "to the moles and the bats," and transferred their loyalties to the gods of their conquerors.

Jeremiah had in a measure prepared Judah for the approaching calamity by predicting it. He had also spiritualized the people's thought of God, and had so universalized him that the doings of other nations were interpreted as in reality directed by him. Therefore, Judah's captivity, instead of destroying her religious beliefs, transformed and strengthened them in a way that has enabled her to preserve her distinctiveness ever since.

The period of the Babylonian exile was thus, in reality, a period of momentous transitions. It turned a settled people into world-wanderers, an agricultural people into a race of merchants and tradesmen. It changed a nation into a religious sect, and developed a literature that made them a people of a Book, administered by a specialized priesthood through an elaborate legalistic and ceremonial system.

The directing mind in the whole situation was Ezekiel's. He was the son of a priest of Jerusalem, and was himself trained for the priesthood. He was carried into captivity in 597 B.C., and while in Babylonia received his call. It came in the form of a vision. The most impressive feature of it was its symbolism of the absolute sovereignty and spirituality of God. Called to be a messenger to the people in exile, he combined the functions of prophet and priest.

As prophet, he predicted the destruction of Jerusalem, and dwelt in detail upon the sins that made her destruction inevitable. After the downfall of the city his messages turned to consolation and hope. In keeping with his conception of the sovereignty of God, he interpreted all history in the light of God's ruling providence. It was for the honor of God's name that Jerusalem had been destroyed; and it would be for the honor of his name that Judah would be restored, that the nations might know that Jehovah was God. Fearing lest his people should be lost in despondency and the overwhelming influence of paganism, he became their pastor, ministering to them individually and in little groups, and developing what became the synagogue system of Judaism.

As priest, he felt keenly the disciplinary and educational value of ritual and ceremony in the nurture and advancement of religion. Hence, he emphasized the Sabbath and feast days; he formulated and enforced laws of ceremonial cleanness and separateness; and, in preparation for Judah's return to Jerusalem, he worked out elaborate plans for the reconstruction of the city and the rehabilitation of religion there.

He was prophet and priest, educator and apocalyptist, and is worthily described as "the father of Judaism," and "the most influential of prophets."

VISION OF EZEKIEL

From a painting by Paul F. Poole

"And I looked, and, behold, a whirlwind came out of the north, a great cloud, and a fire flashing continually, and a brightness was about it, and out of the midst thereof as the color of amber, out of the midst of the fire. Also out of the midst thereof came the likeness of four living creatures."

EZEKIEL

From a fresco by Michelangelo

The prophet has here turned from the roll which he has been studying to follow for a moment the demonstrations which the divine messenger is giving. One can imagine that the prophet is here looking at the plan of the new Jerusalem traced by the divine finger upon the pedestal beside him. The plan of the new Temple grows before him. He sees the orderly array of the priests, he hears the chanting of the choirs, he beholds the rising clouds of incense and the smoke of sacrifice. Out of this vision Ezekiel will formulate plans by which the scattered nation of Israel shall become a compact and zealous church of Jehovah.

EZEKIEL

A VISION OF GOD'S GLORY

LIVING CREATURES APPEAR IN THE STORM

NOW it came to pass in the thirtieth year, in the fourth month, in the fifth day of the month, as I was among the captives by the river Chebar,[8] that the heavens were opened, and I saw visions of God.

And I looked, and, behold, a whirlwind came out of the north, a great cloud, and a fire flashing continually, and a brightness was about it, and out of the midst thereof as the color of amber, out of the midst of the fire.[9]

Also out of the midst thereof came the likeness of four living creatures. And this was their appearance: They had the likeness of a man; and every one had four faces, and every one had four wings. And their feet were straight feet; and the sole of their feet was like the sole of a calf's foot; and they sparkled like the color of burnished brass. And they had the hands of a man under their wings on their four sides; and they four had their faces and their wings thus: Their wings were joined one to another; they turned not when they went; they went every one straight forward.

As for the likeness of their faces, they four had the face of a man; and the face of a lion, on the right side; and they four had the face of an ox, on the left side; they four also had the face of an eagle. Thus were their faces; and their wings were stretched upward; two wings of every one were joined one to another, and two covered their bodies. And they went every one straight forward: whither the spirit was to go, they went; and they turned not when they went.

As for the likeness of the living creatures, their appearance was like burning coals of fire, like the appearance of torches:

THE VISION OF EZEKIEL

From a painting by Raphael

This is the attempt of a great artist to visualize that which it is impossible to picture—the glory of the omnipotent God. Ezekiel describes Jehovah wholly in symbols, symbols that represent strength, swiftness, intelligence and majesty. The four living creatures that embody these elements are the ox, the eagle, the cherub, and the lion. These symbols were perpetuated in the New Testament by the writer of the Book of Revelation, who, like Ezekiel, conceived of them as the attendants of Divinity. Early in the Christian centuries, however, they became associated with the writers of the four Gospels, so that throughout Christian history they have become the emblems of the Evangelists, those inspired writers through whom the nature of God and his Son has been most clearly revealed: the cherub, or man, for Matthew, the lion for Mark, the ox for Luke, and the eagle for John.

These symbols are found in almost every church of the Old World, either as a part of the mosaic decoration, carvings on pulpits and altars, or blazoned on the windows.

it went up and down among the living creatures; and the fire was bright, and out of the fire went forth lightning. And the living creatures ran and returned as the appearance of a flash of lightning.

Now as I beheld the living creatures, behold one wheel upon the earth beside the living creatures, for each of the four faces thereof. The appearance of the wheels and their work was like the color of a beryl: and they four had one likeness; and their appearance and their work was as it were a wheel within a wheel. When they went, they went upon their four sides: they turned not when they went. And their rims, they were so high that they were dreadful; and their rims were full of eyes[10] round about. And when the living creatures were lifted up from the earth, the wheels were lifted up. Whithersoever the spirit was to go, they went; thither was the spirit to go; and the wheels were lifted up beside them: for the spirit of the living creatures was in the wheels.

And the likeness of the firmament upon the heads of the living creatures was like the color of the terrible ice stretched forth over their heads above.

When they went, I heard the noise of their wings like the noise of great waters, like the voice of the Almighty, the voice of speech, like the noise of a host: when they stood, they let down their wings. And there was a voice from the firmament that was over their heads.

Above the firmament that was over their heads was the likeness of a throne, as the appearance of a sapphire stone: and upon the likeness of the throne was a likeness as the appearance of a man upon it above. And I saw as the color of amber, as the appearance of fire round about within it, from the appearance of his loins even upward; and from the appearance of his loins even downward, I saw as it were the appearance of fire, and it had brightness round about him. As the appearance of the bow that is in the cloud in the day of rain, so was the appearance of the brightness round about. This was the appearance of the likeness of the glory of the Lord.

Ezekiel Receives His Message

When I saw it, I fell upon my face, and I heard a voice of one that spoke.

And he said to me, "Son of man, stand upon thy feet, and I will speak to thee."

Then the Spirit entered into me when he spoke to me, and set me upon my feet; and I heard him that spoke to me.

And he said to me: "Son of man, I send thee to the children of Israel, to a rebellious nation, that have rebelled against me: they and their fathers have transgressed against me, even to this very day. For they are impudent children and stiff-hearted. I send thee to them; and thou shalt say to them, 'Thus saith the Lord.' And they, whether they will hear, or whether they will forbear (for they are a rebellious house), yet shall know that there hath been a prophet among them. And thou, son of man, be not afraid of them, neither be afraid of their words, though briers and thorns be with thee, and thou dost dwell among scorpions: be not afraid of their words, nor be dismayed at their looks, though they be a rebellious house. And thou shalt speak my words to them, whether they will hear, or whether they will forbear: for they are most rebellious.

©*Curtis & Cameron*

EZEKIEL

From a fresco by John S. Sargent

This picture suggests that the prophet is here thinking through the problems of his nation, in the presence of Jehovah and under his inspiration.

"But thou, son of man, hear what I say to thee: be not thou rebellious like that rebellious house: open thy mouth, and eat what I give thee."

And when I looked, behold, a hand was sent to me; and, lo, a roll of a book was therein; and he spread it before me: and it was written within and on the back; and there were written therein lamentations, and mourning, and woe. Moreover he said to me, "Son of man, eat what thou findest; eat this roll, and go, speak to the house of Israel." So I opened my mouth, and he made me eat this roll. Then did I eat it; and it was as sweet as honey in my mouth.

Then the Spirit took me up, and I heard behind me a voice of a great rushing, saying, "Blessed be the glory of the Lord from his place." I heard also the noise of the wings of the living creatures that touched one another, and the noise of the wheels beside them, a noise of a great rushing.

So the Spirit lifted me up, and took me away, and I went in bitterness, in the heat of my spirit; but the hand of the Lord was strong upon me. Then I came to them of the captivity at Tel-abib, that dwelt by the river Chebar, and I sat where they sat; and remained there dumfounded among them seven days.

And it came to pass at the end of seven days that the word of the Lord came to me, saying:

"I have made thee a watchman to the house of Israel: therefore hear the word of my mouth, and give them warning from me. When I say to the wicked, 'Thou shalt surely die'; and thou givest him not warning, nor speakest to warn the wicked from his wicked way, to save his life; the same wicked man shall die in his iniquity; but his blood will I require at thy hand. Yet if thou warn the wicked, and he turn not from his wickedness, nor from his wicked way, he shall die in his iniquity; but thou hast delivered thy soul."

THE SLOW PROCESS OF RESTORATION

False prophets were trying to persuade the Jews that their captivity would be short. Ezekiel knew better.

A VISION OF THE SCATTERING OF THE JEWS

"And thou, son of man, take thee a sharp knife, take thee a barber's razor, and cause it to pass upon thy head and upon thy beard: then take thee balances to weigh, and divide the hair. Thou shalt burn with fire a third part in the midst of the city, when the days of the siege are fulfilled: and thou shalt take a third part, and smite about it with a knife; and a third part thou shalt scatter in the wind; and I will draw out a sword after them.

"Thou shalt also take thereof a few in number, and bind them in thy skirts. Then take of them again, and cast them into the midst of the fire, and burn them in the fire; for thereof shall a fire come forth into all the house of Israel.

"Then thou shalt say to all the house of Israel, 'Thus saith the Lord God: This is Jerusalem. A third part of thee shall die with the pestilence, and with famine shall they be consumed in the midst of thee; and a third part shall fall by the sword round about thee; and I will scatter a third part into all the winds, and I will draw out a sword after them.'"

A Vision of Israel's Exile, Led by Their Prince

The word of the Lord also came to me, saying: "Son of man, prepare thee goods for removal, and remove by day in their sight; and thou shalt remove from thy place to another place in their sight. And thou shalt bring forth thy goods by day in their sight, as goods for removal: and thou shalt go forth at even in their sight, as they that go forth into captivity. Dig thou through the wall in their sight, and carry out thereby.[11] In their sight shalt thou bear it upon thy shoulders, and carry it forth in the twilight. Thou shalt cover thy face, that thou see not the ground; for I have set thee for a sign to the house of Israel."

And I did so as I was commanded: I brought forth my goods by day, as goods for removal, and in the even I digged through the wall with my hand; I brought it forth in the twilight, and I bore it upon my shoulder in their sight.

In the morning came the word of the Lord to me, saying: "Son of man, hath not the house of Israel, the rebellious house, said to thee, 'What doest thou?' Say thou to them, 'Thus saith the Lord God, This burden concerneth the prince in Jerusalem, and all the house of Israel that are among them.' Say, 'I am your sign: like as I have done, so shall it be done to them: they shall remove and go into captivity. And the prince that is among them shall bear upon his shoulder in the twilight, and shall go forth; they shall dig through the wall to carry out thereby; he shall cover his face, that he see not the ground with his eyes. My net also will I spread upon him, and he shall be taken in my snare: and I will bring him to Babylon to the land of the Chaldeans; yet shall he not see it, though he shall die there.' "[12]

And the word of the Lord came to me, saying: "Son of man, what is that proverb that ye have in the land of Israel, saying,

> 'The days are prolonged,
> And every vision faileth'?

Tell them therefore: 'Thus saith the Lord God, I will make this proverb to cease, and they shall no more use it as a proverb in Israel'; but say to them,

> 'The days are at hand,
> And the fulfilment of every vision.'

For there shall be no more any vain vision nor flattering divination in the house of Israel. For I am the Lord: I will speak, and the word that I shall speak shall come to pass; it shall be no more prolonged."

The Death of Ezekiel's Wife Provides a Sign

A pathetic incident in his own personal life gave him the opportunity to reveal the truth.

Also the word of the Lord came to me, saying: "Son of man, behold, I take away from thee the desire of thine eyes with a stroke: yet neither shalt thou mourn nor weep, neither shall thy tears run down. Forbear to cry; make no mourning for the dead; bind thy turban upon thee, and put on thy shoes upon thy feet, and cover not thy lips, and eat not the bread of men."

So I spoke to the people in the morning; and at even my wife died; and I did in the morning as I was commanded.

And the people said to me, "Wilt thou not tell us what these things are to us, that thou doest?"

Then I answered them: "The word of the Lord came to me, saying, 'Speak to the house of Israel: Thus saith the Lord God: Behold, I will profane my sanctuary, the excellency of your strength, the desire of your eyes, and that which your soul pitieth; and your sons and your daughters whom ye have left behind shall fall by the sword. And ye shall do as I have done: ye shall not cover your lips, nor eat the bread of men; and your turbans shall be upon your heads, and your shoes upon your feet: ye shall not mourn nor weep; but ye shall pine away for your iniquities, and mourn one toward another. Thus Ezekiel is to you a sign: according to all that he hath done shall ye do.'"

THE DEATH OF EZEKIEL'S WIFE

She is mine,
My fair white lamb, mine only one; whilst thou
Hast many in thy calm fold on the hill
Of frankincense and myrrh, Lord: be content
To lead thy flock where shining waters sleep,
And leave the poor man in the wilderness
His one ewe lamb!

No weak tears
May fall upon the sacred fire; no sound
Of breaking human heart may mar the full
Majestic music of a Prophet's voice,
Speaking to all the ages from the mount
Of cloud and vision.

To speak for God—with such strange calm as God
Can give to dying men, or men with hearts
More dark than death could make them.

By my ruined home
I stand to speak for God, and stretch my hands,
Emptied of their sweet treasure, in God's Name
To all the people.

And when at length
The evening-time of my long day shall come,
And God shall give me leave to lay aside
The prophet's mournful mantle for the robe
Of joy and light—when at his gate I find
An everlasting entrance, there my love
Shall meet me, smiling.

                                           —*H. E. Lewis*

EZEKIEL'S IDEAL HOLY CITY

The prophecy now presents an elaborate ideal plan for reconstructing the Holy City, with greatly enlarged dimensions, revised and purified worship, a renovated and reconsecrated priesthood and a reallotment of the twelve tribes in the land of Israel. The government was to be in the hands of a prince, whose chief concern was to be for the purity of the sacred ceremonies. Instead of the dry Valley of the Kidron skirting the temple hill was to be a flowing stream of crystal water. This is one of the earliest and noblest visions of an ideal commonwealth to be found in all literature.

The Holy City Shall Be Served by Holy Priests

"The priests the Levites, the sons of Zadok,[13] that kept the charge of my sanctuary when the children of Israel went astray from me, they shall come near to me to minister to me, and they shall stand before me to offer to me the fat and the blood," saith the Lord God. "They shall enter into my sanctuary, and they shall come near to my table, to minister to me, and they shall keep my charge.

"And it shall come to pass, that when they enter in at the gates of the inner court, they shall be clothed with linen garments; and no wool shall come upon them, while they minister in the gates of the inner court, and within. They shall have linen turbans upon their heads, and shall have linen breeches upon their loins; they shall not gird themselves with anything that causeth sweat. And when they go forth into the outer court, even into the outer court to the people, they shall put off their garments wherein they ministered, and lay them in the holy chambers, and they shall put on other garments; and they

Gustave Doré

EZEKIEL PROPHESYING

shall not sanctify the people with their garments. "Neither shall they shave their heads, nor suffer their locks to grow long; they shall only poll their heads. Neither shall any priests drink wine, when they enter into the inner court. Neither shall they take for their wives a widow, nor her that is put away; but they shall take maidens of the lineage of the house of Israel, or a widow that had a priest before.

"And they shall teach my people the difference between the holy and profane, and cause them to discern between the unclean and the clean.[14] And in controversy they shall stand in judgment; and they shall judge it according to my judgments: and they shall keep my laws and my statutes in all mine assemblies; and they shall hallow my sabbaths."

Into This Purified City Shall God Reënter

Afterward he brought me to the gate, even the gate that looketh toward the east; and, behold, the glory of the God of Israel came from the way of the east: and his voice was like a noise of many waters: and the earth shone with his glory. And it was according to the appearance of the vision which I saw, even according to the vision that I saw when I came to destroy the city: and the visions were like the vision that I saw by the river Chebar; and I fell upon my face.

And the glory of the Lord came into the house by the way of the gate whose prospect is toward the east. So the spirit took me up, and brought me into the inner court; and, behold, the glory of the Lord filled the house.

And I heard him speaking to me out of the house; and the man stood by me. And he said to me, "Son of man, this is the place of my throne and the place of the soles of my feet, where I will dwell in the midst of the children of Israel forever.

"Thou, son of man, show the house to the house of Israel, that they may be ashamed of their iniquities: and let them measure the pattern. And if they be ashamed of all that they have done, show them the form of the house, and the fashion thereof, and the goings out thereof, and the comings in thereof, and all the forms thereof, and all the ordinances thereof, and all the forms thereof, and all the laws thereof; and write it in their sight, that they may keep the whole form thereof, and all the ordinances thereof, and do them.

"This is the law of the house: Upon the top of the mountain the whole limit thereof round about shall be most holy. Behold, this is the law of the house."

Then he brought me back the way of the gate of the outward sanctuary which looketh toward the east; and it was shut.

Then said the Lord to me, "This gate shall be shut; it shall not be opened, and no man shall enter in by it; because the Lord the God of Israel hath entered in by it, therefore it shall be shut.

"It is for the prince; the prince shall sit in it to eat bread before the Lord.

A Vision of Sabbath Keeping in the Renewed Jerusalem

"The gate of the inner court facing the east shall be shut the six working days; but on the sabbath it shall be opened, and on the day of the new moon it shall be opened.

"And the prince shall enter by the way of the porch of that gate without, and shall stand by the post of the gate, and the priests shall prepare his burnt offering and his peace offerings, and he shall worship at the threshold of the gate: then he shall go out; but the gate shall not be shut until evening.

"Likewise the people of the land shall worship at the door of this gate before the Lord on the sabbaths and on the new moons."

A Vision of the River of the Waters of Life

The only stream that is actually near the city of Jerusalem is the Brook Kidron, a dreary, dirty little brook, dry most of the year, which flows among cemeteries down into the desert. But in the prophet's vision of the happy future, it becomes a river of waters of life, copious and beautiful from its source in the sanctuary, and giving life and healing wherever its waters go.

Afterward he brought me again to the door of the house; and, behold, waters issued out from under the threshold of the house eastward, for the front of the house faced the east; and the waters came down from under, from the right side of the house at the south side of the altar. Then he brought me out by way of the north gate, and led me about by the way without to the outer gate, by the way that looketh eastward; and, behold, there ran out waters on the right side. When the man that had the line in his hand went forth eastward, he measured a thousand cubits, and he brought me through the waters; the waters were to the ankles. Again he measured a thousand, and brought me through the waters; the waters were to the knees. Again he measured a thousand, and brought me through the waters; the waters were to the loins. Afterward he measured a thousand; and it was a river that I could not pass over; for the waters were risen, waters to swim in, a river that could not be passed over. And he said to me, "Son of man, hast thou seen this?"

Then he brought me, and caused me to return to the bank of the river. Now when I had returned, behold, at the bank of the river were very many trees on the one side and on the other. Then he said to me: "These waters issue out toward the east country, and go down into the desert, and go into the [Dead] Sea; which being brought forth into the sea, the waters shall be sweetened. And it shall come to pass, that every thing that liveth, which moveth, whithersoever the rivers shall come, shall live; and there shall be a very great multitude of fish, because these waters shall come thither: for they shall be healed; and every thing shall live whither the river cometh. And it shall come to pass, that the fishers shall stand by it: from En-gedi even unto En-eglaim shall be a place to spread forth nets; their fish shall be according to their kinds, as the fish of the great sea, exceeding many. But the miry places thereof and the marshes thereof shall not be sweetened; they shall be given to salt. And by the river upon the bank thereof, on this side and on that side, shall grow all trees for food, neither shall the fruit thereof be consumed; it shall bring

THE DEAD SEA

This shore of the Dead Sea, nearly 1,300 feet below the level of the Mediterranean, is nearer the center of the earth than any other place in the world. The water is so shallow just here that the men in the boat might wade out a long distance if they could only stand upright in it; but this salt water is so very buoyant that one can neither walk in it up to his waist nor sink into it. In the north-eastern part of this sea the water is 1,300 feet deep.

forth new fruit every month, because the waters thereof issued out of the sanctuary; and the fruit thereof shall be for food, and the leaf thereof for medicine.

A Vision of the New Kingdom

"I will make them one nation in the land upon the mountains of Israel; and one king shall be king to them all: and they shall be no more two nations, neither shall they be divided into two kingdoms any more at all: neither shall they defile themselves any more with their idols, nor with their detestable things, nor with any of their transgressions: but I will save them out of all their dwelling places, wherein they have sinned, and will cleanse them: so shall they be my people, and I will be their God. And David my servant shall be king over them; and they all shall have one shepherd: they shall also walk in my judgments, and observe my statutes, and do them. And they shall dwell in the land that I have given to Jacob my servant, wherein your fathers have dwelt; and they shall dwell therein, even they, and their children, and their children's children forever: and my servant David shall be their prince forever.

"Moreover I will make a covenant of peace with them; it shall be an everlasting covenant with them: and I will place them, and multiply them, and will set my sanctuary in the midst of them forevermore. My tabernacle also shall be with them: yea, I will be their God, and they shall be my people. And the heathen shall know that I the Lord do sanctify Israel, when my sanctuary shall be in the midst of them forevermore.

A Vision of the Strangers Who Shall Help Rebuild the Holy City

"And it shall come to pass that ye shall divide the land by lot for an inheritance to you and to the strangers that sojourn among you, who shall have children among you. And they shall be to you as the home-born among the children of Israel;

they shall have inheritance with you among the tribes of Israel. And it shall come to pass that in whatsoever tribe the stranger sojourneth there shall ye give him his inheritance," saith the Lord.

"And the name of the city from that day shall be: The Lord Is There."

THE WATERS FROM THE EASTERN GATE

"And, behold, waters issued out from under the threshold of the house eastward."

East the forefront of habitations holy
Gleamed to Engedi, shone to Eneglaim;
Softly thereout and from thereunder slowly
Wandered the waters, and delayed, and came.

Then the great stream, which, having seen, he
　　　showeth,
Hid from the wise, but manifest to him,
Flowed and arose, as when Euphrates floweth,
Rose from the ankles till a man might swim.

Even with so soft a surge and an increasing,
Drunk of the sand and thwarted of the clod,
Stilled, and astir, and checked, and never-ceasing,
Spreadeth the great wave of the grace of God;

Bears to the marshes and the bitter places
Healing for hurt, and for their poisons, balm;
Isle after isle in infinite embraces
Floods and enfolds and fringes with the palm.

—*F. W. H. Myers*

ISAIAH, PROPHET OF THE MESSIAH

In later Isaiah are the great prophecies that consoled the people of Israel during their exile. The keynote of the entire message is struck in the opening words:

"Comfort ye, comfort ye my people," saith your God.
"Speak ye comfortingly to Jerusalem,
And cry to her that her warfare is accomplished."

There are two great thoughts in this "Evangelist of the Old Testament."

The first is the thought of God. He is "the Holy One of Israel." He is the only God who exists, the Creator of heaven and earth, the God of history and of prophecy, whose purposes are infinite, cannot be resisted, and are all in behalf of his people. Just now he has chosen Cyrus the Persian as his shepherd and king to gather his scattered flock, and to fulfil his pleasure concerning Jerusalem. The second thought is of the Servant of Jehovah. The kingdom has been destroyed; so we no longer read of a Davidic king to prosper Israel's cause. Now God's will is to be done by a servant. At first Israel is that servant:

"He said to me: 'Thou art my servant;
O Israel, in whom I will be glorified.'"

Later, Israel seems to be personified in an individual, the Man of Sorrows, of whose travail comes an infinite satisfaction.

It is a book of shadow and sunshine, a book of redemption and glory, a book of triumph through suffering.

A HYMN OF THE HOLY ONE OF ISRAEL

"COMFORT ye, comfort ye my people," saith your God.
"Speak ye comfortingly to Jerusalem,
And cry to her that her warfare is accomplished,
That her iniquity is pardoned;
For she hath received of the Lord's hand
Double for all her sins."
The voice of him that crieth:

"Prepare ye in the wilderness the way of the Lord;
Make straight in the desert a highway for our God!
Every valley shall be lifted up,
Every mountain and hill shall be made low;
The crooked shall be made straight,
The rough places plain!
The glory of the Lord shall be revealed,
And all flesh shall see it together;
For the mouth of the Lord hath spoken it."

The voice said, "Cry!"
And he said, "What shall I cry?
All flesh is grass,
And all the goodliness thereof is as the flower of the field.
The grass withereth, the flower fadeth,
Because the spirit of the Lord bloweth upon it.
Surely the people is grass.
The grass withereth, the flower fadeth,
But the word of our God shall stand forever."

O Zion, that bringest good tidings,
Get thee up into the high mountain!
O Jerusalem, that bringest good tidings,
Lift up thy voice with strength!
Lift it up, be not afraid!
Say to the cities of Judah:
"Behold your God!
Behold, the Lord God will come with strong hand,
And his arm shall rule for him;
Behold, his reward is with him,
And his work before him.
He shall feed his flock like a shepherd:
He shall gather the lambs with his arm,
And carry them in his bosom,
And shall gently lead those that have their young."

Who hath measured the waters in the hollow of his hand,
And meted out heaven with the span,
And comprehended the dust of the earth in a measure,
And weighed the mountains in scales,
And the hills in a balance?
Who hath directed the spirit of the Lord?
Or being his counselor hath taught him?
With whom took he counsel, and who instructed him,
And taught him in the path of justice,
And taught him knowledge,
And showed to him the way of understanding?

Behold, the nations are as a drop of a bucket,
And are counted as the small dust of the balance;
Behold, he taketh up the isles as a very little thing.
And Lebanon is not sufficient to burn,
Nor the beasts thereof sufficient for a burnt offering.
All the nations before him are as nothing;
They are accounted by him as less than nothing, and vanity.

To whom then will ye liken God?
Or what likeness will be compared to him?
The workman melteth a graven image,
And the goldsmith spreadeth it over with gold,
And casteth silver chains.
He that is so impoverished that he hath no oblation
Chooseth a tree that will not rot;
He seeketh to him a skilful workman
To prepare a graven image, that shall not be moved.

Have ye not known? have ye not heard?
Hath it not been told you from the beginning?
Have ye not understood from the foundations of the earth?
It is he that sitteth above the circle of the earth,
And the inhabitants thereof are as grasshoppers;

That stretcheth out the heavens as a curtain,
And spreadeth them out as a tent to dwell in;
That bringeth the princes to nothing;
He maketh the judges of the earth as vanity.
Yea, they shall not be planted;
Yea, they shall not be sown;
Yea, their stock shall not take root in the earth.
And he shall also blow upon them, and they shall wither,
And the whirlwind shall take them away as stubble.

"To whom then will ye liken me, or shall I be equal?"
Saith the Holy One.
Lift up your eyes on high,
And behold who hath created these things,
That bringeth out their host by number;
He calleth them all by name;
By the greatness of his might, and because he is strong in
　　　　power,
Not one faileth.
Why sayest thou, O Jacob,
And speakest, O Israel,
"My way is hid from the Lord,
And my judgment is passed over from my God"?

Hast thou not known? hast thou not heard
That the everlasting God, the Lord,
The Creator of the ends of the earth,
Fainteth not, neither is weary?
There is no searching of his understanding.
He giveth power to the faint;
And to them that have no might he increaseth strength.
Even the youths shall faint and be weary,
And the young men shall utterly fall.
But they that wait upon the Lord shall renew their strength;
They shall mount up with wings as eagles;

They shall run, and not be weary;
They shall walk, and not faint.

THE FALL OF BABYLON

Come down, and sit in the dust, O virgin daughter of Babylon, sit on the ground: there is no throne, O daughter of the Chaldeans; for thou shalt no more be called "tender and delicate."

Take the millstones, and grind meal: uncover thy locks, pass over the rivers. Thy nakedness shall be uncovered, yea, thy shame shall be seen. Sit thou silent, and get thee into darkness, O daughter of the Chaldeans: for thou shalt no more be called "the lady of kingdoms." And thou saidst, "I shall be a lady forever": so that thou didst not lay these things to thy heart, neither didst remember the latter end of it. Therefore hear now this, thou that art given to pleasures, that dwellest carelessly, that sayest in thy heart, "I am, and none else besides me; I shall not sit as a widow, neither shall I know the loss of children." But these two things shall come to thee in a moment in one day, the loss of children, and widowhood: they shall come upon thee in their perfection for the multitude of thy sorceries, and for the great abundance of thine enchantments.

For thou hast trusted in thy wickedness: thou hast said, "None seeth me." Thy wisdom and thy knowledge, it hath perverted thee; and thou hast said in thy heart, "I am, and none else besides me." Therefore shall evil come upon thee; thou shalt not know from whence it ariseth: and mischief shall fall upon thee; thou shalt not be able to put it off: and desolation shall come upon thee suddenly, which thou shalt not know. Stand now with thine enchantments, and with the multitude of thy sorceries, wherein thou hast labored from thy youth; if so be thou shalt be able to profit, if so be thou mayest prevail.

Thou art wearied in the multitude of thy counsels. Let now the astrologers, the star-gazers, the monthly prognosticators, stand up, and save thee from these things that shall come upon thee. Behold, they shall be as stubble; the fire shall burn them; they shall not deliver themselves from the power of the flame: there shall not be a coal to warm at, nor fire to sit before it.

Thus shall they be to thee with whom thou hast labored, even thy merchants, from thy youth: they shall wander every one to his quarter; none shall save thee.

Go ye forth of Babylon,
Flee ye from the Chaldeans;

with a voice of singing declare ye, tell this, utter it even to the end of the earth. Say ye:

"The Lord hath redeemed his servant Jacob:
And they thirsted not when he led them through the
deserts:
He caused the waters to flow out of the rock for them:
He clave the rock also, and the waters gushed out.
There is no peace, saith the Lord, to the wicked."

THE SERVANT WHO SUFFERS AND IS SATISFIED

Behold, my servant shall deal prudently;
He shall be exalted and extolled,
And be very high.

As many were astonished at thee
(His visage was so marred more than any man,
And his form more than the sons of men),
So shall he sprinkle many nations.

Kings shall shut their mouths at him;
For that which had not been told them shall they see,
And that which they had not heard shall they consider.

Who hath believed our report?
And to whom is the arm of the Lord revealed?
For he shall grow up before him like a tender plant,
And as a root out of a dry ground.

He hath no form nor comeliness;
And when we shall see him, there is no beauty that we
        should desire him.

He is despised and rejected of men;
A man of sorrows, and acquainted with grief:
And we hid, as it were, our faces from him;
He was despised, and we esteemed him not.
Surely he hath borne our griefs,
And carried our sorrows:
Yet we did esteem him stricken,
Smitten of God, and afflicted!

He was wounded for our transgressions,
He was bruised for our iniquities:
The chastisement of our peace was upon him,
And by his stripes we are healed.

All we like sheep have gone astray;
We have turned every one to his own way;
And the Lord hath laid on him
The iniquity of us all.

He was oppressed, and he was afflicted,
Yet he opened not his mouth:
He is brought as a lamb to the slaughter,
And as a sheep before her shearers is dumb,
So he openeth not his mouth.

He was taken from prison and from judgment,
And who shall declare his generation?

For he was cut off from the land of the living:
For the transgression of my people was he stricken.

And he made his grave with the wicked,
And with the rich, in his death;
Because he had done no violence,
Neither was any deceit in his mouth.

Yet it pleased the Lord to bruise him;
He hath put him to grief.
When thou shalt make his soul an offering for sin,
He shall see his posterity, he shall prolong his days,
And the pleasure of the Lord shall prosper in his hand.
He shall see of the travail of his soul, and be satisfied:
By his knowledge shall my righteous servant justify many;
For he shall bear their iniquities.

Therefore will I divide him a portion with the great,
And he shall divide the spoil with the strong;
Because he poured out his soul unto death,
And he was numbered with the transgressors:
And he bore the sin of many,
And made intercession for the transgressors.

OBADIAH

PROPHET OF HOPE IN THE HOUR OF GLOOM

DOWN the throats of the treacherous and cruelly exultant Edomites, Obadiah thrust Israel's defiance, and with it her invincible hope. Then, there is silence; and we hear his voice no more.

But, in that one cry, there is the intensity of accumulated passion, the pent-up force of centuries of hatred. The blood feud between Israel and Edom is perhaps the longest in history. It began on the day that Jacob deceived and supplanted his brother Esau. It continued throughout the careers of both races, projecting itself into the Christian era in the hated rule of the Herods, and ended only with the overthrow of Israel by Rome.

Commanding as she did both the ports of the Gulf of Akaba and the caravan routes from Arabia to Gaza and Damascus, the very location of Edom was such as to maintain perpetual animosity between herself and Israel. A hundred miles by about twenty of rugged and mountainous territory, grandly picturesque with cliffs and chasms and tangled hills and slim valleys; climbing eastward to the rocky stretches of the eastern plateau, dropping precipitately westward to the desert "Arabah"; well supplied with living springs and streams of water, with cornfields and vineyards, high and lifted up in the clefts of rocks reached only through narrow and deep defiles; such, in brief, was the location of Edom. Thus impregnably situated, and in control of the southeastern trade routes, she had been a constant source of bitterness to Israel.

And this antagonism, arising out of the conflicting material and national interests of both, was intensified into the deepest hatred by the added conflict in their ideals. For Edom was essentially materialistic in all her aims. Secure in the fastnesses of her hills, she pursued after wealth and grandeur with a vigor that made her worldly-wise men a byword and a proverb.

Israel, on the other hand, despite her manifold weaknesses, had pursued after the ideal of a knowledge of God. Consequently, her sorrow was turned to the gall of bitterness when Edom, hated Edom, vengefully leagued with pagan Babylon to destroy Judah. "Remember, O Lord," wrote a psalmist years later, "the children of Edom in the days of Jerusalem; who said, 'Rase it! Rase it, even to the foundation thereof!'" But, in the very hour almost of Judah's desolation and Edom's vaunting, Obadiah cried aloud his prediction of Edom's doom and Israel's restoration. Were Edom never so high in the security of hills, the Lord would yet bring her down; complete beyond recovery would be her ruin; but the remnant of Israel would return to their land in security and power. Such was the triumphant hope of this swift and fleeting voice among the prophets!

OBADIAH

THE DOOM OF EDOM

THUS saith the Lord God concerning Edom: "We have
heard a rumor from the Lord, and an ambassador is
sent among the nations, saying, 'Arise ye, and let us
rise up against her in battle.'"
Behold, I have made thee small among the nations:
Thou art greatly despised.
The pride of thy heart hath deceived thee,
Thou that dwellest in the clefts of the rock,
Whose habitation is high;
That saith in his heart,
"Who shall bring me down to the ground?"
Though thou exalt thyself as the eagle,
And though thou set thy nest among the stars,
Thence will I bring thee down, saith the Lord.

EDOM'S BRIEF REJOICING

If thieves came to thee, if robbers by night
(How art thou cut off!),
Would they not steal only till they had enough?
If grape-gatherers came to thee,
Would they not leave some gleaning grapes?
How are the things of Esau searched out!
How are his hidden things sought up!

All the men of thy confederacy
    Have brought thee even to the border:
The men that were at peace with thee
    Have deceived thee and prevailed against thee.

They that eat thy bread lay a snare under thee:
 There is no understanding in him.
Shall I not in that day, saith the Lord,
Destroy the wise men out of Edom,
And understanding out of the mount of Esau?
And thy mighty men, O Teman, shall be dismayed,
So that every one of the mount of Esau may be cut off
  by slaughter.

For thy violence against thy brother Jacob
Shame shall cover thee,
And thou shalt be cut off forever.
In the day that thou stoodest on the other side,
In the day that the strangers carried away captive his
  substance,
And foreigners entered into his gates,
And cast lots upon Jerusalem,
Even thou wast as one of them.
But thou shouldst not have looked on the day of thy
  brother
In the day that he became a captive;
Neither shouldst thou have rejoiced over the children of
  Judah
In the day of their destruction;
Neither shouldst thou have spoken proudly
In the day of distress.[15]

Neither shouldst thou have stood in the crossway,
To cut off those of his that did escape;
Neither shouldst thou have delivered up those of his that
  did remain
In the day of their calamity.

For the day of the Lord is near
Upon all the nations:

As thou hast done, it shall be done to thee;
Thy dealings shall return upon thine own head.
For as ye have drunk upon my holy mountain,
So shall all the nations drink continually;
Yea, they shall drink, and swallow down,
And shall be as though they had not been.

THE TRIUMPH OF ZION

But in mount Zion shall be those that escape,
And it shall be holy,
And the house of Jacob shall possess their possessions.
And the house of Jacob shall be a fire,
And the house of Joseph a flame,
And the house of Esau for stubble,
And they shall burn among them and devour them,
And there shall not be any remaining of the house of
       Esau;
For the Lord hath spoken it.
And they of the South shall possess the mount of Esau,
And they of the lowland the Philistines;
And they shall possess the field of Ephraim, and the field
       of Samaria,
And Benjamin shall possess Gilead.
And the captives of this host of the children of Israel
Shall possess that which belongeth to the Canaanites,
Even unto Zarephath;
And the captives of Jerusalem, that are in Sepharad,
Shall possess the cities of the South.
And saviors shall come upon mount Zion
To judge the mount of Esau;
And the kingdom shall be the Lord's.

HAGGAI AND ZECHARIAH

In reading of the rebuilding of the Temple under Zerubbabel one learns how the inspiration for the work came from the cheering words of two prophets. Haggai was an old man who had seen the first temple, and Zechariah was his younger helper.

We will not quote further from the earlier prophet, but the words of Zechariah are so picturesque that four of his visions of the coming days of purity and peace are quoted below. In the first, God's law is pictured pursuing the evildoer. In the second, God's angels are seen on horseback, returned after going to and fro in the earth. They report that the earth is still and at rest, and one of them obtains from God the promise that Zion shall be comforted. In the third, the prophet sees Wickedness, under the figure of a woman, carried off in a barrel to Babylonia, whence she came. In the fourth, four celestial chariots go forth to the four winds to protect Jerusalem against any invader, and return in peace.

VISIONS OF WARNING AND CHEER

The Vision of the Flying Roll

THEN I turned, and lifted up mine eyes, and looked, and, behold, a flying roll. And he said to me, "What seest thou?"

And I answered, "I see a flying roll; the length thereof is twenty cubits, and the breadth thereof ten cubits."

Then said he to me, "This is the curse that goeth forth over the face of the whole earth: for every one that stealeth shall be cut off as on this side according to it; and every one that sweareth shall be cut off as on that side according to it.

"I will bring it forth," saith the Lord of hosts, "and it shall enter into the house of the thief, and into the house of him that sweareth falsely by my name: and it shall remain in the midst of his house, and shall consume it with the timber thereof and the stones thereof."

HAGGAI

From a fresco by Sargent

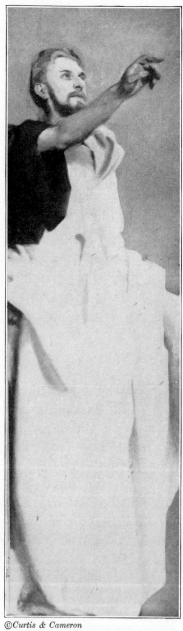

ZECHARIAH

From a fresco by Sargent

A Vision of God's Horsemen

The prophet dates his vision "in the second year of Darius," a time of revolts in various provinces of the Medo-Persian empire. Just now these rebellions had temporarily subsided, but hope of eventual release was suggesting itself to the freedom-loving people of Judah.

I saw by night, and, behold, a man riding upon a red horse, and he stood among the myrtle trees that were in the bottom; and behind him were there red horses, speckled and white.

Then said I, "O my lord, what are these?"

And the angel that talked with me said to me, "I will show thee what these be."

And the man that stood among the myrtle trees answered and said, "These are they whom the Lord hath sent to walk to and fro through the earth."

And they answered the angel of the Lord that stood among the myrtle trees, and said, "We have walked to and fro through the earth; and, behold, all the earth sitteth still, and is at rest."

Then the angel of the Lord answered and said, "O Lord of hosts, how long wilt thou not have mercy on Jerusalem and on the cities of Judah, against which thou hast had indignation these threescore and ten years?"[16]

And the Lord answered the angel that talked with me with good words and comfortable words.

So the angel that communed with me said to me: "Cry thou, saying, 'Thus saith the Lord of hosts: I am jealous for Jerusalem and for Zion with a great jealousy. And I am very sore displeased with the heathen that are at ease; for I was but a little displeased, and they helped forward the affliction. Therefore thus saith the Lord: I am returned to Jerusalem with mercies: my house shall be built in it, saith the Lord of hosts, and a line shall be stretched forth upon Jerusalem.' Cry yet, saying, 'Thus saith the Lord of hosts: My cities through prosperity shall yet be spread abroad; and the Lord shall yet comfort Zion, and shall yet choose Jerusalem.'"

The Vision of the Woman in a Barrel

Then the angel that talked with me went forth, and said to me, "Lift up now thine eyes, and see what is this that goeth forth."

And I said, "What is it?"

And he said, "This is a barrel that goeth forth." He said moreover, "And this is a woman sitting in the midst of the barrel." And he said, "This is Wickedness." And he cast her down into the midst of the barrel: and he cast a weight of lead upon the mouth thereof.

Then lifted I up mine eyes, and saw, and, behold, there came forth two women, and the wind was in their wings. Now they had wings like the wings of a stork; and they lifted up the barrel between earth and heaven.

Then said I to the angel that talked with me, "Whither do these bear the barrel?"

And he said to me, "To build her a house in the land of Shinar: and when it is prepared, she shall be set there in her own place."

The Vision of the Four Chariots

And I turned and lifted up mine eyes, and looked, and, behold, there came four chariots out from between the two mountains; and the mountains were mountains of brass. In the first chariot were red horses; and in the second chariot black horses; and in the third chariot white horses; and in the fourth chariot grizzled and bay horses.

Then I answered and said to the angel that talked with me, "What are these, my lord?"

And the angel answered and said to me, "These are the four spirits of the heavens, that go forth from standing before the Lord of all the earth. The black horses which are therein go forth into the north country; and the white go forth after them; and the grizzled go forth toward the south country."

And the bay went forth, and sought to go that they might walk to and fro through the earth; and he said, "Get you hence, walk to and fro through the earth."

So they walked to and fro through the earth.

Then cried he upon me, and spoke to me, saying, "Behold, they that go toward the north country have quieted my spirit in the north country."

Facing the four winds of heaven, chariots go forth to fulfil God's judgments upon the nations that had oppressed Israel. The prophet was comforted because those who first went departed northward, to bring retribution upon Assyria.

MALACHI

From a painting by James J. Tissot

MALACHI

We know what were the conditions that Nehemiah and Ezra endeavored to correct. The people had already begun to neglect the temple that Zerubbabel had rebuilt, and were cheating in making their offerings to Jehovah. They were divorcing their Jewish wives and marrying among the heathen, oppressing the poor, and living greedily.

Against these evils arose a prophet. Malachi means "My Messenger." This author was truly a "messenger" from Jehovah, but he promises a greater yet to come.

Here is his argument: God loves Israel, but Israel has forgotten God and is slighting his worship. Some powerful messenger must come, a second Elijah in sternness and patience, to bring Israel back to its God.

A DIVINE MESSENGER PROMISED

BEHOLD, I will send my messenger,
And he shall prepare the way before me:
And the Lord, whom ye seek,
Shall suddenly come to his temple.
But who may endure the day of his coming?
And who shall stand when he appeareth?
For he is like a refiner's fire
And like fullers' soap:
And he shall sit as a refiner and purifier of silver,
And he shall purify the sons of Levi,
And refine them as gold and silver,
That they may offer to the Lord an offering in righteous-
  ness.
Then shall the offering of Judah and Jerusalem
Be pleasant to the Lord,
As in the days of old,
And as in former years.

I will come near to you to judgment;
And I will be a swift witness

95

©*Curtis & Cameron*

MALACHI
From a fresco by John S. Sargent

Against the sorcerers, and against the adulterers,
And against false swearers,
And against those who oppress the hireling in his wages,
The widow and the fatherless;
That turn aside the stranger from his right,
And fear not me, saith the Lord of hosts.
For I am the Lord, I change not;
Therefore ye, sons of Jacob, are not consumed.

THE BLESSING OF REMEMBERING GOD

"Will a man rob God?
Yet ye have robbed me.

But ye say, 'Wherein have we robbed thee?'
In tithes and offerings.
Ye are cursed with a curse,
For ye have robbed me,
Even this whole nation.
Bring ye all the tithes into the storehouse,
That there may be food in my house,
And prove me now herewith,"
Saith the Lord of hosts,
"If I will not open you the windows of heaven,
And pour you out a blessing,
That there shall not be room enough to receive it."

Then they that feared the Lord spoke often one with
        another;
And the Lord hearkened and heard.
And a book of remembrance was written before him,
Of them that feared the Lord,
And that thought upon his name.
"And they shall be mine," saith the Lord of hosts,
"In the day when I make up my jewels."

A SECOND ELIJAH

Behold, I will send you Elijah the prophet
Before the coming of the great and dreadful day of the
        Lord:
And he shall turn the heart of the fathers to the children,
And the heart of the children to their fathers,
Lest I come and smite the earth with a curse.

JOEL AND OBADIAH

From a fresco by John S. Sargent

Joel hides his averted face under his heavy mantle as if unwilling to see the doom that was destined to overthrow his nation. Obadiah grasps his head in both hands as if his brain were reeling under the shock of his visions. They see looming large upon the horizon those menacing forms which became so clear to later prophets. In their present agony, they see no hope, but later we shall hear the comforting words, "Thou wilt keep him in perfect peace whose mind is stayed on thee."

JOEL

Joel was a prophet of Judea, and particularly of Jerusalem. The date of his prophesying is uncertain; but as he mentions the Greeks, and speaks of the walls of the city as standing, he probably lived near the close of the Persian period. The occasion of his prophecies was, first, the recent occurrence of a devastating invasion of locusts, and, secondly, a time a few months later, when the land had begun to recover its fruitfulness again. He describes the visitation with marvelous realism and without exaggeration, as various modern writers testify. He makes fine use of the lessons of the plague to point his people to the saving power of the Lord and to the outpouring of the Spirit that is to come on all the people.

THE OVERCOMING OF DISASTER

THE ONCOMING OF THE LOCUSTS

THAT which the palmer-worm hath left hath the lo-
cust eaten;
And that which the locust hath left hath the canker-worm
eaten;
And that which the canker-worm hath left hath the cater-
pillar eaten.[17]
For a nation is come up on my land,
Strong, and without number;
Whose teeth are the teeth of a lion,
And he hath the cheek teeth of a lioness.
He hath laid my vine waste,
And barked my fig tree:
He hath made it clean bare, and cast it away;
The branches thereof are made white.

Blow ye the trumpet in Zion,
Sound an alarm in my holy mountain:
Let all the inhabitants of the land tremble:
For the day of the Lord cometh,

A SWARM OF LOCUSTS FLYING OVER JERUSALEM

Photograph by American Colony, Jerusalem

Infinite in number, the locusts devour everything living. In the prophet's vision they typify the invading enemies of Israel.

For it is nigh at hand:
A day of darkness and of gloominess,
A day of clouds and of thick darkness,
As the morning spread upon the mountains!
A great people and a strong:
There hath not been ever the like,
Neither shall be any more after it,
Even to the years of many generations.
A fire devoureth before them,
And behind them a flame burneth.
The land is like the garden of Eden before them,
And behind them a desolate wilderness;
Yea, and nothing shall escape them.

The appearance of them is like the appearance of horses,
And like horsemen so shall they run.
Like the noise of chariots on the tops of mountains shall
        they leap,
Like the noise of a flame of fire that devoureth the stubble,
Like a strong people set in battle array.
Before their face the people shall be much pained:
All faces shall gather blackness.

They shall run like mighty men;
They shall climb the wall like men of war;
And they shall march every one in his ways,
And they shall not break their ranks.
Neither shall one thrust the other;
They shall walk every one in his path;
And when they fall upon the sword, they shall not be
        wounded.
They shall run to and fro in the city;
They shall run up on the wall;
They shall climb up into the houses;
They shall enter in at the windows like a thief.

Sir Edwin Landseer

KING OF THE FOREST
"Be not afraid, ye beasts of the field."

The earth shall quake before them;
The heavens shall tremble;
The sun and the moon shall be dark,
And the stars shall withdraw their shining:
And the Lord shall utter his voice before his army;
For his host is very great;
For he is strong that executeth his word:
For the day of the Lord is great and very terrible;
And who can abide it?

The Outcry of the People

Therefore also now, saith the Lord,
Turn ye to me with all your heart,
And with fasting, and with weeping, and with mourning;
And rend your heart, and not your garments,
And turn to the Lord your God;
For he is gracious and merciful,
Slow to anger, and of great kindness.
Who knoweth if he will turn,
And repent and leave a blessing behind him?

Blow the trumpet in Zion!
Sanctify a fast, call a solemn assembly:
Gather the people,
Sanctify the congregation,
Assemble the elders, gather the children.
Let the bridegroom go forth from his chamber,
And the bride out of her pavilion.
Let the priests, the ministers of the Lord,
Weep between the porch and the altar,
And let them say, "Spare thy people, O Lord,
And give not thy heritage to reproach,
That the heathen should rule over them.
Wherefore should they say among the people,
'Where is their God?'"

After the Departure of the Locusts

Then will the Lord be jealous for his land,
And pity his people.
Yea, the Lord will answer and say to his people,
"Behold, I will send you grain, and wine, and oil,
And ye shall be satisfied therewith;
And I will no more make you a reproach among the
heathen."

THE OLD LACE MAKER

From a painting by Nikolaas Maes

As old age makes the day's task more and more wearisome, this old saint turns to the passage in Joel, "And it shall come to pass, that whosoever shall call on the name of the Lord shall be delivered."

Fear not, O land, be glad and rejoice;
For the Lord will do great things.
Be not afraid, ye beasts of the field:
For the pastures of the wilderness do spring,
For the tree beareth its fruit,
The fig tree and the vine do yield their strength.
Be glad then, ye children of Zion,
And rejoice in the Lord your God;
For he giveth you the former rain moderately;
He causeth to come down for you the rain,
The former rain and the latter rain, in the first month.
The floors shall be full of wheat,
And the vats shall overflow with wine and oil.
I will restore to you the years that the locust hath eaten,
The canker-worm, and the caterpillar, and the palmer-
        worm,
My great army which I sent among you.
And ye shall eat in plenty, and be satisfied,
And praise the name of the Lord your God,
Who hath dealt wondrously with you.
My people shall never be put to shame;
And ye shall know that I am in the midst of Israel;
That I am the Lord your God, and there is none else.
My people shall never be put to shame.

And it shall come to pass afterward,
That I will pour out my spirit upon all flesh:
And your sons and your daughters shall prophesy;
Your old men shall dream dreams;
Your young men shall see visions.
And also upon the menservants and upon the handmaids
In those days will I pour out my spirit.
And it shall come to pass,
That whosoever shall call on the name of the Lord shall
        be delivered.

A Host of Peace Enters Jerusalem

The poet, in his trust that God will relieve the city from its foes, imagines a processional about to enter the rebuilt gates after its deliverance.

In that day shall this song be sung in the land of Judah:

We have a strong city;
Salvation will God appoint for walls and bulwarks.
Open ye the gates,
That the righteous nation that keepeth the truth may
　　enter in.
Thou wilt keep him in perfect peace whose mind is stayed
　　on thee,
Because he trusteth in thee.
Trust ye in the Lord forever,
For in the Lord Jehovah is everlasting strength.

ANTICIPATION OF THE MESSIAH

BEHOLD, THY KING COMETH!

Still the hope that a king would arise to deliver the Hebrews did not die; and in this song the longed-for deliverer is pictured as having already won the victory, returning in triumph to his capital.

REJOICE greatly, O daughter of Zion!
Shout, O daughter of Jerusalem!
Behold, thy King cometh to thee:
He is just, and having salvation;
Lowly, and riding upon an ass,
On a colt, the foal of an ass.
I will cut off the chariot from Ephraim
And the horse from Jerusalem,
And the battle-bow shall be cut off.
He shall speak peace to the heathen;
And his dominion shall be from sea even to sea,
And from the River even to the ends of the earth.
As for thee also, by the blood of thy covenant,
I have sent forth thy prisoners out of the pit wherein is
　　　　no water.
Turn you to the stronghold, ye prisoners of hope:
Even today do I declare, "I will render double unto thee."

THERE SHALL BE ONE LORD

Ezekiel speaks of the River of Life as flowing from the Temple down to the Dead Sea. This prophetic writer sees that stream flowing both to the western and the eastern seas, and perennially, summer and winter.

And it shall come to pass in that day,
That the light shall not be clear, nor dark;

107

"AT EVENING–TIME IT SHALL BE LIGHT"

But it shall be one day that is known to the Lord,
Not day, nor night;
But it shall come to pass,
That at evening-time it shall be light.

And it shall be in that day
That living waters shall go out from Jerusalem;
Half of them toward the eastern sea,
And half of them toward the western sea;
In summer and in winter shall it be.
And the Lord shall be King over all the earth:
In that day there shall be one Lord, and his name one.

PROPHETS

Made of unpurchasable stuff,
They went the way when ways were rough;
They, when the traitors had deceived,
Held the long purpose, and believed;
They, when the face of God grew dim,
Held thro' the dark and trusted him—
Brave souls that fought the mortal way
And felt that faith could not betray.

Give thanks for heroes that have stirred
Earth with the wonder of a word;
But all thanksgiving for the brerd
Who have blent destiny with deed—
Souls of the high heroic birth,
Souls sent to poise the shaken earth;
And then called back to God again
To make heaven possible for men.

JUSTICE

From a painting by Raphael

Raphael presents to us in this picture the well-known symbols.   Justice is a goddess seated upon the clouds of heaven.   By this he means to say that Justice is a divine attribute.   This idea is still further emphasized by the heavenly cherubs that surround her. The goddess carries in her left hand the balances, which here are evenly poised, symbol that justice is nothing if not exact, equable, impartial.   The face of the goddess is turned away because she must be no respecter of persons.   In her right hand she carries a sword, symbol of the divine power that will execute the judgment awarded by the scales.

SOCIAL IDEALS OF THE HEBREWS

SOCIAL IDEALS OF THE HEBREWS

"Love the Lord Thy God . . . and Thy Neighbor
as Thyself"

IT has been said that the discovery that the great teachers
of the Jews were above all else social teachers and reformers is revolutionizing the study of the Bible. We
have come to see that the Bible is not only a religious book,
but a social book. It has not merely one great aim, but two.
It shows men how they may come to know God and find life
and freedom in his service. It also shows how they may live
in right relations with their fellow-men, and thus develop
that fair and happy social order which we call the Kingdom
of God.

In Volume Two we may read how the prophets, during the
troublous days of Israel's decline, were ever insisting that
only as men showed their love to God by right social living
could they have any assurance of peace and success. We may
also read how the world-wide Kingdom, which had its heart
in Israel, is a kingdom of brotherhood.

The following sayings, chiefly from the prophets, are chosen to bring out, first, the passionate hatred of injustice
and oppression in these great men; and, second, the means
that they foresaw by which oppression and injustice may be
brought to an end, and the kingdom of Heaven may triumph.

The sins that are here described, and the miseries and
sorrows that result from them, are startlingly modern. Many
of these indictments might have been drawn up by some of
the most passionate social reformers of our own day.

GOD'S ATTITUDE TOWARD SOCIAL INIQUITY

HIS UNCOMPROMISING JUSTICE

I

THE Lord shall be for a sanctuary;
But for a stone of stumbling and for a rock of offense
to both the houses of Israel,
And for a gin and for a snare to the inhabitants of Jerusalem.

II

Thou hast been a strength to the poor,
A refuge to the needy in his distress,
A refuge from the storm,
A shadow from the heat,
When the blast of the terrible ones is as a storm against
the wall.

III

Thus saith the Lord of hosts:

These are the things that ye shall do:
Speak ye every man the truth to his neighbor;
Execute the judgment of truth and peace in your
gates;
And let none of you imagine evil in his heart against
his neighbor;
And love no false oath.

IV

He bringeth down them that dwell on high;
The lofty city, he layeth it low;
He layeth it low, even to the ground;

He bringeth it even to the dust.
The foot shall tread it down; even the feet of the poor,
And the steps of the needy.

The way of the just is uprightness;
Thou, O Most Upright, dost weigh the path of the just.
Yea, in the way of thy justice, O Lord, have we waited
        for thee;
The desire of our soul is to thy name,
And to the remembrance of thee.

With my soul have I desired thee in the night;
Yea, with my spirit within me will I seek thee early;
For when thy judgments are in the earth,
The inhabitants of the world will learn righteousness.

V

Their land is full of silver and gold,
Neither is there any end to their treasures;
Their land is also full of horses,
Neither is there any end to their chariots;
Their land also is full of idols;
They worship the work of their own hands,
That which their own fingers have made.

The loftiness of man shall be bowed down,
And the haughtiness of men shall be made low,
And the Lord alone shall be exalted,
And the idols shall he utterly abolish.

VI

Hear the word of the Lord,
O king of Judah, that sittest upon the throne of David,
Thou and thy servants and thy people that enter in by
        these gates.

Thus saith the Lord:
Execute ye justice and righteousness,
And deliver the spoiled out of the hand of the oppressor;
And do no wrong, do no violence
To the stranger, the fatherless and the widow;
Neither shed innocent blood in this place.
For if ye do this thing indeed,
Then there shall enter in by the gates of this house kings
        sitting upon the throne of David,
Riding in chariots and on horses,
He and his servants and his people.

VII

I, even I, am he that comforteth you.
Who art thou, that thou shouldst be afraid of a man that
        shall die,
And of the son of man that shall be made as grass;
And forgettest the Lord thy Maker,
Who hath stretched forth the heavens,
And laid the foundations of the earth;
And hast feared continually every day
Because of the oppressor, as if he were ready to destroy?
And where is the fury of the oppressor?
The captive exile hasteneth that he may be loosed,
And that he should not die in the pit,
Nor that his bread should fail.

But I am the Lord thy God,
That divided the sea, whose waves roared.
The Lord of hosts is his name.
And I have put my words in thy mouth,
And I have covered thee in the shadow of my hand,
That I may plant the heavens,
And lay the foundations of the earth,
And say to Zion, "Thou art my people."

CORRUPT LEGISLATION

From a fresco by Elihu Vedder

On the right the factory chimneys are belching smoke. Prosperity is in full blast. An elderly figure who evidently controls the money box and the bags at his feet, the profits of the roaring mills, has taken his seat beside the wanton figure of Justice. An open Book of the Law is on his lap, but the aim of this master of industry is to know the law only to evade it, and he places the bag of gold in the pan of the scales while he looks intently at the face of Justice to note the effect. The eyes of the goddess are unbandaged. She desires to see, for she is a respecter of persons and not an impartial executive.

On the other side of the picture the factories stand cold and empty. A youthful figure presents his argument to the goddess—the argument of the empty distaff and the useless spindle. But Justice, seated under her fruitful vine, enthroned between cornucopias that are bursting with gold, refuses to listen to any plea that has not a golden luster.

This picture is a symbol of the age-old conflict between justice and greed, between the right to live and work, and the desire to possess and dominate.

PROTESTS AGAINST CORRUPTION

AGAINST INDIFFERENCE TO SOCIAL EVILS

I

YEA, the stork in the heaven knoweth her appointed
    times;
And the turtledove and the crane and the swallow ob-
    serve the time of their coming,
But my people know not the judgment of the Lord.

117

II

They have healed the hurt of the daughter of my
   people slightly,
Saying, "Peace, peace," when there is no peace.

Were they ashamed when they had committed abomination? nay, they were not at all ashamed, neither could they blush; therefore they shall fall among them that fall: at the time that I visit them they shall be cast down, saith the Lord.

Thus saith the Lord, Stand ye in the ways, and see, and ask for the old paths, where is the good way, and walk therein, and ye shall find rest for your souls.

But they said, "We will not walk therein."

Also I set watchmen over you, saying, "Hearken to the sound of the trumpet."

But they said, "We will not hearken."

The Lord hath come to me, and I have spoken to you, rising early and speaking; but ye have not hearkened. And the Lord hath sent to you all his servants the prophets, rising early and sending them; but ye have not hearkened, nor inclined your ear to hear.

III

The harvest is past,
The summer is ended,
And we are not saved.
Is there no balm in Gilead?
Is there no physician there?

IV

Oh that I had in the wilderness a
  lodging place of wayfaring men;
That I might leave my people, and
  go from them.

V

In that day did the Lord God of
    hosts call to weeping,
And to mourning, and to baldness,
    and to girding with sackcloth;
And behold, joy and gladness,
Slaying oxen and killing sheep,
Eating flesh and drinking wine:
"Let us eat and drink,
For tomorrow we shall die."

AGAINST THOSE WHO MISTREAT THE LABORER

I

The Lord will enter into judgment with the elders of
    his people,
And the princes thereof;
For ye have eaten up the vineyard:
The spoil of the poor is in your houses.
What mean ye that ye beat my people to pieces,
And grind the faces of the poor?

II

Woe to him that buildeth a town with blood,
And establisheth a city by iniquity!
Behold, it is not from the Lord of hosts,
That the people shall labor in the very fire,
And the people wear themselves out for very vanity!
But the earth shall be filled with the knowledge of the
    glory of the Lord,
As the waters cover the sea.

III

Woe to him [King Jehoiakim] that buildeth his house
    by unrighteousness,

And his chambers by wrong!
That useth his neighbor's service without wages,
And giveth him not for his work;
That saith, "I will build me a wide house and large
  chambers";
And cutteth him out windows;
And it is ceiled with cedar, and painted with vermi-
  lion.
Shalt thou reign, because thou inclosest thyself in cedar?

Did not thy father [King Josiah] eat and drink, and
  exercise justice?
Then it was well with him.
He judged the cause of the poor and needy:
Then it was well with him.
"Was not this to know me?" saith the Lord.
But thine eyes and thy heart are not but for thy
  covetousness,
And to shed innocent blood, and for oppression,
And for violence, to do it.

AGAINST THOSE WHO DEFRAUD THE POOR

I

There are those that remove the landmarks:
They violently take away flocks, and feed thereof;
They drive away the ass of the fatherless;
They take the widow's ox for a pledge;
They turn the needy out of the way.

The poor of the earth hide themselves together.
Behold, as wild asses in the desert,
They go forth to their work, rising early for food;
The wilderness yieldeth food for them and for
  their children.

They reap every one his grain in the field;
And they gather the vintage of the wicked.
They cause the naked to lodge without clothing,
That they have no covering in the cold.
They are wet with the showers of the mountains,
And embrace the rock for want of a shelter.

There are those that pluck the fatherless from the
     breast,
And take a pledge of the poor:
They cause him to go naked without clothing;
And they take away the sheaf from the hungry,
Who make oil within their walls,
And tread their winepresses, and suffer thirst.

Men groan from out of the city,
And the soul of the wounded crieth out.
They are of those that rebel against the light;
They know not the ways thereof,
Nor abide in the paths thereof.

The murderer riseth with the light;
He killeth the poor and needy;
And in the night he is as a thief.

The eye also of the adulterer waiteth for the
     twilight,
Saying, "No eye shall see me":
And he disguiseth his face.
In the dark they dig through houses,
Which they had marked for themselves in the
     daytime.
They know not the light:
For the morning is to them as the shadow of death;
For they know the terrors of darkness.

II

Hear this, O ye that swallow up the needy,
Even to make the poor of the land to fail,
Saying: "When will the new moon be gone, that we
   may sell grain?
And the sabbath, that we may set forth wheat
(Making the measure small, and the shekel great,
And falsifying the balances by deceit);
That we may buy the poor for silver,
And the needy for a pair of shoes;
Yea, and sell the refuse of the wheat?"

III

Woe to him that coveteth an evil covetous-
   ness to his house,
That he may set his nest on high,
That he may be delivered from the power of
   evil!
Thou hast consulted shame to thy house
By cutting off many people,
And thou hast sinned against thy soul.
For the stone shall cry out of the wall,
And the beam out of the timber shall answer it.

IV

Forasmuch as your treading is upon the poor,
And ye take from them burdens of wheat:
Ye have built houses of hewn stone,
But ye shall not dwell in them;
Ye have planted pleasant vineyards,
But ye shall not drink wine of them.
For I know your manifold transgressions and
   your mighty sins,
Ye that afflict the just,

That take a bribe,
And that turn aside the poor in the gate from
          their right.
Therefore the prudent shall keep silence in that time;
For it is an evil time.
Seek good, and not evil, that ye may live;
And so the Lord, the God of hosts, shall be with
          you, as ye have spoken.
Hate the evil, and love the good,
And establish judgment in the gate.
It may be that the Lord of hosts
Will be gracious to the remnant of Joseph.
Therefore the Lord, the God of hosts, the Lord,
          saith thus:
"Wailing shall be in all streets,
And they shall say in all the highways, 'Alas! alas!'
They shall call the husbandman to mourning,
And such as are skilful of lamentation to wailing.
In all vineyards shall be wailing,
For I will pass through thee," saith the Lord.

Woe unto you that desire the day of the Lord!
To what end is it for you?
The day of the Lord is darkness, and not light:
As if a man did flee from a lion,
And a bear met him;
Or went into the house, and leaned his hand on
          the wall,
And a serpent bit him.
Shall not the day of the Lord be darkness, and
          not light?
Even very dark, and no brightness in it?

"The people of the land have used oppression, and exer-
cised robbery, and have vexed the poor and needy: yea,

they have oppressed the stranger wrongfully. And I sought for a man among them, that should make up the hedge, and stand in the gap before me for the land, that I should not destroy it: but I found none.

"Therefore have I poured out mine indignation upon them; I have consumed them with the fire of my wrath: their own way have I recompensed upon their heads," saith the Lord God.

Thus speaketh the Lord of hosts, saying, "Execute true judgment, and show mercy and compassion every man to his brother: and oppress not the widow, nor the fatherless, the stranger, nor the poor; and let none of you imagine evil against his brother in his heart."

But they refused to hearken, and pulled away the shoulder, and stopped their ears, that they should not hear.

Yea, they made their hearts as an adamant stone, lest they should hear the law, and the words which the Lord of hosts hath sent in his spirit by the former prophets: therefore came a great wrath from the Lord of hosts.

THE NEED FOR MEN

God give us men! A time like this demands
Strong minds, great hearts, true faith, and willing hands;
Men whom the lust of office does not kill;
Men whom the spoils of office cannot buy;
Men who possess opinions and a will;
Men who have honor; men who will not lie;
Men who can stand before a demagogue
And damn his treacherous flatteries without winking;
Tall men, sun-crowned, who live above the fog
In public duty and in private thinking.

For while the rabble with their thumb-worn creeds,
Their large professions and their little deeds,
Mingle in selfish strife, lo, Freedom weeps!
Wrong rules the land, and waiting justice sleeps!
—*J. G. Holland*

AGAINST INJUSTICE

Behold, the Lord's hand is not shortened,
        that it cannot save,
Nor his ear heavy, that it cannot hear.
But your iniquities have separated between
        you and your God,
And your sins have hid his face from you,
That he will not hear.

For your hands are defiled with blood,
And your fingers with iniquity:
Your lips have spoken lies;
Your tongue hath muttered perverseness.
None calleth for justice,
Nor any pleadeth for truth:
They trust in vanity, and speak lies;
They conceive mischief, and bring forth iniquity.
They hatch adders' eggs,
And weave the spider's web:
He that eateth of their eggs dieth,
And that which is crushed breaketh out into a viper.
Their webs shall not become garments,
Neither shall they cover themselves with
        their works:
Their works are works of iniquity,
And the act of violence is in their hands.
Their feet run to evil,
And they make haste to shed innocent blood.
Their thoughts are thoughts of iniquity:
Wasting and destruction are in their paths.
The way of peace they know not,
And there is no justice in their goings.
They have made them crooked paths:
Whatsoever goeth therein shall not know peace.

Therefore is judgment far from us,
Neither doth justice overtake us:
We wait for light, but behold obscurity;
For brightness, but we walk in darkness.
We grope for the wall like the blind,
Yea, we grope as if we had no eyes.
We roar all like bears,
And mourn sadly like doves.
We look for justice, but there is none;
For salvation, but it is far from us.

AGAINST CORRUPT JUDGES

I

Ye who turn judgment to wormwood,
And cast down righteousness to the earth,
Seek him that maketh the Pleiades and
        Orion,
And turneth the shadow of death into the
        morning,
And maketh the day dark with night;
That calleth for the waters of the sea, and
        poureth them out
Upon the face of the earth:
The Lord is his name.

Shall horses run upon the rock?
Will one plow there with oxen?
For ye have turned judgment into gall,
And the fruit of righteousness into hemlock.

II

Hear, I pray you, O heads of Jacob,
And ye princes of the house of Israel;
Is it not for you to know justice?

Who hate the good, and love the evil;
Who pluck off their skin from them,
And their flesh from off their bones;
Who also eat the flesh of my people,
And flay their skin from off them.
They break their bones, and chop them in
       pieces,
As for the pot, and as flesh within the cal-
       dron.
Then shall they cry to the Lord, but he
       will not hear them;
He will even hide his face from them at
       that time,
Because they have behaved themselves ill
       in their doings.

III

Woe to them that decree unrighteous de-
       crees,
And to the writers that write perverseness:
To turn aside the needy from judgment,
And to take away the right of the poor of
       my people,
That widows may be their spoil,
That they may make the fatherless their
       prey!

And what will ye do in the day of visitation,
And in the desolation which shall come
       from far?
To whom will ye flee for help?
And where will ye leave your glory?
Without me they shall bow down under
       the prisoners,
They shall fall under the slain.

For all this his anger is not turned away,
But his hand is stretched out still!

AGAINST BRIBERY AND GRAFT

I

Thy princes are rebellious,
And companions of thieves.
Every one loveth bribes,
And followeth after rewards.
They judge not the fatherless;
Neither doth the cause of the widow come
    to them.

II

Hear this, I pray you, ye heads of the house
    of Jacob,
And ye princes of the house of Israel,
Who abhor justice,
And pervert all equity;
Who build up Zion with blood,
And Jerusalem with iniquity.
The heads thereof judge for reward,
And the priests thereof give oracles for a
    hire,
And her prophets thereof divine for money:
Yet will they lean upon the Lord, and say,
"Is not the Lord among us?
No evil can come upon us."

Therefore shall Zion for your sakes
Be plowed as a field,
And Jerusalem shall become heaps of ruins,
And the mountain of the house as the high
    places of the forest.

AGAINST THE SINS OF WEALTH AND LUXURY

I

Woe to them that join house to house,
And lay field to field,
Till there be no more room,
That they may be placed alone in the midst of
    the land!
In mine ears saith the Lord of hosts,
"Of a truth many houses shall be desolate,
Even great and fair, without inhabitant."

Woe to them that rise up early in the morning,
That they may follow strong drink,
That continue till night, till wine inflame
    them![18]
And the harp and the viol,
The tabret and flute, and wine, are in their
    feasts;
But they regard not the work of the Lord,
Neither consider the operation of his hands.
Therefore my people are gone into captivity
Because they have no knowledge;
Their nobles are famished,
And their multitude dried up with thirst.

Woe to them that are mighty to drink wine,
And men of strength to mingle strong drink!

II

Woe to them that are at ease in Zion,
That trust in the mount of Samaria;
That put far away the evil day,
And cause the seat of violence to come near;
That lie upon beds of ivory,

And stretch themselves upon their couches;
That eat the lambs out of the flock,
And the calves out of the midst of the stall;
That chant to the sound of the viol,
And invent to themselves instruments of music,
      like David;
That drink wine in bowls,
And anoint themselves with the chief ointments:
But they are not grieved for the affliction of
      Joseph.

AGAINST INTEMPERANCE

I

"Come ye," say they, "I will fetch wine,
And we will fill ourselves with strong drink;
And tomorrow shall be as this day—
And much more abundant!"

II

Woe to him that giveth his neighbor drink;
To thee that puttest thy bottle to him,
And makest him drunken also
That thou mayest gloat on his nakedness!
Thou art filled with shame—not with glory;
Drink also thou, and stagger.
The cup of the Lord's right hand shall come
      round to thee,
And foul shame shall be on thy glory.
For the violence done to Lebanon shall cover
      thee,
The destruction of beasts shall affright thee,
Because of men's blood, and the violence to
      the land,
To the city and all that dwell therein.

III

The people have erred through wine;
Through strong drink they are out of the way.
The priest and the prophet have erred through
     strong drink;
They are swallowed up of wine;
They are out of the way through strong drink;
They err in vision, they stumble in judgment.

IV

Woe to the crown of pride,
To the drunkards of Ephraim,
Whose glorious beauty is a fading flower,
Which are on the head of the fat valley[19] of them
     that are overcome with wine!
Behold, the Lord hath a mighty and strong one,
Which as a tempest of hail and a destroying storm,
As a flood of mighty waters overflowing,
Shall cast down to the earth with the hand.
The crown of pride, the drunkards of Ephraim,
Shall be trodden under feet:
And the glorious beauty,
Which is on the head of the fat valley,
Shall be a fading flower,
And as the hasty fruit before the summer;
Which when he that looketh upon it seeth,
While it is yet in his hand he eateth it up.

AGAINST IDOLATRY

I

Seest thou not what they do in the cities of
     Judah,
And in the streets of Jerusalem?

The children gather wood,
And the fathers kindle the fire,
And the women knead their dough,
To make cakes to the queen of heaven,[20]
And to pour out drink offerings to other gods,
That they may provoke me to anger.

Do they provoke me to anger?
Do they not provoke themselves to the con-
    fusion of their own faces?

II

Then said he to me, "Son of man, lift up thine eyes now
the way toward the north."

So I lifted up mine eyes the way toward the north, and
behold, northward at the gate of the altar this image of
jealousy in the entry.

He said furthermore to me, "Son of man, seest thou
what they do? even the great abominations that the house
of Israel committeth here, that I should go far off from my
sanctuary? but turn thee yet again, and thou shalt see
greater abominations."

And he brought me to the door of the court; and when
I looked, behold a hole in the wall.

Then said he to me, "Son of man, dig now in the wall."
And when I had digged in the wall, behold a door.

And he said to me, "Go in, and behold the wicked
abominations that they do here."

So I went in and saw; and behold, every form of creep-
ing things, and abominable beasts, and all the idols of the
house of Israel, portrayed upon the wall round about. And
there stood before them seventy men of the elders of the
house of Israel, and in the midst of them stood Jaazaniah
the son of Shaphan, with every man his censer in his hand;
and a thick cloud of incense went up.

DEVOTEES WORSHIPING COBRA IDOLS

Everywhere in India one sees these objects of popular veneration. Usually they are placed under the village tree so that the villagers may easily come to present their offerings, milk and ghi (clarified butter) and the petals of the marigold. These are poured or placed on the representation of the divinity. No matter how small the offering, it is always acceptable.

As the cobra is to be feared because of its tooth of death, so these idols represent those malignant influences of the unseen world which man must propitiate if he would continue to be fortunate. Low-caste religion is a religion of fear.

Then said he to me, "Son of man, hast thou seen what the ancients of the house of Israel do in the dark, every man in the chambers of his imagery? for they say, 'The Lord seeth us not; the Lord hath forsaken the earth.'"

He said also to me, "Turn thee yet again, and thou shalt see greater abominations that they do."

Then he brought me to the door of the gate of the Lord's house which was toward the north; and behold, there sat women weeping for Tammuz [Adonis].[21]

Then said he to me, "Hast thou seen this, O son of man? turn thee yet again, and thou shalt see greater abominations than these."

And he brought me into the inner court of the Lord's house, and behold, at the door of the temple of the Lord, between the porch and the altar, were about twenty-five men, with their backs toward the temple of the Lord, and their faces toward the east; and they worshiped the sun toward the east.

Then he said to me: "Hast thou seen this, O son of man? Is it a light thing to the house of Judah that they commit the abominations which they commit here? for they have filled the land with violence, and have returned to provoke me to anger: and, lo, they put the branch to their nose. Therefore will I also deal in fury: mine eye shall not spare, neither will I have pity: and though they cry in mine ears with a loud voice, yet will I not hear them."

III

What profiteth the graven image
That the maker thereof hath graven it;
The molten image, and a teacher of lies,
That the maker of his work trusteth therein,
To make dumb idols?

Woe to him that saith to the wood, "Awake!"
To the dumb stone, "Arise!" Shall this teach?
Behold, it is laid over with gold and silver,
And there is no breath at all in the midst
    of it.
But the Lord is in his holy temple:
Let all the earth keep silence before him.

Thy calf, O Samaria, hath cast thee off;
Mine anger is kindled against them:
How long will it be ere they attain to inno-
    cency?

For from Israel was it also:
The workman made it; therefore it is not God:

MODERN WAYSIDE IDOLS, SOUTH INDIA

But the calf of Samaria [22] shall be broken
    in pieces.
For they have sown the wind,
And they shall reap the whirlwind.

It hath no stalk:
The bud shall yield no meal:
If so be it yield, the strangers shall swallow it up.

Because Ephraim hath made many altars to sin, altars shall be to him to sin.

I have written to him the great things of my law, but they were counted as a strange thing.

They sacrifice flesh for the sacrifices of mine offerings, and eat it; but the Lord accepteth them not. Now will he remember their iniquity, and visit their sins: they shall return to Egypt.

For Israel hath forgotten his Maker, and buildeth temples; and Judah hath multiplied fenced cities: but I will send a fire upon his cities, and it shall devour the palaces thereof.

I found Israel like grapes in the wilderness; I saw your fathers as the first-ripe in the fig tree at her first time: but they went to Baal-peor, and separated themselves to that shame; and their abominations were according as they loved.

AGAINST SINS IN GOD'S HOUSE

I

"Behold, ye trust in lying words, that cannot profit. Will ye steal, murder, and commit adultery, and swear falsely, and burn incense to Baal, and walk after other gods whom ye know not; and come and stand before me in this house, which is called by my name, and say, 'We are delivered to do all these abominations'? Is this house, which is called by my name, become a den of robbers in your eyes? Behold, even I have seen it," saith the Lord.

"And now, because ye have done all these works," saith the Lord, "and I spoke to you, rising up early and speaking, but ye heard not; and I called you, but ye answered not: therefore will I do to this house, which is called by my name, wherein ye trust, and to the place which I gave to you and to your fathers, as I have done to Shiloh. I will cast you out of my sight, as I have cast out all your brethren, even all the descendants of Ephraim. Therefore pray not thou for this people, neither lift up cry nor prayer for them, neither make intercession to me: for I will not hear thee."

II

Now go: write it before them on a tablet,
And note it in a book,
That it may be for the time to come forever and ever:
That this is a rebellious people, lying children,
Children that will not hear the law of the Lord:
Who say to the seers, "See not,"
And to the prophets, "Prophesy not to us right things,

Speak to us smooth things, prophesy deceits;
Get you out of the way,
Turn aside out of the path,
Cause the Holy One of Israel to cease from before us.''

Because ye despise this word,
And trust in oppression and perverseness, and stay thereon,
Therefore this iniquity shall be to you as a breach ready
   to fall,
The swelling out in a high wall,
Whose breaking cometh suddenly in an instant.
And he shall break it as the breaking of the potter's vessel
   that is broken in pieces;
He shall not spare;
So that there shall not be found in the bursting of it a
   potsherd
Wherewith to take fire from the hearth,
Or to take water withal out of the pot.

AGAINST FALSE PROPHETS

I

The prophet that hath a dream, let him tell a dream;
And he that hath my word let him speak my word faith-
   fully.
What is the chaff to the wheat?
Is not my word like as a fire?
And like a hammer that breaketh the rock in pieces?

Therefore, behold, I am against the prophets that steal
   my words every one from his neighbor.
Behold, I am against the prophets that use their tongues,
   and say, ''He saith.''
Behold, I am against them that prophesy false dreams,
And do tell them, and cause my people to err

By their lies, and their lightness:
Yet I sent them not, nor commanded them;
Therefore they shall not profit this people at all.

II

Set thy face against the daughters of thy people,
Who prophesy out of their own heart;
And prophesy thou against them,
And say, "Thus saith the Lord God:
Woe to the women that sew pillows upon all elbows,
And make kerchiefs for the head of persons of every stature
      to hunt souls!

"Will ye hunt the souls of my people,
And will ye save the souls alive that come to you?
And will ye pollute me among my people
For handfuls of barley and for pieces of bread,
To slay the souls that should not die,
And to save the souls alive that should not live,
By your lying to my people that hear your lies?
Because with lies ye have made the heart of the righteous sad,
Whom I have not made sad,
And strengthened the hands of the wicked,
That he should not return from his wickedness,
By promising him life:
Therefore ye shall see no more vanity,
Nor divine divinations,
For I will deliver my people out of your hand,
And ye shall know that I am the Lord."

III

A wonderful and horrible thing is committed in the land:
the prophets prophesy falsely, and the priests bear rule by
their means; and my people love to have it so: and what
will ye do in the end thereof?

There is a conspiracy of her prophets in the midst thereof, like a roaring lion ravening the prey: they have devoured souls; they have taken the treasure and precious things; they have made her many widows in the midst thereof.

And her prophets have daubed them with untempered mortar, seeing vanity, and divining lies to them, saying, "Thus saith the Lord God," when the Lord hath not spoken.

AGAINST THE SINS OF THE NORTHERN NATION

I

O Ephraim, what shall I do to thee? O Judah, what shall I do to thee? for your goodness is as a morning cloud, and as the early dew it goeth away. Therefore have I hewed them by the prophets; I have slain them by the words of my mouth: and thy judgments are as the light that goeth forth. For I desired mercy, and not sacrifice; and the knowledge of God more than burnt offerings. But they like men have transgressed the covenant: there have they dealt treacherously against me.

Gilead is a city of them that work iniquity, and is polluted with blood. And as troops of robbers wait for a man, so the company of priests murder in the way toward Shechem.

When I would have healed Israel, then the iniquity of Ephraim was discovered, and the wickedness of Samaria: for they commit falsehood; and the thief cometh in, and the troop of robbers spoileth without. And they consider not in their hearts that I remember all their wickedness: now their own doings have beset them about; they are before my face. They make the king glad with their wickedness, and the princes with their lies.

In the day of our king, the princes have made him sick with bottles of wine; he stretched out his hand with scorners.

ANARCHY

From a fresco by Elihu Vedder

The artist has pictured anarchy by using the symbols of the three furies. The central figure has the snaky locks which frighten the beholder. In one hand she bears the wine cup, the source of her frenzy, in the other the firebrand with which to consume the world. Everywhere one sees the results of anarchy. The tree in the background is dead, the work of the builder is wantonly destroyed, the strings of the lyre are snapped, the scrolls of the poet are trampled under foot, the wheels of industry are broken.

For they have made ready their heart like an oven, while they lie in wait: their baker sleepeth all the night; in the morning it burneth as a flaming fire.

They are all hot as an oven, and have devoured their judges; all their kings are fallen: there is none among them that calleth to me.

II

Ephraim hath mixed himself among the people;
Ephraim is a cake not turned.
Strangers have devoured his strength, and he knoweth it not;
Yea, gray hairs are here and there upon him, yet he knoweth it not.
And the pride of Israel testifieth to his face,
And they do not return to the Lord their God,

Nor seek him for all this.
Ephraim also is like a silly dove without heart:
They call to Egypt,
They go to Assyria.
When they shall go, I will spread my net upon them;
I will bring them down as the fowls of the heaven;
I will chastise them, as their congregation hath heard.

Woe to them! for they have fled from me.
Destruction to them! because they have transgressed
          against me.
Though I have redeemed them, yet have they spoken
          lies against me.
And they have not cried to me with their heart,
When they howled upon their beds;
They assemble themselves for grain and wine,
And they rebel against me.
Though I have bound and strengthened their arms,
Yet do they imagine mischief against me.

They return, but not to the Most High:
They are like a deceitful bow;
Their princes shall fall by the sword for the rage of
          their tongue:
This shall be their derision in the land of Egypt.

AGAINST THE CARELESS WOMEN OF ISRAEL

Rise up, ye women that are at ease;
Hear my voice, ye careless daughters;
Give ear to my speech.
Many days and years shall ye be troubled,
          ye careless women;
For the vintage shall fail,
The gathering shall not come.

THE NIGHT WATCH
From a painting by Briton Rivière

Tremble, ye women that are at ease;
Be troubled, ye careless ones;
Strip you, and make you bare,
And gird sackcloth upon your loins.
They shall smite upon the breasts
For the pleasant fields,
For the fruitful vine.

Upon the land of my people shall come up
        thorns and briers,
Yea, upon all the houses of joy in the
        joyous city;
Because the palaces shall be forsaken,
The multitude of the city shall be left,
The forts and towers shall be for dens forever,
A joy of wild asses,
A pasture of flocks;
Until the Spirit be poured upon us from on high,
And the wilderness be a fruitful field,
And righteousness remain in the fruitful field.

AGAINST ALL KINDS OF INIQUITY

I

Cursed be he that removeth his neighbor's landmark.
Cursed be he that maketh the blind to wander out of the
        way.
Cursed be he that twisteth the justice due to the sojour-
        ner, fatherless, and widow.
Cursed be he that smiteth his neighbor in secret.
Cursed be he that taketh a bribe to slay an innocent person.

II

I have seen violence and strife in the city.
Day and night they go about it upon the walls thereof.

Mischief also and sorrow are in the midst of it;
Wickedness is in the midst thereof;
Deceit and guile depart not from her streets.

III

Among my people are found wicked men: they lie in
wait, as he that setteth snares; they set a trap, they catch
men. As a cage is full of birds, so are their houses full of
deceit. They have become fat, they shine; yea, they over-
pass the deeds of the wicked. They judge not the cause of
the fatherless, and the right of the needy do they not defend.

"Shall not I visit for such things?" saith the Lord: "shall
not my soul be avenged on such a nation as this?"

IV

Woe to them that draw iniquity with cords of
falsehood,
And sin as it were with a cart rope;
That say, "Let him make speed,
And hasten his work, that we may see it.
Let the counsel of the Holy One of Israel
Draw nigh and come, that we may know it!"

Therefore hell hath enlarged herself,
And opened its mouth without measure;
And their glory and their multitude,
And their pomp, and he that rejoiceth, shall de-
scend into it.
Then shall lambs feed there as in their pasture,
And fatlings shall feed among the waste places.

V

The good man is perished out of the earth,
And there is none upright among men:
They all lie in wait for blood;
They hunt every man his brother with a net.

ISAIAH
From a painting by James J. Tissot

That they may do evil with both hands earnestly,
The prince asketh, and the judge is ready for a reward;
And the great man, he uttereth his mischievous
          desire:
Thus they weave it together.
The best of them is as a brier,
The most upright is sharper than a thorn hedge.
The day of thy watchmen and thy visitation
          cometh:
Now shall be their perplexity.

Trust ye not in a friend;
Put ye not confidence in a guide;
Keep the doors of thy mouth
From her that lieth in thy bosom.

For the son dishonoreth the father;
The daughter riseth up against her mother;
The daughter-in-law against her mother-in-law;
A man's enemies are the men of his own house.

For from the least of them even to the greatest of them
every one is given to covetousness; and from the prophet
even to the priest every one dealeth falsely. They have
healed also the hurt of my people slightly, saying, "Peace,
peace"; when there is no peace.

Hear the word of the Lord, ye children of Israel: for the
Lord hath a controversy with the inhabitants of the land,
because there is no truth, nor mercy, nor knowledge of God
in the land. By swearing, and lying, and killing, and steal-
ing, and committing adultery, they break out, and blood
toucheth blood. Therefore shall the land mourn, and every
one that dwelleth therein shall languish, with the beasts of
the field, and with the fowls of heaven; yea, the fishes of
the sea also shall be taken away.

GOOD GOVERNMENT

From a fresco by Elihu Vedder

Good government sits enthroned in conscious security and power. Her well-arranged robes, her braided hair, her majestic pose, indicate the reign of order. The left hand holds her wand of office, and the right a tablet whose inscription shows the source of her power. On her head is a living wreath. Behind her, towers the tree of life with its thick, protecting branches. The lions crouching under her throne may well typify evil forces subdued and to be led. Her attendants are two youthful figures whose wings show their heavenly origin. One holds the sword of righteous action, the other the bridle of self-restraint.

THE TRIUMPH OF JUSTICE

THE COVENANT WITH DEATH SHALL FAIL

HEAR the word of the Lord, ye scorn-
ful men,
Rulers of this people which is in Jerusalem!
Because ye have said, "We have made a
covenant with death,
And with hell are we at agreement;
When the overflowing scourge shall pass
through, it shall not come to us;
For we have made lies our refuge,
And under falsehood have we hidden ourselves"[23]:
Therefore thus saith the Lord God:

147

"Behold, I lay in Zion for a foundation a
    stone, a tried stone,
A precious corner stone, a sure foundation.
He that believeth shall not make haste.
Justice also will I lay to the measuring line,
And righteousness to the plummet.
Hail shall sweep away the refuge of lies,
And the waters shall overflow the hiding place.
Your covenant with death shall be annulled,
And your agreement with hell shall not stand:
When the overflowing scourge shall pass through,
Then shall ye be trodden down by it."

SECRET INIQUITY SHALL DECLINE

Forasmuch as this people draw near me with their mouth,
And with their lips do honor me,
But have removed their heart far from me,
And their fear toward me is taught by the precept of men;
Therefore, behold, I will proceed to do a marvelous work
    among this people,
Even a marvelous work and a wonder;
For the wisdom of their wise men shall perish,
And the understanding of their prudent men shall be hid.

Woe to them that seek deep to hide their counsel from the
    Lord,
And their works are in the dark,
And they say, "Who seeth us?" and "Who knoweth us?"
Surely your turning of things upside down shall be esteemed
    as the potter's clay;
For shall the work say of him that made it, "He made
    me not"?
Or shall the thing framed say of him that framed it, "He
    had no understanding"?

Is it not a very little while,
And Lebanon shall be turned into a fruitful field,
And the fruitful field shall be esteemed as a forest?
In that day shall the deaf hear the words of the book,
And the eyes of the blind shall see out of obscurity and
     out of darkness.
The meek also shall increase their joy in the Lord,
And the poor among men shall rejoice in the Holy One of
     Israel.
For the terrible one is brought to nought,
And the scorner is consumed,
And all that watch for iniquity are cut off.

GOD WILL PUNISH THE INIQUITOUS

I am sought of them that asked not for me;
I am found of them that sought me not.
I said, "Behold me, behold me!" to a nation
     that was not called by my name.
I have spread out my hands all day to a rebel-
     lious people,
Who walketh in a way that was not good,
After their own thoughts;
A people that provoketh me to anger continually
     to my face;
That sacrificeth in gardens,
And burneth incense upon altars of brick;
Who remain among the graves,
And lodge in the secret places;
Who eat swine's flesh,
And broth of abominable things is in their vessels;
Who say, "Stand by thyself;
Come not near me, for I am holier than thou!"
These are a smoke in my nose,
A fire that burneth all the day.

Behold, it is written before me:
"I will not keep silence,
But will recompense, even recompense into their
      bosom,
Your iniquities and the iniquities of your
      fathers together," saith the Lord,
"Who have burned incense upon the mountains,
And blasphemed me upon the hills:
Therefore will I measure their former work into
      their bosom."

GOD WILL RESCUE HIS FAITHFUL

Come, my people, enter thou into thy chambers,
And shut thy doors about thee;
Hide thyself as it were for a little moment,
Until the indignation be overpast.
For lo, the Lord cometh out of his place
To punish the inhabitants of the earth for their iniquity:
The earth also shall disclose her blood,
And shall no more cover her slain.

He openeth also their ear to instruction,
And commandeth that they return from iniquity.
If they hearken and serve him,
They spend their days in prosperity,
And their years in pleasures.
But if they hearken not, they perish by the sword,
And they die without knowledge.

METHODS OF SECURING THE SOCIAL GOOD

INDIVIDUAL RIGHTEOUSNESS

THE PRACTICE OF GOODNESS

SOW to yourselves in righteousness, reap in mercy,
Break up your fallow ground;
For it is time to seek the Lord,
Till he come and rain righteousness upon you!

THE PATHWAY OF PENITENCE

And they shall say, "Cast ye up, cast ye up, prepare the
　　way![24]
Take up the stumbling block out of the way of my people!"

For thus saith the high and lofty One that inhabiteth
　　eternity:
"I dwell in the high and holy place,
With him also that is of a contrite and humble spirit,
To revive the spirit of the humble,
And to revive the heart of the contrite ones.
I have seen his ways, and will heal him;
I will lead him also, and restore comforts to him and to
　　his mourners.
I create the fruit of the lips:
'Peace, peace to him that is far off,
And to him that is near,'" saith the Lord God;
"And I will heal him."

But the wicked are like the troubled sea, when it cannot rest.
"There is no peace," saith my God, "to the wicked."

Mercy More to be Desired than Fasting

Behold, on the day of your fast ye find
    pleasure,
And ye exact all money lent on pledge.
Behold, ye fast for strife and contention,
And to smite with the fist of wickedness.
Ye shall not fast as ye do this day,
To make your voice to be heard on high.
Is it such a fast that I have chosen,
A day for a man to afflict his soul?
Is it to bow down his head like a bulrush,
And to spread sackcloth and ashes under
    him?
Wilt thou call this a fast,
And an acceptable day to the Lord?

Is not this the fast that I have chosen:
To loose the bands of wickedness,
To undo the heavy burdens,
And to let the oppressed go free,
And that ye break every yoke?
Is it not to deal thy bread to the hungry,
And to bring the poor that are cast out to
    thy house?
When thou seest the naked that thou cover
    him,
And that thou hide not thyself from thine
    own flesh?
Then shall thy light break forth as the morning,
And thy healing shall spring forth speedily;
And thy righteousness shall go before thee;
The glory of the Lord shall be thy rearward.
Thou shalt cry, and he shall say, "Here
    am I."

The Sacrifices of Righteousness

"To what purpose is the multitude of your sac-
    rifices?" saith the Lord.
"I am full of the burnt offerings of rams,
And the fat of fed beasts;
And I delight not in the blood of bullocks,
Or of lambs and of he-goats.
When ye come to appear before me,
Who hath required this at your hand, to tread
    my courts?
Bring no more vain oblations;
Incense is an abomination to me;
The new moons and sabbaths, the calling of
    assemblies:
I cannot bear iniquity along with the solemn
    meeting.

"Your new moons and your appointed feasts my
    soul hateth;
They are a trouble to me;
I am weary to bear them.
And when ye spread forth your hands,
I will hide mine eyes from you.
Even when ye make many prayers,
I will not hear:
Your hands are full of blood.

"Wash you, make you clean.
Put away the evil of your doings from before
    mine eyes.
Cease to do evil,
Learn to do good:
Seek justice, relieve the oppressed,
Judge the fatherless, plead for the widow.

"Come now, and let us reason together," saith
the Lord.
"Though your sins be as scarlet, they shall be
as white as snow;
Though they be red as crimson, they shall be as
wool.
If ye be willing and obedient, ye shall eat the
good of the land:
But if ye refuse and rebel, ye shall be devoured
by the sword;
For the mouth of the Lord hath spoken it."

Justice Between Man and Man

Amend your ways and your doings,
And I will cause you to dwell in this place.
Trust ye not in lying words, saying, "The temple of the
Lord,
The temple of the Lord, the temple of the Lord, are these!"
For if ye thoroughly amend your ways and your doings,
If ye thoroughly execute justice between a man and his
neighbor,
If ye oppress not the stranger, the fatherless, and the widow,
And shed not innocent blood in this place,
Neither walk after other gods to your hurt;
Then will I cause you to dwell in this place,
In the land that I gave to your fathers forever and ever.

Return from Backsliding

Turn, O ye backsliding children,
For I am married to you;
And I will take you, one of a city,
And two of a family,
And I will bring you to Zion,
And I will give you shepherds according to my heart,
Who shall feed you with knowledge and understanding.

But I said: "How shall I put thee among the children,
And give thee a pleasant land,
A goodly heritage of the hosts of nations?"

And I said, "Thou shalt call me 'My Father';
And shalt not turn away from me.
Return, ye backsliding children,
And I will heal your backslidings."

"Behold, we come to thee,
For thou art the Lord our God."

Faith in God

Cursed be the man that trusteth in man,
And maketh flesh his arm,
And whose heart departeth from the Lord.
For he shall be like the heat in the desert,
And shall not see when good cometh,
But shall inhabit the parched places in the
        wilderness,
In a salt land and not inhabited.

Blessed is the man that trusteth in the Lord,
And whose hope the Lord is.
For he shall be as a tree planted by the waters,
And that spreadeth out her roots by the river,
And shall not see when heat cometh,
But her leaf shall be green;
And shall not be anxious in the year of drought,
Neither shall cease from yielding fruit.

THE RULE OF A GOOD KING

The Solitary Kingly Conqueror

Israel's king is seen coming in lonely triumph from Edom, the land of the sons of Esau, their treacherous enemies, and from Bozrah, its capital.

Who is this that cometh from Edom,
In crimsoned garments from Bozrah?
This that is glorious in his apparel,
Traveling along in the greatness of his
  strength?

"I, that speak in righteousness,
Mighty to save."

Wherefore art thou red in thy apparel,
And thy garments like his that treadeth in
  the wine vat?

"I have trodden the winepress alone,
And of the people there was none with me:
Yea, I trod them in mine anger,
And trampled them in my fury;
And their blood is sprinkled upon my gar-
  ments,
And I have stained all my raiment.
For a day of vengeance was in my heart,
And the year of my redeemed is come.
I looked, but there was none to help,
And I wondered that there was none to up-
  hold:
Therefore mine own arm brought salvation
  to me,
And my wrath, it upheld me.
So I trod down the people in mine anger,
And broke them to pieces in my fury,
And I poured out their blood on the earth."

A Vision of the King of Peace

Behold, a King shall reign in righteousness,
And princes shall rule with judgment.

And a man shall be as a refuge from the wind,
And a covert from the tempest;
As rivers of water in a dry place,
As the shadow of a great rock in a weary land.

Then justice shall dwell in the wilderness,
And righteousness remain in the fruitful field,
And the work of righteousness shall be peace;
And the effect of righteousness, quietness and
　　　security forever.
And my people shall dwell in a peaceful habitation,
And in sure dwellings, and in quiet resting places.

Blessed are ye that sow beside all waters,
That send forth thither the feet of the ox and
　　　the ass.

Visions of a Shepherd King to Come

I

But thou, Beth-lehem Ephrathah,
Though thou be little among the thousands of Judah,
Yet out of thee shall he come forth unto me that is to
　　　be ruler in Israel,
Whose goings forth have been from of old, from everlasting.
Therefore shall he give them up, until she who beareth
　　　shall have borne.
Then the remnant of his brethren shall return with the
　　　children of Israel.
And he shall stand and shepherd his flock in the strength
　　　of the Lord,
In the majesty of the name of the Lord his God.
And they shall abide!
For now shall he be great to the ends of the earth,
And this man shall be our peace.

A SHEPHERD BY THE JORDAN RIVER

II

I will set up one shepherd over them,
And he shall feed them,
Even my servant David.

I will make with them a covenant of peace,
And will cause the evil beasts to cease out of the land;
They shall dwell safely in the wilderness,
And sleep in the woods.
I will make them and the places round about my hill a
      blessing,
And I will cause the shower to come down in its season;
There shall be showers of blessing.

And they shall be safe in their land;
And they shall know that I am the Lord,
When I have broken the bars of their yoke,
And have delivered them out of the hand of those that
      served themselves with them.

III

I will gather the remnant of my flock out of all countries
      whither I have driven them,
And will bring them again to their folds,
And they shall be fruitful and increase.
And I will set up shepherds over them who shall feed them,
And they shall fear no more,
Nor be dismayed, neither shall they be lacking.

Behold, the days come that I will raise unto David a
      righteous branch,
And a King shall reign and prosper,
And shall execute judgment and justice in the earth.
In his day Judah shall be saved,

And Israel shall dwell safely;
And this is his name whereby he shall be called:
THE LORD OUR RIGHTEOUSNESS.

RECESSIONAL

God of our fathers, known of old,
    Lord of our far-flung battle line,
Beneath whose awful Hand we hold
    Dominion over palm and pine—
Lord God of Hosts, be with us yet,
Lest we forget—lest we forget!

The tumult and the shouting dies;
    The Captains and the Kings depart:
Still stands thine ancient sacrifice,
    An humble and a contrite heart.
Lord God of Hosts, be with us yet,
Lest we forget—lest we forget!

Far-called, our navies melt away;
    On dune and headland sinks the fire:
Lo, all our pomp of yesterday
    Is one with Nineveh and Tyre!
Judge of the Nations, spare us yet,
Lest we forget—lest we forget!

If, drunk with sight of power, we loose
    Wild tongues that have not thee in awe,
Such boastings as the Gentiles use,
    Or lesser breeds without the Law—
Lord God of Hosts, be with us yet,
Lest we forget—lest we forget!

For heathen heart that puts her trust
    In reeking tube and iron shard,
All valiant dust that builds on dust,
    And, guarding, calls not thee to guard,
For frantic boast and foolish word—
Thy mercy on thy People, Lord!

                —*Rudyard Kipling*

THE IDEAL SOCIAL SERVANT: THE MESSIAH

As the fulfilment of the hope of a heroic king was delayed, another vision was given to some of the greater prophets. They dreamed of a deliverer who should accomplish his work, not by war and bloodshed, but through sacrifice, suffering, and death. He was called "the servant of Jehovah," because his whole-hearted obedience and loyalty to God were such a contrast to the infidelity of his people; and because of his thorough devotion, ultimately he should be raised to high reward and should see the satisfaction of all his hopes. Sometimes Israel itself—that is, the faithful remnant of Israel—is thought of as Jehovah's servant; but it is evident that always there was the anticipation that there would be an individual as the head of his people.

In the Maccabean time this servant, whether the reference be to the loyal people of Israel or to their head, is known as "the Son of Man."

The two great thoughts as to the deliverer—the servant who was a man of sorrows, and the King who was to be "numbered with the great"— are brought together in the famous passage in the Book of Isaiah, quoted in this volume under "The Servant Who Suffers and Is Satisfied." [25]

ISRAEL, JEHOVAH'S SERVANT

I

BUT thou, Israel, art my servant,
    Jacob whom I have chosen,
The children of Abraham my friend;
Thou whom I have taken from the ends of the earth,
And called thee from the uttermost parts thereof,
And said to thee: "Thou art my servant;
I have chosen thee, and not cast thee away."
Fear thou not, for I am with thee;
Be not dismayed, for I am thy God.
I will strengthen thee, yea, I will help thee;
Yea, I will uphold thee with the right hand of my
    righteousness.
Behold, all they that are incensed against thee

Shall be ashamed and confounded;
They that strive with thee shall perish:
They that war against thee
Shall be as nothing, and as a thing of nought.
For I the Lord thy God will hold thy right hand,
Saying unto thee, "Fear not, I will help thee."

II

Ye are my witnesses, saith the Lord,
And my servant whom I have chosen;
That ye may know and believe me,
And understand that I am he.
Before me there was no God formed,
Neither shall there be after me.
I, even I, am the Lord,
And beside me there is no savior.
I have declared, and have saved,
And I have showed, and there was no strange god
   among you.
Therefore ye are my witnesses, that I am God.

III

Fear not, O Jacob my servant,
And thou, Jeshurun [Beloved], whom I have chosen.
For I will pour water upon the thirsty land,
And floods upon the dry ground:
I will pour my spirit upon thy family,
And my blessing upon thy offspring;
And they shall spring up among the grass,
As willows by the water-courses.

IV

Remember these, O Jacob and Israel, for thou art my
   servant;
I have formed thee, thou art my servant;
O Israel, thou shalt not be forgotten of me!

I have blotted out, as a thick cloud, thy transgressions,
And, as a cloud, thy sins:
Return to me, for I have redeemed thee.

Sing, O ye heavens, for the Lord hath done it!
Shout, ye lower parts of the earth!
Break forth into singing, ye mountains,
O forest, and every tree therein;
For the Lord hath redeemed Jacob,
And glorified himself in Israel.

THE SERVANT WHO LEARNS AND WHO SUFFERS

The Lord God hath given me the tongue of them that are
    taught,
That I should know how to speak a word in season, to him
    that is weary.
He wakeneth me morning by morning,
He wakeneth mine ear to hear, as they that are taught:
The Lord God hath opened mine ear,
And I was not rebellious, neither turned away backward.

I gave my back to the smiters,
And my cheeks to those who plucked off the hair;
I hid not my face from insult and spitting:
For the Lord God will help me,
Therefore shall I not be confounded.
Therefore I have set my face like flint,
And I know that I shall not be put to shame.

He is near who justifieth me: who will contend with me?
Who is mine adversary? Let him draw near to me!
Behold, the Lord God will help me; who is he that shall
    condemn me?

Lo, they all shall grow old like a garment:
The moth shall eat them up.

Who is among you that feareth the Lord,
That obeyeth the voice of his servant?
That walketh in darkness,
And hath no light?
Let him trust in the name of the Lord,
And stay upon his God.

THE SERVANT OF MEEKNESS AND CONSTANCY

Behold my servant, whom I uphold,
My chosen, in whom my soul delighteth:
I have put my spirit upon him;
He shall bring forth justice to the Gentiles.

He shall not cry, nor lift up,
Nor cause his voice to be heard in the street.
A bruised reed shall he not break,
And smoking flax shall he not quench.
He shall bring forth justice to truth:
He shall not fail nor be discouraged,
Till he have set justice in the earth;
And the isles shall wait for his law.

THE SERVANT ANOINTED FOR HIS TASK

The spirit of the Lord God is upon me;
Because the Lord hath anointed me
To preach good tidings to the meek;
He hath sent me to bind up the broken-hearted,
To proclaim liberty to the captives,
And the opening of the prison to them that are
        bound;

To proclaim the year of the Lord's favor,
And the day of vengeance of our God [26];
To comfort all that mourn;
To appoint unto them that mourn in Zion,
To give them a garland for ashes,
     The oil of joy for mourning,
     The garment of praise for the spirit of
          heaviness:
That they may be called trees of righteousness,
The planting of the Lord,
That he may be glorified.

THE PROMISED LAND

O little Land of lapping seas,
　　Of vineyards, vales and hills;
Of tender rains and rainbow plains,
　　Of deserts and of rills;
O little Land of mounting crags,
　　Of lonely height and deep;
A world away thy children stray
　　And long, and wait, and weep.

I know the golden oranges
　　Englobed beneath the moon;
The sky that spills 'twixt seas and hills
　　Its shining draught of noon;
The vines that bind our holy hills
　　With grapes like jewels set;
The silver-green of olive sheen
　　Oh, can my soul forget?

O little Land of holy men
　　Of fearless dream and deed,
From clime to clime the storms of time
　　Have strewn thy hardy seed;
And fearless still and holy still,
　　We sang through hate and shame;
With faith we fought, with deed and thought
　　And God's enduring name.

My heart is singing like a bird
　　Of home that still may be,
And joys I dared to leave, and spared,
　　Hold out their arms to me.
We cannot sleep in cushioned ease
　　Nor yield to martial will,
But we must hear God's trumpet clear
　　Sound peace upon his Hill.
　　　　　　　　—*Jessie E. Sampter*

By permission of The Bloch Publishing Company

PATRIOTIC POETRY

LOVE OF TRIBE AND COUNTRY

TRIBAL SONGS

Of Reuben

REUBEN, thou art my first-born,
My might, and the beginning of my strength,
The excellency of dignity, and the excellency of
    power:
Unstable as water, thou shalt not excel.[27]

Let Reuben live and not die;
And let not his men be few.

Of Judah

I

Judah [Praise], thou art he whom thy brethren shall
    praise:
Thy hand shall be on the neck of thine enemies;
Thy father's children shall bow down before thee.

Judah is a lion's whelp.
From the prey, my son, thou art gone up;
He stooped down, he couched as a lion,
And as an old lion; who shall rouse him up?

The scepter shall not depart from Judah,
Nor a lawgiver from between his feet,
As long as men come to Shiloh;
And to him shall the gathering of the people be.

Binding his foal to the vine,
And his ass's colt to the choice vine,

He washed his garments in wine,
And his clothes in the blood of grapes:
His eyes shall be red with wine,
And his teeth white with milk.

II

Hear, Lord, the voice of Judah,
And bring him to his people.
Let his hands be sufficient to him,
And be thou a help to him from his enemies.

OF ZEBULUN

I

Zebulun shall dwell at the haven of the sea,
And he shall be for a haven of ships;
And his border shall be unto Sidon.

II

Rejoice, Zebulun, in thy going out,
And, Issachar, in thy tents.
They shall call the people to the mountain:
There they shall offer sacrifices of righteousness;
For they shall suck of the abundance of the seas,
And of treasures hid in the sands.

OF ISSACHAR

Issachar is a strong ass,
Couching down between two burdens:
For he saw that rest was good,
And the land that it was pleasant;
And he bowed his shoulder to bear,
And became a servant to tribute.

OF DAN

I

Dan [Judge] shall judge his people,
As one of the tribes of Israel.

Dan shall be a serpent by the way,
An adder in the path,
That biteth the horse's heels,
So that his rider shall fall backward.

II

Dan is a lion's whelp;
He shall leap from Bashan.

OF GAD

I

Gad [Troop], a troop shall troop upon him,
But he shall overcome at the last.

II

Blessed be he that enlargeth Gad.
He dwelleth like a lion,
And teareth the arm with the crown of the head.
And he provided the first part for himself,
Because there, in a portion of the lawgiver, was
        he seated,
And he came with the heads of the people.
He executed the justice of the Lord,
And his judgments with Israel.

OF ASHER

I

Out of Asher his bread shall be fat,
And he shall yield royal dainties.

II

Let Asher be blessed with children;
Let him be acceptable to his brethren,
And let him dip his foot in oil.
Thy shoes shall be iron and brass;
And as thy days, so shall thy strength be.

Of Naphtali

I

Naphtali is a hind let loose:
He giveth goodly words.

II

O Naphtali, satisfied with favor,
And full with the blessing of the Lord,
Possess thou the west and the south.

Of Joseph

I

Joseph is a fruitful bough,
A fruitful vine by a well,
Whose branches run over the wall.
The archers have sorely grieved him,
And shot at him, and hated him:
But his bow abode in strength,
And the arms of his hands were made strong
By the hands of the Mighty One of Jacob,
(From thence is the shepherd, the stone of Israel);
Even by the God of thy father, who shall help thee,
And by the Almighty, who shall bless thee
With blessings of heaven above.
The blessings of thy father have prevailed
Above the blessings of my progenitors
To the utmost bound of the everlasting hills:
They shall be on the head of Joseph,
And on the crown of the head of him that was
　　　separate from his brethren.

II

Blessed of the Lord be his land,
For the precious things of the heavens, for the dew,

And for the deep that coucheth beneath,
And for the precious fruits brought forth by the sun,
And for the precious things put forth by the moon,
And for the chief things of the ancient mountains,
And for the precious things of the lasting hills,
And for the precious things of the earth and fulness
       thereof,
And for the good will of him that dwelt in the bush.
Let the blessing come upon the head of Joseph,
And upon the top of the head of him that was sepa-
      rated from his brethren.

His glory is like the firstling of his bullock,
And his horns are like the horns of the wild ox:
With them he shall push the people together
To the ends of the earth.
And they are the ten thousands of Ephraim,
And they are the thousands of Manasseh.

OF BENJAMIN

I

Benjamin shall ravin as a wolf:
In the morning he shall devour the prey,
And at night he shall divide the spoil.

II

The beloved of the Lord shall dwell securely by him,
And the Lord shall cover him all day long,
And he shall dwell between his shoulders.

OF LEVI

Let thy Urim and Thummim be with the Holy One,
Whom thou didst prove at Massah,
And with whom thou didst strive at the waters of
      Meribah:

For they have observed thy word,
And kept thy covenant.
They shall teach Jacob thy judgments,
And Israel thy law:
They shall put incense before thee,
And whole burnt sacrifice upon thine altar.
Bless, Lord, his substance,
And accept the work of his hands.

Of Israel

There is none like the God of Jeshurun,
Who rideth upon the heaven for thy help,
And in his excellency on the sky.
The eternal God is thy refuge,
And underneath are the everlasting arms:
And he shall thrust out the enemy from before thee,
And shall say, "Destroy!"
Israel then shall dwell in safety, alone.
The fountain of Jacob shall be upon a land of corn
        and wine;
Also his heavens shall drop down dew.
Happy art thou, O Israel:
Who is like thee, O people saved by the Lord,
The shield of thy help,
And the sword of thine excellency!

NATIONAL ASPIRATIONS

Conquest

A Prose Poem

If ye shall diligently keep all these commandments that
I command you, to do them, to love the Lord your God, to
walk in all his ways, and to cleave to him; then will the Lord
drive out all these nations from before you, and ye shall

1V-175

"I WILL OPEN RIVERS IN HIGH PLACES"

possess nations greater and mightier than yourselves. Every place whereon the sole of your foot shall tread shall be yours: from the wilderness, and Lebanon, from the river, the river Euphrates, even to the uttermost sea shall your border be. There shall no man be able to stand before you, for the Lord your God shall lay the fear of you and the dread of you upon all the land that ye shall tread upon, even as he hath said to you.

Happiness and Splendor

The Lord their God shall save them in that day—
As the flock of his people;
For they shall be as the jewels of a crown,
Lifted up as an ensign upon his land.
For how great is his goodness!
And how great is his beauty!
Grain shall make the young men cheerful,
And new wine the maidens.

A Song in the Night

Ye shall have a song, as in the night when a holy solemnity
    is kept,
And gladness of heart, like his who goeth with a flute,
To come into the mountain of the Lord,
To the Mighty One of Israel.
And the Lord will cause his glorious voice to be heard,
And will show the lighting down of his arm.

The Land of Plenty

When the poor and needy seek water, and
    there is none,
And their tongue faileth for thirst,
I the Lord will hear them:
I the God of Israel will not forsake them
I will open rivers in high places,

And fountains in the midst of the valleys:
I will make the wilderness a pool of water,
And the dry land springs of water.
I will plant in the wilderness the cedar,
The acacia, and the myrtle, and the oil tree:
I will set in the desert the fir tree,
And the pine, and the box tree together;
That they may see, and know.
And consider, and understand together,
That the hand of the Lord hath done this,
And the Holy One of Israel hath created it.

OUR MOTHER COUNTRY

Rejoice ye with Jerusalem,
And be glad with her, all ye that love her!
Rejoice for joy with her, all ye that mourned over her;
For behold, I will extend peace to her like a river,
And the glory of the Gentiles like a flowing stream;
Then her sucklings also shall be borne on her side,
And be caressed upon her knees.
As one whom his mother comforteth, so will I comfort you;
And ye shall be comforted in Jerusalem.

THE CITY BESIDE ITS RIVER

Thine eyes shall see Jerusalem,
A quiet habitation, a tent that shall not
    be taken down:
Not one of the pegs thereof shall ever be
    removed,
Neither shall any of the cords thereof be broken.

But there the Lord will be with us in majesty,
A place of broad rivers and streams,
Wherein shall go no galley with oars,
Neither shall gallant ship pass thereby.

For the Lord is our Judge,
The Lord is our Lawgiver,
The Lord is our King:
He will save us.

THE HOLY NATION

Ye have seen how I bore you on eagles' wings,
And brought you to myself.
Now therefore, if ye will obey my voice indeed,
And keep my covenant,
Then ye shall be mine own possession above
      all peoples;
For all the earth is mine.
And ye shall be to me a kingdom of priests,
And a holy nation.

RUINS OF JERUSALEM

From a painting by James J. Tissot

The patriot Nehemiah rides about the ruins of his nation's capital and allows the full meaning of its destruction to sink into his soul. He hears in imagination the weeping prophet Jeremiah, "How doth the city sit solitary, that was full of people! How is she become a widow, she that was great among the nations!" The desolation had been all that the prophets and the poets had sung; but Nehemiah could also see the rising wall that was to bring to the city peace and prosperity again.

THE SORROWS OF A PEOPLE WHO FORGET GOD

DESOLATE JERUSALEM

HOW doth the city sit solitary, that was full of people!
How is she become a widow, she that was great
among the nations!
She that was a princess among the provinces, how is
she become tributary!

She weepeth sore in the night, and her tears are on
her cheeks;
Among all her lovers, she hath none to comfort her;
All her friends have dealt treacherously with her,
they are become her enemies.

Judah is gone into captivity because of affliction,
and because of great servitude;
She dwelleth among the heathen, she findeth no rest;
All her persecutors overtook her, between the straits.

The ways of Zion do mourn, because none come to
the solemn feasts;
All her gates are desolate, her priests do sigh;
Her maidens are afflicted, and she is in bitterness.

Her adversaries are the head, her enemies prosper;
For the Lord hath afflicted her, for the multitude of
her transgressions;
Her children are gone into captivity, before the enemy.

And from the daughter of Zion all her beauty is
departed;

Her princes are become like harts that find no pasture;
And they are gone without strength before the pur-
suer.

Is it nothing to you, all ye that pass by?
Behold, and see if there be any sorrow like my sorrow which is done to me,
Wherewith the Lord hath afflicted me in the day of
his fierce anger.

The Lord hath trodden under foot all my mighty
men in the midst of me;
He hath called an assembly against me to crush my
young men;
The Lord hath trodden the virgin, the daughter of
Judah, as in a winepress.

For these things I weep; mine eye, mine eye runneth
down with water,
Because the comforter that should relieve my soul is
far from me;
My children are desolate, because the enemy pre-
vaileth.

Zion spreadeth forth her hands, and there is none to
comfort her;
The Lord hath commanded concerning Jacob that his
adversaries should be around him;
Jerusalem is among them as an unclean thing.

I called for my lovers, but they deceived me;
My priests and mine elders gave up the ghost in the
city;
While they sought their food to refresh their souls.

THE SHEPHERD SMITTEN AND THE SHEEP SCATTERED

Awake, O sword, against my shepherd,
And against the man that is my fellow;
Smite the shepherd, and the sheep shall be scattered,
And I will turn my hand upon the little ones.

And it shall come to pass, that in all the land
Two parts therein shall be cut off and die,
But the third shall be left therein.
And I will bring the third part through the fire,
And will refine him as silver is refined,
And will try them as gold is tried.

They shall call on my name, and I will hear them:
I will say, "It is my people";
And they shall say, "The Lord is my God."

THE DARKENING OF JOY

I

The new wine mourneth,
The vine languisheth,
All the merry-hearted do sigh.
The mirth of tabrets ceaseth,
The noise of them that rejoice endeth,
The joy of the harp ceaseth.
They shall not drink wine with a song:
Strong drink shall be bitter to them that drink it.
The city of confusion is broken down;
Every house is shut up, that no man may come in.
There is a crying amidst the wine in the streets,
All joy is darkened,
The mirth of the land is gone.

When thus it shall be in the midst of the land
    among the people,
There shall be as the shaking of an olive tree,
And as the gleaning grapes when the vineyard is
    done.
They shall lift up their voice,
They shall sing for the majesty of the Lord,
They shall cry aloud from the sea.

Wherefore glorify ye the Lord in the fires,
Even the name of the Lord God of Israel in the isles
    of the sea.

II

I will take from them the voice of mirth, and the
    voice of gladness;
The voice of the bridegroom, and the voice of the
    bride;
The sound of the millstones, and the light of the
    candle.

III

And the daughter of Zion is left as a cottage in a
    vineyard,
As a lodge in a garden of cucumbers,
As a besieged city.

IV

The harvest of the field is perished.
The vine is dried up,
And the fig tree languisheth;
The pomegranate tree, the palm tree also, and
    the apple tree,
Even all the trees of the field are withered;
Because joy is withered away from the sons of men.

THE DESTRUCTION OF THE BEAUTIFUL
HOUSE OF GOD

Oh, that thou wouldst rend the heavens,
That thou wouldst come down,
That the mountains might flow at thy presence!
As when the melting fire burneth,
The fire causeth the waters to boil,
To make thy name known to thine adversaries,
That the nations may tremble at thy presence!

When thou didst terrible things which we looked
      not for,
Thou camest down;
The mountains flowed down at thy presence;
For since the beginning of the world men have not
      heard,
Nor perceived by the ear,
Neither hath the eye seen, O God, besides thee,
What he hath prepared for him that waiteth for him.

Thou meetest him that rejoiceth and worketh
      righteousness,
Those that remember thee in thy ways:
Behold, thou art wroth, for we have sinned;
In them have we continued; and shall we be saved?
But we are all as an unclean thing,
And all our righteousnesses are as filthy rags;
And we all do fade like a leaf,
And our iniquities, like the wind, have driven
      us away.
And there is none that calleth upon thy name,
That stirreth up himself to take hold of thee;
For thou hast hid thy face from us,
And hast consumed us, because of our iniquities.

©*Keystone View Co.*

THE JEWS' WAILING PLACE, JERUSALEM

The wall of huge stones on the right is the western retaining wall of the Temple area. It rises some twenty feet above the present level and descends probably fifty feet into the ground. It was not built by Solomon but by King Herod the Great. Nevertheless, the size and magnificence of the stones help perpetuate the old legend of the Talmud that Solomon had the help of the jinns or desert demons in building the Temple. As the little old Mohammedan woman whose fig orchard one may enter through the door at the back of the picture once said, "Devils put these stones here."

The Jews who live in Jerusalem have made it their pious duty to weep over these stones and to recall the downfall of their beloved nation. Every afternoon some mourners are to be found here. On Friday the courtyard is filled with them. They are mostly aged people who are pensioned by western Jews in order that they may live here and keep alive the traditions of the race. Some of the wailing is perfunctory, some of it seems to be genuine. The wailer reads from a little copy of the Book of Lamentations or the Psalms or the Prophets, usually with his face half hidden in one of the giant cracks in the old wall. The scene becomes pathetic only when we recall the long tragedy of Jewish history and realize that behind this great piece of Herodian engineering lies the spot most sacred in all the world to a Jew.

But now, Lord, thou art our Father;
We are the clay, and thou art our potter;
And we all are the work of thy hand.
Behold, see, we beseech thee:
We are all thy people.
Thy holy cities are a wilderness,
Zion is a wilderness, Jerusalem a desolation.

Our holy and our beautiful house,
Where our fathers praised thee,
Is burned with fire,
And all our pleasant things are laid waste.

AT THE JEWS' WAILING PLACE

With heads bowed down, they stand with streaming eyes,
    Before the ruined wall, whose grimy stones
Are crumbling with the weight of centuries,
    And read their Mincha-prayer in mournful tones.

Their garb proclaims them men of many lands:
    Those dwell amid the northern snows, and these
Have wandered far from Yemen's burning sands,
    Or sought their way across the western seas.

Not here alone do wailing figures stand!
    Not here alone do tears of sorrow flow!
In every clime they beat, with clenchèd hand
    Against the stones of Israel's wall of woe.

In every land there rises, stern and great,
    This selfsame wail of torment and of fears,
Its courses laid with stones of scorn and hate,
    And bonded with cement of blood and tears.
                 —*Louis Federleicht*

THE WOES OF UNFAITHFUL ISRAEL

Thus hath the Lord God showed to me;
And behold, he formed locusts in the beginning of the
    shooting up of the latter-growth;
And lo, it was the latter-growth after the king's mowings.
And it came to pass that when they had made an end of
    eating the grass of the land,
Then I said, "O Lord God, forgive, I beseech thee:
By whom shall Jacob rise? for he is small!"
Then the Lord repented for this:
"It shall not be," saith the Lord.

Thus hath the Lord God showed to me:
And behold, the Lord God called to contend by fire;
And it devoured the great deep
And did eat up a part of the land.
Then I said, "O Lord God, cease, I beseech thee:
By whom shall Jacob rise? for he is small!"
Then the Lord repented of this:
"This also shall not be," saith the Lord.

Thus he showed me;
And behold, the Lord stood upon a wall made by a
        plumb line, with a plumb line in his hand.
And the Lord said to me, "Amos, what seest thou?"
And I said, "A plumb line."

And the Lord said: "Behold, I will set a plumb line
        in the midst of my people Israel;
I will not again pass by them any more.
And the high places of Isaac shall be desolate,
And the sanctuaries of Israel shall be laid waste;
And I will rise against the house of Jeroboam with
        the sword."

Thus the Lord God showed to me:
And behold, a basket of summer fruit.
And he said, "Amos, what seest thou?"
And I said, "A basket of summer fruit."

And the Lord said to me: "The end is come upon my
        people Israel;
I will not again pass by them any more.
And the songs of the temple shall be howlings in that
        day.
There shall be many dead bodies in every place;
They shall cast them forth with silence."

WANDERING SHEEP

Give glory to the Lord your God,
Before he cause darkness,
And before your feet stumble upon the dark
      mountains,
And, while ye look for light, he turn it into the
      shadow of death,
And make it gross darkness.

Where is the flock that was given thee, thy
      beautiful flock?
What wilt thou say when he shall punish thee?
And if thou say in thy heart, "Wherefore come
      these things upon me?"
For the greatness of thine iniquity are thy heels
      made bare.

Can the Ethiopian change his skin,
Or the leopard his spots?
Then may ye also do good,
That are accustomed to do evil.
Therefore will I scatter them,
As the stubble that passeth away by the wind of
      the wilderness.

THE REFUGEES IN EGYPT AND IN ASSYRIA

We have given the hand to the Egyptians,
And to the Assyrians, that we might be
      satisfied with food.
Princes are hanged up by their hand;
The faces of elders were not honored.
They took the young men to grind the mill,
And the children stumbled under the wood.

The elders have ceased from the gate,
The young men from their music.
The joy of our heart is ceased;
Our dance is turned into mourning.
The crown is fallen from our head:
Woe to us! for we have sinned.
For this our heart is faint;
For these things our eyes are dim;
Because of the mountain of Zion, which is desolate:
Jackals walk upon it.

THE DOUBT OF THE DARK

He calleth to me out of Seir:
"Watchman, what of the night?
Watchman, what of the night?"
The watchman said,
"The morning cometh,
And also the night.
If ye will inquire, inquire.
Return, come."

THE CRY OF AN EXILED PEOPLE

Shepherd thy people with thy staff,
The flock of thy heritage which dwell solitarily
In the wood, in the midst of Carmel.
Let them feed in Bashan and Gilead, as in the days of
          old.
As in the days of thy coming out from the land of Egypt,
Will I show them marvelous things.

A CRY TO THE HEAVENLY FATHER

Look down from heaven,
And behold from the habitation of thy holiness
          and of thy glory:

ISAIAH MOURNING OVER HIS PEOPLE
From a drawing by Gustave Doré

Where is thy zeal and thy strength,
The yearning of thy heart and of thy mercies
        toward me?
Are they restrained?

Doubtless thou art our Father,
'Though Abraham be ignorant of us,
And Israel acknowledge us not.
Thou, O Lord, art our Father, our Redeemer:
Thy name is from everlasting.

GOD WILL NOT FORGET HIS PEOPLE

GOD WITH US

Now behold, the Lord bringeth up upon them
The waters of the River, strong and many,
Even the king of Assyria and all his glory:
And it shall come up over all its channels,
And go over all its banks;
And it shall pass through Judah;
It shall overflow and go over, it shall reach even to
        the neck;
But the stretching out of his [God's] wings shall
        fill the breadth of thy land,
For God is with us.

Associate yourselves, O ye peoples, yet ye shall be
        broken in pieces;
And give ear, all ye of far countries:
Gird yourselves, yet ye shall be broken in pieces;
Gird yourselves, yet ye shall be broken in pieces.
Take counsel together, and it shall come to nought;
Speak the word, and it shall not stand:
For God is with us.

God Our Defender

In that day shall the Lord defend the inhabitants of
    Jerusalem:
He that is feeble among them at that day shall be as
    David,
And the house of David shall be as God, as the angel of
    the Lord before them.
I will pour upon the house of David,
And upon the inhabitants of Jerusalem, the spirit of grace
    and of supplications:
They shall look upon me whom they have pierced,
And they shall mourn for him, as one mourneth for his only
    son,
And shall be in bitterness for him, as one that is in bitter-
    ness for his first-born.
In that day shall there be a great mourning in Jerusalem,
As the mourning of Hadadrimmon[28] in the valley of Me-
    giddon.

The Mercy of Our God

It is of the Lord's mercies that we are not consumed,
Because his compassions fail not.
They are new every morning:
Great is thy faithfulness.

"The Lord is my portion," saith my soul:
"Therefore will I hope in him."
The Lord is good to them that wait for him,
To the soul that seeketh him.

It is good for a man that he should both hope
And quietly wait for the salvation of the Lord.
It is good for a man
That he bear the yoke in his youth.

He sitteth alone and keepeth silence,
Because he hath laid it upon him.
He giveth his cheek to him that smiteth him;
He is filled with reproach.

For the Lord will not cast off forever.
For though he cause grief, yet will he have com-
    passion
According to the multitude of his mercies.
For he doth not afflict willingly,
Nor grieve the children of men.

God Our Redeemer

But now, thus saith the Lord that created thee, O
    Jacob,
And he that formed thee, O Israel:
"Fear not, for I have redeemed thee;
I have called thee by thy name, thou art mine.

"When thou passest through the waters, I will be with
    thee;
And through the rivers, they shall not overflow thee:
When thou walkest through the fire, thou shalt not
    be burned;
Neither shall the flame kindle upon thee."

God, the Defender, with the Staff of Doom

The Lord will cause his glorious voice to be heard,
And will show the lighting down of his arm,
With the indignation of his anger,
And with the flame of a devouring fire,
With scattering, and tempest, and hailstones.
For, through the voice of the Lord,
Shall the Assyrian be beaten down,
Who smote with a rod.

And in every place where the staff of doom shall pass,
Which the Lord shall lay upon him,
It shall be with tabrets and harps;
And in battles with the brandishing of his arm he
      shall fight with them.

THE EXILE'S LIGHT
From a drawing by Lilien
Permission of B. W. Huebsch

"Thy word is a lamp unto my feet and a light unto my path."

"In 'The Exile's Light' the head of an old man is seen looking up from a Bible, his hand resting lovingly on its open page. The table on which the book rests, as well as the shelf behind with the candles, gives a horizontality to the composition, broken by the vertical tapers in the foreground and back. A cleverly conceived border of ram's horns and palms, objects used on Atonement Day, frames the illustration. When darkness and danger threaten him, when poverty and despair oppress him, when life is a burden and hope well-nigh abandoned, this Book, this sacred Word of the Law, is his sole light, his comfort and his guide."

"THE CEDARS OF LEBANON WHICH HE HATH PLANTED"

The cedars grew in the beautiful mountains to the north, the ideal paradise of the Hebrew race. This region, not always in the possession of Israel, had about it the idealism of distance and inaccessibility. From these mountains trees were brought in the days of glory under Solomon for the building of the Lord's house, and again these forests were drawn upon in the time of the rebuilding of the Temple. Israel is often referred to in the prophets under the symbolism of the cedar. It is also mentioned frequently in the Psalms.

The cedars of Lebanon are so near extinction, due to wanton deforestation, that only this small grove remains. The whole region has, consequently, lost much of its ancient fertility and beauty.

THE DOOM
OF WORLDLY NATIONS

These doom songs are not to be judged merely for the hatred they display, a hatred that has been known in our own day in time of war and oppression. The Jews also saw, in the approaching destruction of their foes, evidences of the working out of an Infinite Justice. There is always a dignity about these foreseeings of ruin; they sound on the ear with solemnity, like a knell, over the fate of those who rose up against the peaceful and the humble, and did them wrong.

JEHOVAH'S DAY OF JUDGMENT

I

THE day of the Lord of hosts shall be
  Upon every one that is proud and lofty;
Upon every one that is lifted up, and he shall be
    brought low;
Upon all the cedars of Lebanon, that are high and
    lifted up;
Upon all the oaks of Bashan,
Upon all the high mountains,
Upon all the hills that are lifted up,
Upon every high tower,
Upon every fenced wall,
Upon all the ships of Tarshish,
Upon all pleasant watchtowers.
The loftiness of man shall be bowed down,
The haughtiness of men shall be made low,
And the Lord alone shall be exalted
In that day;
And the idols he shall utterly abolish.
They shall go into the holes of the rocks
And into the caves of the earth,

For fear of the Lord,
And for the glory of his majesty,
When he ariseth to shake terribly the earth.

In that day shall a man cast away his idols of silver
and his idols of gold,
Which they made each one for himself to worship,
To the moles and to the bats;
To go into the clefts of the rocks,
And into the tops of the ragged rocks,
For fear of the Lord,
And for the glory of his majesty,
When he ariseth to shake terribly the earth.

II

Put ye in the sickle, for the harvest is ripe;
Come get you down, for the press is full, the vats
overflow;
For their wickedness is great.

Multitudes, multitudes in the valley of decision!
For the day of the Lord is near in the valley of
decision.
The sun and the moon shall be darkened,
And the stars shall withdraw their shining.
The Lord also shall roar out of Zion,
And utter his voice from Jerusalem;
And the heavens and the earth shall shake;
But the Lord will be the hope of his people,
And the strength of the children of Israel.
So shall ye know that I am the Lord your God,
Dwelling in Zion, my holy mountain;
Then shall Jerusalem be holy,
And there shall no strangers pass through her any
more.

III

Behold, the Lord maketh the earth empty,
And he maketh it waste,
And turneth it upside down,
And scattereth abroad the inhabitants thereof.
And it shall be, as with the people, so with the
      priest;
As with the servant, so with his master;
As with the maid, so with her mistress;
As with the lender, so with the borrower;
As with the taker of usury, so with the giver of
      usury to him.
The land shall be utterly emptied,
And utterly spoiled,
For the Lord hath spoken this word.

The earth mourneth and fadeth away,
The world languisheth and fadeth away,
The haughty people of the earth do languish.
The earth also is defiled under the inhabitants
      thereof;
Because they have transgressed the laws,
Changed the ordinance, broken the everlasting
      covenant.
Therefore hath the curse devoured the earth,
And they that dwell therein are desolate;
Therefore the inhabitants of the earth are burned,
And few men left.

ODE ON THE COMING DESTRUCTION OF BABYLON

THE SUMMONS AGAINST BABYLON

Lift ye up a banner upon the high mountain!
Lift up the voice to them!

Wave the hand, that they may go into the gates of
      the nobles.
I have commanded my consecrated ones,
I have also called my mighty ones for mine anger,
Even them that rejoice in my majesty.
The noise of a multitude in the mountains, like as of a
      great people!
A tumultuous noise of the kingdoms of the nations
      gathered together!
The Lord of hosts mustereth the host for the battle.

The Approach of Babylon's Conquerors

They come from a far country,
From the end of heaven,
Even the Lord and the weapons of his indignation,
To destroy the whole land.
Howl ye; for the day of the Lord is at hand;
It shall come as a destruction from the Almighty.
Therefore shall all hands be faint,
And every man's heart shall melt:
And they shall be afraid;
Pangs and sorrows shall take hold of them;
They shall stare one at another;
Their faces shall be as flames.

The Dark Day of the Conquest

Behold, the day of the Lord cometh,
Cruel, both with wrath and fierce anger,
To lay the land desolate:
And he shall destroy the sinners thereof out of it.
For the stars of heaven and the constellations thereof
      shall not give their light;
The sun shall be darkened in his going forth,
And the moon shall not cause her light to shine.
I will punish the world for its evil,

And the wicked for their iniquity;
I will cause the arrogancy of the proud to cease,
And I will lay low the haughtiness of the terrible.
I will make a man more rare than fine gold,
Even a man than the gold wedge of Ophir.
Therefore I will shake the heavens,
And the earth shall remove out of her place,
In the wrath of the Lord of hosts,
And in the day of his fierce anger.

The Flight of the Babylonians

They shall be like the chased roe,
And like a sheep which no man taketh up:
They shall every man turn to his own people,
And flee every one to his own land.
Every one that is found shall be thrust through:
And every one that is taken shall fall by the sword.
Their children also shall be dashed to pieces before
        their eyes;
And their houses shall be spoiled.
Behold, I will stir up the Medes against them,
Who shall not regard silver;
And as for gold, they shall not delight in it.
Their bows also shall dash the young men in pieces;
And they shall have no pity on the little ones:
Their eye shall not spare the children.

The Utter Ruin of the City

And Babylon, the glory of kingdoms,
The beauty of the Chaldeans' pride,
Shall be as when God overthrew Sodom and Go-
        morrah.
It shall never be inhabited,
Neither shall it be dwelt in from generation to
        generation:

LIONS AMONG RUINS

From a painting by Briton Rivière

"The wild beasts shall cry in their desolate houses, and dragons in their pleasant palaces. Her time is near to come and her days shall not be prolonged."

Neither shall the Arabian pitch tent there;
Neither shall the shepherds make their fold there.
But wild beasts of the desert shall lie there;
Their houses shall be full of doleful creatures;
And owls shall dwell there,
And satyrs shall dance there.
The wild beasts of the islands shall cry in their
        desolate houses,
And dragons[29] in their pleasant palaces.
Her time is near to come
And her days shall not be prolonged.

THE DOOM OF BABYLON

How hath the oppressor ceased!
The golden city ceased!
The Lord hath broken the staff of the wicked,
And the scepter of the rulers;
He who smote the peoples in wrath
With a continual stroke,
That ruled the nations in anger,
Is persecuted, and none hindereth.

The whole earth is at rest, and is quiet:
They break forth into singing!
Yea, the fir trees rejoice at thee,
And the cedars of Lebanon, saying,
"Since thou art laid low,
No woodsman is come up against us."

Hell from beneath thee is moved for thee
To meet thee at thy coming:
It stirreth up the dead for thee,
Even all the chief ones of the earth;
It hath raised up from their thrones

All the kings of the nations.
All they shall speak and say to thee,
"Art thou also become weak as we?
Art thou become like us?"
Thy pomp is brought down to the grave,
And the noise of thy viols:
The worm is spread under thee,
And the worms cover thee.

How art thou fallen from heaven,
O Lucifer,[30] son of the morning!
How art thou cut down to the ground,
That didst weaken the nations!
For thou saidst in thy heart: "I will ascend
          into heaven,
I will exalt my throne above the stars of God.
I will sit also on the mount of assembly,
In the depths of the north:
I will ascend above the heights of the clouds;
I will be like the Most High."
Yea, thou art brought down to hell,
To the depths of the pit.

They that see thee shall stare upon thee,
And consider thee, saying:
"Is this the man that made earth to tremble,
That did shake kingdoms;
That made the world as a wilderness,
And destroyed the cities thereof?
That opened not the house of his prisoners?"
All the kings of the nations, even all of them,
          lie in glory,
Every one in his own house.
But thou art cast forth from thy grave like an
          abominable branch,

BABYLON FALLEN

From a drawing by Gustave Doré

"And Babylon, the glory of kingdoms, the beauty of the Chaldeans' pride, shall be as when God overthrew Sodom and Gomorrah. It shall never be inhabited."

And like the raiment of those that are slain,
  thrust through with the sword;
That go down to the stones of the pit,
Like a dead body trampled under feet.
Thou shalt not be joined with them in burial,
Because thou hast destroyed thy land,
And slain thy people.
The offspring of evildoers shall never be named.

BABYLON

The many-colored domes
Yet wore one dusky hue;
The cranes upon the mosque
Kept their night-clatter still,
When through the gate the early traveler passed;
 And when, at evening, o'er the swampy plain
  The bittern's boom came far,
  Distinct in darkness seen
Above the low horizon's lingering light,
Rose the near ruins of old Babylon.

Once from her lofty walls the charioteer
Looked down on swarming myriads; once she flung
 Her arches o'er Euphrates' conquered tide,
And through her brazen portals when she poured
 Her armies forth, the distant nations looked
 As men who watch the thundercloud in fear,
Lest it should burst above them. She was fallen!
The Queen of cities, Babylon, was fallen!

Low lay her bulwarks; the black scorpion basked
 In the palace courts; within the sanctuary
  The she-wolf hid her whelps.
 Is yonder huge and shapeless heap, what once
 Hath been the aerial gardens, height on height
Rising like Media's mountains crowned with wood,
 Work of imperial dotage? Where the fame
 Of Belus? Where the Golden Image now,
 Which at the sound of dulcimer and lute,
 Cornet and sackbut, harp and psaltery,
  The Assyrian slaves adored?
 A labyrinth of ruins, Babylon

Spreads o'er the blasted plain;
The wandering Arab never sets his tent
Within her walls; the shepherd eyes afar
Her evil towers, and devious drives his flock.
Alone unchanged, a free and bridgeless tide,
Euphrates rolls along,
Eternal nature's work.

—*Robert Southey*

THE DOOM OF EGYPT

It is plain to see that the crocodile, the emblem of Egypt, is "the monster in the seas" concerning which this prophecy of destruction is uttered.

And it came to pass in the twelfth year, in the twelfth month, in the first day of the month, that the word of the Lord came to me, saying, "Son of man, take up a lamentation for Pharaoh king of Egypt, and say to him:

"'Thou art like a young lion of the nations:
And thou art like a monster in the seas;
And thou camest forth with thy rivers,
And troubledst the waters with thy feet,
And fouledst their rivers.

"'Thus saith the Lord God:
I will therefore spread out my net over thee
With a company of many peoples;
And they shall bring thee up in my net.
Then will I leave thee upon the land,
I will cast thee forth upon the open field,
And will cause all the fowls of the heaven to
settle upon thee,
I will fill the beasts of the whole earth with thee.
I will lay thy flesh upon the mountains,
And fill the valleys with thy height.
I will also water with thy blood
The land wherein thou swimmest, even to the
mountains:

THE PYRAMIDS OF EGYPT

And the rivers shall be full of thee.
And when I shall put thee out, I will cover the
      heaven,
And make the stars thereof dark;
I will cover the sun with a cloud,
And the moon shall not give her light.
All the bright lights of heaven will I make dark
      over thee,
And set darkness upon thy land, saith the Lord
      God.'"

THE DOOM OF THE BEAUTIFUL
PRINCE OF TYRE

Moreover the word of the Lord came to me, saying, "Son
of man, take up a lamentation for the king of Tyre,[31] and say
to him:
  "'Thus saith the Lord God:
Thou sealest up the measure, full of wisdom, and
      perfect in beauty.
Thou hast been in Eden, the garden of God:
Every precious stone was thy covering,
The sardius, the topaz, and the diamond,
The beryl, the onyx, and the jasper,
The sapphire, the emerald, and the carbuncle, and gold:
The workmanship of thy tabrets and of thy pipes was
      prepared in thee,
In the day that thou wast created.
Thou art the anointed cherub that covereth:
And I have set thee, so thou wast upon the holy
      mountain of God;
Thou hast walked up and down in the midst of the
      stones of fire.
Thou wast perfect in thy ways from the day that
      thou wast created,

Till iniquity was found in thee.
By the multitude of thy merchandise they have filled
      the midst of thee with violence,
And thou hast sinned:

"'Therefore will I cast thee as profane out of the
      mountain of God;
And I will destroy thee, O covering cherub,
From the midst of the stones of fire.
Thy heart was lifted up because of thy beauty,
Thou hast corrupted thy wisdom by reason of thy
      brightness:
I will cast thee to the ground,
I will lay thee before kings,
That they may behold thee.
Thou hast defiled thy sanctuaries
By the multitude of thine iniquities,
In the iniquity of thy traffic;
Therefore will I bring forth a fire from the midst
      of thee,
It shall devour thee;
And I will bring thee to ashes upon the earth
In the sight of all them that behold thee.
All they that know thee among the peoples shall be
      astonished at thee:
Thou shalt be a terror,
And never shalt thou be any more.'"

THE UTTER RUIN OF TYRE

And they shall destroy the walls of Tyre,[32]
And break down her towers;
I will also scrape her dust from her,
And make her like the top of a rock.
It shall be a place for spreading of nets in the midst
      of the sea.

THE DOOM OF THE ENEMIES OF GOD

And it shall be as when a hungry man dreameth,
    and, behold, he eateth;
But he awaketh, and his soul is empty:
Or as when a thirsty man dreameth, and, behold,
    he drinketh;
But he awaketh, and, behold, he is faint,
And his soul hath appetite:
So shall the multitude of all the nations be,
That fight against mount Zion.

TYRE

High on the stately wall,
    The spear of Arvad hung;
Through corridor and hall
    Gemaddin's war note rung.
Where are they now? the note is o'er;
Yes, for a thousand years or more
Five fathom deep beneath the sea
Those halls have lain all silently;
Naught listing save the mermaid's song,
While rude sea monsters roam the corridors along.

Far from the wandering East
    Tubal and Javan came,
And Araby the blest,
    And Kedar, mighty name.
Now on that shore, a lonely guest,
Some dripping fisherman may rest,
Watching on rock or naked stone
His dark net spread before the sun,
Unconscious of the dooming lay,
That broods o'er that dull spot, and there shall
    brood for aye.
—*Richard Hurrell Froude*

THE RUINS OF TYRE

You are looking south from the end of the rocky peninsula on which Tyre is situated. Across the little bay of Tyre you can see the Phœnician coast lying with its fringe of trees and the misty foothills of Lebanon. Acre and Mount Carmel are off the picture to the right.

Ancient Tyre was built on a rocky island half a mile from the coast. Her bulwark was the sea; her wealth was won from the sea, either by her fisheries, or by her manufactures of Tyrian purple, or by her masters of the galleys. She was the head of a proud empire; her sails whitened every sea, even the stormy seas that encompass Britain and the Azores. Her colonists dotted the entire circle of the Mediterranean.

As Ezekiel sang in his song, "The Wreck of the Goodly Ship Tyre":

"Thy builders have perfected thy beauty.
They have made all thy planks of fir trees from Senir;
They have taken cedars from Lebanon to make masts for thee.
Of the oaks of Bashan have they made thine oars;
They have made thy benches of ivory inlaid with boxwood,
    brought out of the isles of Kittim.
Of fine linen with broidered work from Egypt was thy sail
That it might be to thee for an ensign;
Blue and purple from the isles of Elishah was thine awning.
The inhabitants of Sidon and Arvad were thy rowers:
Thy wise men, O Tyre, that were in thee were thy pilots."

Portions of the wreckage of this goodly vessel are to be seen in the foreground of the picture. They are the columns from some resplendent temple built in the days of her glory—of red granite and gray from the cataract of Egypt. For not only did the destruction foreseen by Ezekiel come upon her, but many another storm of war has strewn her coast with the wreckage of her greatness. The Assyrians took the city in 664 B.C.; the Chaldeans besieged it for thirteen years; Alexander the Great utterly destroyed it in 332, after a siege of seven months; Antigonus took the rebuilt city in 314; it was conquered by Egypt, by the Seleucids, by the Romans, by the Saracens, and by the Crusaders. Its form changes like that of the Old Man of the Sea, but it still continues to live. Today there are more than seven thousand people dwelling on the identical site of old Tyre. It was the ruins and rubbish of ancient Tyre that furnished material for the gigantic mole built by Alexander the Great during his memorable siege. We must remember that Tyre was at that time completely surrounded by prodigious walls which were said to have been one hundred and fifty feet high towards the mainland. Aided by his Phœnician and Cyprian allies who blockaded the harbor, Alexander finally succeeded in laying a causeway two hundred feet wide out to the island.

THE RUINS OF TYRE

"It shall be a place for spreading of nets in the midst of the sea."

THE MESSIANIC ERA

From a fresco by John S. Sargent

"All they gather themselves together, they come to thee: thy sons shall come from far, and thy daughters shall be nursed at thy side. . . . A little one shall become a thousand, and a small one a strong nation."

THE GLORIOUS FUTURE

Our own literature is full of dreams of a Golden Age. We love to read of Utopia, of the New Atlantis, of the City in the Sun, of the Land of Beulah. The Bible has its anticipations of a Better Country, and it contains no more eloquent and moving passages than the songs that tell of a time when social evils shall be done away with, and the full purpose of the God of righteousness shall be fulfilled.

Naturally, many of these poems tell of Israel's Return from Captivity; but there are many that have a wider sweep and have been a comfort to men of other races, because they seem to point to God's greater purpose, in many lands and to the end of time.

It is to be noted that it is upon a real earth that the new heaven is to be builded. Life is to be truly worth living in the Glorious Age. The land is for all; families live together in settled habitations of their own, under their own vine and fig tree; and the joy is of a happy people who rejoice in the work of their hands. It is a millennium of fruitful, well-rewarded labor.

Yet spiritual blessings crown it all. It is the Lord God who is to be the everlasting light and glory of the people whom he shall redeem.

"All thy children shall be taught of the Lord,
And great shall be the peace of thy children."

A TRIUMPHAL ODE UPON THE RETURN

ARISE, shine; for thy light is come,
And the glory of the Lord is risen upon thee.
For, behold, the darkness shall cover the earth,
And gross darkness the people;
But the Lord shall arise upon thee,
And his glory shall be seen upon thee.
Gentiles shall come to thy light,
And kings to the brightness of thy rising.

Lift up thine eyes round about, and see:
All they gather themselves together, they come to
        thee;

THE GLORY OF LEBANON

Lebanon presents some of the most picturesquely beautiful scenery in the world. This lofty range, or chain, of mountains is about one hundred miles in length and twenty-five in breadth and, commencing in rolling foothills, rises in peaks five to ten thousand feet in height. The moist winds from the Mediterranean and the balmy breezes from the south make the western and southern slopes beautiful, for the substance of the range is such that, as it crumbles away, it makes a fertile soil where trees, vines and flowers flourish.

Thy sons shall come from far,
And thy daughters shall be nursed at thy side.
Then shalt thou see and be radiant,
And thy heart shall fear and be enlarged;
Because the abundance of the sea shall be turned
    to thee,
The forces of the Gentiles shall come to thee.

The multitude of camels shall cover thee,
The dromedaries of Midian and Ephah;
All they from Sheba shall come;
They shall bring gold and incense,
And they shall show forth the praises of the
    Lord.
All the flocks of Kedar shall be gathered to thee,
The rams of Nebaioth shall minister to thee;
They shall come up with acceptance on mine
    altar,
And I will glorify the house of my glory.
Who are these that fly as a cloud,
And like the doves to their windows?
Surely the isles shall wait for me,
And the ships of Tarshish first,
To bring thy sons from afar,
Their silver and their gold with them,
To the name of the Lord thy God,
And to the Holy One of Israel,
Because he hath glorified thee.

And the sons of strangers shall build up thy walls,
And their kings shall minister to thee;
For in my wrath I smote thee,
But in my favor have I had mercy upon thee.
Therefore thy gates shall be open continually;
They shall not be shut day nor night;

That men may bring to thee the wealth of the
        Gentiles,
And their kings led captive.

The glory of Lebanon shall come to thee,
The fir tree, the pine and the box together,
To beautify the place of my sanctuary;
And I will make the place of my feet glorious.
The sons also of them that afflicted thee shall come
        bending unto thee;
And all they that despised thee shall bow down
        at the soles of thy feet;
And they shall call thee, "The City of the Lord,"
"The Zion of the Holy One of Israel."

Whereas thou hast been forsaken,
And hated, so that no man went through thee,
I will make thee an eternal excellency,
A joy of many generations.
Thou shalt suck the milk of the Gentiles,
And shalt suck the breast of kings;
Thou shalt know that I the Lord am thy Savior,
And thy Redeemer, the Mighty One of Jacob.

For brass I will bring gold,
And for iron I will bring silver.
I will also make thy officers peace,
And thy taskmasters righteousness.
Violence shall no more be heard in thy land,
Wasting nor destruction within thy borders;
And thou shalt call thy walls Salvation,
And thy gates Praise.
The sun shall be no more thy light by day;
Neither for brightness shall the moon give light
        to thee;

But the Lord God shall be to thee an everlasting
    light,
And thy God thy glory.
Thy sun shall no more go down,
Neither shall thy moon withdraw itself;
For the Lord will be thine everlasting light,
And the days of thy mourning shall be ended.
Thy people also shall all of them be righteous;
They shall inherit the land forever,
The branch of my planting,
The work of my hands, that I may be glorified.
A little one shall become a thousand,
And a small one a great nation;
I, the Lord, will hasten it in its time.

THE RETURN OF THE PRODIGAL SON

I have surely heard Ephraim bemoaning himself
    thus:
"Thou hast chastised me, and I was chastised,
As a bullock unaccustomed to the yoke:
Turn thou me, and I shall be turned,
For thou art the Lord my God.
Surely after I was turned I repented,
And after I was instructed I smote upon my thigh:
I was ashamed, yea, even confounded,
Because I did bear the reproach of my youth."

"Is Ephraim my dear son?
Is he a pleasant child?
For since I spoke against him, I do earnestly
    remember him still:
Therefore my heart is troubled for him:
I will surely have mercy upon him," saith the
    Lord.

MODERN JEWISH HUSBANDRY

For nearly a century the Jews have been establishing agricultural colonies in the Holy Land. Latterly there seems to be a growing success because of the freer use of capital and the arrival of colonists of greater intelligence and purpose. The plains of Sharon and Phi-listia are now dotted with the red-tiled houses of these newer immigrants.

"Set thee up waymarks,
Make thee high heaps,
Set thy heart toward the highway,
Even the way which thou wentest:
Turn again, O maiden of Israel,
Turn again to these thy cities."
Thus saith the Lord of hosts, the God of Israel:
"Yet shall they use this speech in the land of
      Judah,
And in the cities thereof, when I shall bring again
      their captivity:
'The Lord bless thee, O habitation of justice,
And mountain of holiness!'
And there shall dwell in Judah itself, and in all
      the cities thereof together,
Husbandmen, and they that go forth with flocks.
For I have satiated the weary soul,
And I have replenished every sorrowful soul."

Upon this I awaked, and beheld;
And my sleep was sweet to me.

SONGS OF THE RETURN

I

I will bring the blind by a way that they knew not;
I will lead them in paths that they have not known;
I will make darkness light before them,
And crooked things straight.
These things will I do to them,
And not forsake them.

II

Seek ye out of the book of the Lord, and read:
"No one of these shall fail,

None shall want her mate";
For my mouth it hath commanded,
And his spirit, it hath gathered them.
And he hath cast the lot for them,
And his hand hath divided it to them by line;
They shall possess it forever,
From generation to generation shall they dwell
    therein.

III

I will increase them with men like a flock.
As the holy flock,
As the flock of Jerusalem in their solemn feasts;
So shall the waste cities be filled with flocks of
    men;
And they shall know that I am the Lord.

IV

I am the Lord thy God,
The Holy One of Israel, thy Savior.
I gave Egypt for thy ransom,
Ethiopia and Seba for thee.
Since thou wast precious in my sight,
And honorable, and I have loved thee,
Therefore will I give men for thee,
And people for thy life.

Fear not! for I am with thee:
I will bring thine offspring from the east,
And gather thee from the west;
I will say to the north, "Give up";
And to the south, "Keep not back":
Bring my sons from far,
And my daughters from the ends of the earth,
Even every one that is called by my name;

For I have created him, for my glory;
I have formed him, yea, I have made him.

V

Awake, awake! put on thy strength, O Zion;
Put on thy beautiful garments, O Jerusalem, the
      Holy City.
Shake thyself from the dust, rise, and sit down;
Loose thyself from the bands of thy neck, O
      captive daughter of Zion.
For thus saith the Lord, "Ye have sold your-
      selves for nought,
And ye shall be redeemed without money."

VI

Israel shall be saved in the Lord with an ever-
      lasting salvation;
Ye shall not be ashamed nor confounded, world
      without end.

VII

And he shall set up an ensign for the nations,
And shall assemble the outcasts of Israel,
And gather together the dispersed of Judah
From the four corners of the earth.

VIII

But they shall sit every man under his vine and
      under his fig tree,
And none shall make them afraid;
For the mouth of the Lord hath spoken it.
For all people will walk every one in the name
      of his god,
And we will walk in the name of our God forever
      and ever.

IX

The Lord will have mercy on Jacob,
And will yet choose Israel,
And set them in their own land.
The strangers shall be joined with them,
And they shall cleave to the house of Jacob.
The people shall take them, and bring them to
    their place;
The house of Israel shall possess them in the land
    of the Lord for servants and handmaids;
They shall take them captives, whose captives
    they were;
And they shall rule over their oppressors.

THE RETURN OF THE MOTHER WITH HER CHILDREN

Sing, O childless one, thou that hast not borne;
Break forth into singing, and cry aloud, thou that hast
    not travailed;
For more are the children of the desolate
Than the children of the married wife.
Enlarge the place of thy tent,
And let them stretch forth the curtains of thy habitations;
Spare not; lengthen thy cords,
And strengthen thy stakes:
For thou shalt break forth on the right hand and on
    the left,
And thy family shall inherit the Gentiles,
And make the desolate cities to be inhabited.

Fear not, for thou shalt not be ashamed:
Neither be thou confounded, for thou shalt not be put
    to shame;
For thou shalt forget the shame of thy youth,

And shalt not remember the reproach of thy widowhood
    any more.
For thy Maker is thy husband,
The Lord of hosts is his name;
And thy Redeemer, the Holy One of Israel,
"God of the whole earth," shall he be called.

For the Lord hath called thee as a woman forsaken and
    grieved in spirit,
As a wife of youth, when thou wast rejected.
For a small moment have I forsaken thee,
But with great mercies will I gather thee:
In a little wrath I hid my face from thee for a mo-
    ment,
But with great mercies will I have mercy on thee.

For the mountains shall depart,
And the hills be removed,
But my kindness shall not depart from thee,
Neither shall the covenant of my peace be removed.

O thou afflicted, tossed with tempest, and not comforted:
Behold, I will set thy stones with fair colors,
And lay thy foundation with sapphires;
I will make thy windows of agates,
And thy gates of carbuncles,
And all thy borders of pleasant stones.
All thy children shall be taught of the Lord,
And great shall be the peace of thy children.

SONG FOR THE WATCHMEN OF JERUSALEM

AFTER THE RETURN

How beautiful upon the mountains are the feet of him
That bringeth good tidings, that publisheth peace,

That bringeth good tidings of good, that publish-
    eth salvation,
That saith to Zion, "Thy God reigneth!"

Thy watchmen shall lift up the voice,
With the voice together shall they sing;
For they shall see, eye to eye,
How the Lord shall bring again Zion.

Break forth into joy, sing together,
Ye waste places of Jerusalem:
For the Lord hath comforted his people,
He hath redeemed Jerusalem.

The Lord hath made bare his holy arm
In the eyes of all the nations,
And all the ends of the earth
Shall see the salvation of our God.

A SONG OF GOD'S OWN PRESENCE IN THE RETURN

I will mention the lovingkindnesses of the Lord,
And the praises of the Lord,
According to all that the Lord hath bestowed on
    us,
And the great goodness toward the house of Israel,
Which he hath bestowed on them according to his
    mercies,
According to the multitude of his lovingkindnesses.
For he said, "Surely they are my people,
Children that will not lie";
So he was their Savior:
In all their affliction he was afflicted,
And the angel of his presence saved them:

1V-225

"HO! EVERY ONE THAT THIRSTETH, COME YE TO THE WATERS"

In his love and in his pity he redeemed them,
And he took them up, and carried them, all the
    days of old.

THE RETURN TO JEHOVAH

Ho! every one that thirsteth, come ye to the waters,
And he that hath no money; come ye, buy, and eat;
Yea, come, buy wine and milk
Without money and without price.
Wherefore do ye spend money for that which is not
    bread,
And your labor for that which satisfieth not?
Hearken diligently to me, and eat ye that which is
    good,
And let your soul delight itself in fatness.

Incline your ear, and come unto me;
Hear, and your soul shall live:
And I will make an everlasting covenant with you,
Even the sure mercies of David.
Behold, I have given him for a witness to the people,
A leader and commander to the people.
Behold, thou shalt call a nation that thou knowest not,
And nations that have not known thee shall run to thee,
Because of the Lord thy God,
And for the Holy One of Israel,
For he hath glorified thee.

Seek ye the Lord while he may be found;
Call ye upon him, while he is near:
Let the wicked forsake his way,
And the unrighteous man his thoughts;
And let him return to the Lord,
And he will have mercy upon him;

And to our God,
For he will abundantly pardon.
For my thoughts are not your thoughts,
Neither are your ways my ways, saith the Lord.
But as the heavens are higher than the earth,
So are my ways higher than your ways,
And my thoughts than your thoughts.
For as the rain cometh down, and the snow from
      heaven,
And returneth not thither, but watereth the earth,
And maketh it bring forth and bud,
That it may give seed to the sower,
And bread to the eater:
So shall my word be that goeth forth out of my
      mouth;
It shall not return to me void,
But it shall accomplish that which I please,
And it shall prosper in the thing whereto I sent it.
For ye shall go out with joy,
And be led forth with peace;
The mountains and the hills shall break out before
      you into singing,
And all the trees of the field shall clap their hands.
Instead of the thorn shall come up the fir tree,
And instead of the brier shall come up the myrtle tree;
And it shall be to the Lord for a name [a memorial],
For an everlasting sign which shall not be cut off.

A NEW HEART AND A NEW SPIRIT

I

Although I have cast them far off among the
      nations,
And although I have scattered them among the
      countries,

Yet will I be to them for a little while as a sanc-
      tuary
In the countries where they shall come.
I will even gather you from the peoples,
And assemble you out of the countries where ye
      have been scattered,
And I will give you the land of Israel.

They shall come thither;
And I will give them one heart,
I will put a new spirit within them;
I will take the stony heart out of their flesh,
And I will give them a heart of flesh:
That they may walk in my statutes,
And keep mine ordinances and do them:
They shall be my people,
And I will be their God.

II

Then will I sprinkle clean water upon you, and ye
      shall be clean;
From all your filthiness and from all your idols
      will I cleanse you.

A new heart also will I give you,
And a new spirit will I put within you;
I will take away the stony heart out of your flesh,
And I will give you a heart of flesh.
I will put my spirit within you,
And cause you to walk in my statutes,
And ye shall keep my judgments, and do them.

Ye shall dwell in the land that I gave your fathers;
And ye shall be my people,
And I will be your God.

A VIEW OF JERUSALEM

From an etching by E. M. Lilien

THE BETTER COUNTRY

THE LAND OF BEULAH

AND thou shalt be called by a new name
  Which the mouth of the Lord shall name:
Thou shalt also be a crown of beauty in the hand of
      the Lord,
And a royal diadem in the hand of thy God.
No more shalt thou be termed "Forsaken";
Neither shall thy land any more be termed "Desolate":
But thou shalt be called Hephzi-bah [My Delight Is
      in Her],
And thy land Beulah [Married][33];
For the Lord delighteth in thee,
And thy land shall be married.
For as a young man marrieth a maiden,
So shall thy sons [or, Thy Builder] marry thee:
And as the bridegroom rejoiceth over the bride,
So shall thy God rejoice over thee.
I have set watchmen upon thy walls, O Jerusalem;
Who shall never hold their peace, day nor night:
Ye that make mention of the Lord, keep not silence,
And give him no rest until he establish,
And until he make Jerusalem a praise in the earth.
And they shall call them "The holy people,"
"The redeemed of the Lord":
And thou shalt be called "Sought out,"
"A city not forsaken."

A SONG OF REBUILDING AND REPLANTING

Yea, I have loved thee with an everlasting love;
Therefore with lovingkindness have I drawn thee.

Again I will build thee,
And thou shalt be built, O virgin of Israel:
Thou shalt again be adorned with thy tabrets,
And shalt go forth in the dances of them that make
    merry.
Thou shalt yet plant vines upon the mountains of
    Samaria:
The planters shall plant, and shall eat them as
    common things.

Behold, I will bring them from the north country,
And gather them from the coasts of the earth,
And with them the blind and the lame:
A great company shall return thither.
They shall come with weeping,
And with supplications will I lead them:
I will cause them to walk by the rivers of waters
In a straight way, wherein they shall not stumble;
For I am a father to Israel,
And Ephraim is my first-born.[34]

PROSPERITY TO FARM AND VINEYARD

BUTTER AND HONEY

And it shall come to pass in that day,
That a man shall keep alive a young cow and two
    sheep;
And because of the abundance of milk that they
    shall give he shall eat butter;
For butter and honey shall every one eat that is
    left in the land.

JOY IN THE GARDENS

The Lord shall comfort Zion,
He will comfort all her waste places;

©*Rau Art Studios*

THE PLAIN OF SHARON

Nothing can be more ravishingly brilliant than the Plain of Sharon in spring. The vegetation is lush, a vivid green, and scattered everywhere, as on the pattern of a carpet, are the most gorgeous flowers of all colors, red, blue, and scarlet. There are a dozen shades of anemones; the red predominates, however, the deep red of the "Rose of Sharon."

And he will make her wilderness like Eden,
And her desert like the garden of the Lord:
Joy and gladness shall be found therein,
Thanksgiving and the voice of melody.

THE INHERITANCE OF THE MOUNTAINS

As the new wine is found in the cluster,
And one saith, "Destroy it not, for a blessing is in it";

So will I do for my servants' sake,
That I may not destroy them all.
I will bring forth a nation out of Jacob,
And out of Judah an inheritor of my mountains;
My chosen shall inherit it,
And my servants shall dwell there.
Sharon shall be a fold of flocks,
And the valley of Achor a place for the herds to
　　　lie down in,
For my people that have sought me.

Abundance of Harvests

Behold, the days come that the plowman shall
　　　overtake the reaper,
And the treader of grapes him that soweth seed.
The mountains shall drop sweet wine,
And all the hills shall melt.
I will bring again the captivity of my people of
　　　Israel,
And they shall build the waste cities, and inhabit them;
They shall plant vineyards, and drink the wine
　　　thereof;
They shall also make gardens, and eat the fruit
　　　of them.
I will plant them upon their land,
And they shall no more be pulled up out of their
　　　land, which I have given them.

THE PILLAR OF CLOUD AND OF FIRE

In that day shall the branch of the Lord be beau-
　　　tiful and glorious,
And the fruit of the earth shall be excellent and
　　　comely
For them that are escaped of Israel.

And the Lord will create upon every dwelling
     place of mount Zion,
And upon her assemblies,
A cloud and smoke by day,
And the shining of a flaming fire by night:
For upon all, the glory shall be a defense;
And there shall be a pavilion for a shadow in the
     daytime from the heat,
And for a covert from storm and from rain.

GOD THE CROWN OF HIS PEOPLE

In that day shall the Lord of hosts be for a crown of
    glory,
And for a diadem of beauty to the residue of his people,
And for a spirit of justice to him that sitteth in judgment,
And for strength to them that turn back the battle at
    the gate.

NO MORE CRYING

I

Thou shalt weep no more;
He will be very gracious to thee at the voice of
    thy cry;
When he shall hear it, he will answer thee.

And though the Lord hath given you
The bread of adversity and the water of affliction,
Yet shall not thy teacher be removed into a cor-
    ner any more,
But thine eyes shall see thy teacher.

And thine ears shall hear a word behind thee,
    saying,
"This is the way; walk ye in it!"

When ye turn to the right hand and when ye turn
    to the left.

In that day shall thy cattle feed in large pastures.
The oxen likewise and the young asses that till
    the ground
Shall eat clean provender,
Which hath been winnowed with the shovel and
    with the fan.

And there shall be upon every high mountain and
    upon every high hill,
Rivers and streams of water,
In the day of the great slaughter,
When the towers fall.

Moreover the light of the moon shall be as the
    light of the sun,
And the light of the sun shall be sevenfold,
On the day that the Lord bindeth up the wound
    of his people,
And healeth the hurt of their wound.

II

A voice was heard in Ramah, lamentation, and
    bitter weeping,
Rachel, weeping for her children:
She refuseth to be comforted for her children,
Because they are not.

Refrain thy voice from weeping,
And thine eyes from tears:
For thy work shall be rewarded,
And they shall come again from the land of the enemy.
And there is hope in thy latter end,
That thy children shall come again to their own border.

JOY INSTEAD OF MOURNING

He that scattered Israel will gather him,
And keep him, as a shepherd doth his flock.
For the Lord hath redeemed Jacob,
And ransomed him from the hand of him that was
    stronger than he.
Therefore they shall come and sing in the height of Zion,
And shall flow together to the goodness of the Lord,
For wheat, and for wine, and for oil,
And for the young of the flock and of the herd.
Their soul shall be as a watered garden;
And they shall not sorrow any more at all.
Then shall the maiden rejoice in the dance,
Both young men and old together:
For I will turn their mourning into joy,
And will comfort them, and make them rejoice from
    their sorrow.

THE CITY IMPREGNABLE

Behold, I have created the smith that bloweth the
    coals in the fire,
And that bringeth forth an instrument for his work,
And I have created the waster to destroy.
But no weapon that is formed against thee shall
    prosper,
And every tongue that shall rise against thee in
    judgment thou shalt condemn.
This is the heritage of the servants of the Lord,
And their righteousness is of me.

THE NEW HEAVEN AND EARTH

For, behold, I create new heavens and a new earth;
And the former shall not be remembered,
Nor come into mind.

But be ye glad and rejoice forever in that which I
        create:
For behold, I create Jerusalem a rejoicing,
And her people a joy.
I will rejoice in Jerusalem,
And joy in my people:
And the voice of weeping shall be no more heard in her,
Nor the voice of crying.

There shall no longer be there an infant of days,
Nor an old man that hath not filled out his days:
For the child will die when a hundred years old,
But the sinner, when a hundred years old, shall be
        accursed.

And they shall build houses, and inhabit them;
And they shall plant vineyards, and eat the fruit of them.
They shall not build, and another inhabit;
They shall not plant, and another eat:
For like the days of a tree are the days of my people,
And my chosen shall long enjoy the work of their
        hands.
They shall not labor in vain,
Nor bring forth for trouble;
For they are the family of the blessed of the Lord,
And their offspring with them.
And it shall come to pass that before they call, I
        will answer;
And while they are yet speaking, I will hear.

AS THE STARS FOR EVER AND EVER

At that time shall Michael stand up,
The great prince who standeth for the children of thy
        people;

MICHAEL

From a painting by Raphael

The archangel Michael stands for the protecting power of God, for the divine militancy that will not allow his Holy Ones to suffer.

"And at that time shall Michael stand up, the great Prince who standeth for the children of thy people; and at that time thy people shall be delivered."

And there shall be a time of trouble,
Such as never was since there was a nation even to that
     same time;
At that time thy people shall be delivered,
Every one that shall be found written in the book.
Many of them that sleep in the dust of the earth shall
     awake,
Some to everlasting life, and some to shame and ever-
     lasting contempt.
They that are wise shall shine as the brightness of the
     firmament,
And they that turn many to righteousness as the stars
     for ever and ever.

GOD'S PURPOSES FOR THE WHOLE WORLD

PEACE AMONG THE NATIONS

AND in the last days it shall come to pass
That the mountain of the Lord's house
Shall be established in the top
Of the mountains,
And it shall be exalted above the hills.
People shall flow to it,
And many nations shall come, and say:

"Come, and let us go up to the mountain of the Lord,
And to the house of the God of Jacob;
He will teach us of his ways,
And we will walk in his paths;
For the law shall go forth out of Zion,
And the word of the Lord from Jerusalem."[35]

Then he shall judge among many nations,
And rebuke strong nations afar off:
They shall beat their swords into plowshares,
And their spears into pruning hooks;
Nation shall not lift up sword against nation,
Neither shall they learn war any more.
But they shall sit, every man under his vine
And under his fig tree,
And none shall make them afraid.

ISRAEL AS LIBERATOR

Thus saith the Lord,
The Redeemer of Israel, and his Holy One,

To him whom man despiseth,
To him whom the nation abhorreth,
To a servant of rulers:
"Kings shall see and arise,
Princes also shall worship,
Because of the Lord that is faithful,
And the Holy One of Israel, who hath chosen thee."

Thus saith the Lord:
"In an acceptable time have I heard thee,
And in a day of salvation have I helped thee;
And I will preserve thee,
And give thee for a covenant of the people,
To establish the earth,
To cause to inherit the waste heritages;
That thou mayest say to the prisoners, 'Go forth';
To them that are in darkness, 'Show yourselves.'"

GOD'S PEOPLE, THE LIGHT OF THE NATIONS

Listen, O isles, to me,
And hearken, ye people from afar!
The Lord hath called me from birth.
From my mother's lap hath he made mention of
        my name.
He hath made my mouth like a sharp sword;
In the shadow of his hand hath he hid me.
He made me a polished arrow;
In his quiver hath he hid me.
He said to me, "Thou art my servant,
O Israel, in whom I will be glorified."
But I said, "I have labored in vain;
I have spent my strength for nought, and in vain;
Yet surely my judgment is with the Lord,
And my word is with my God."

And now saith the Lord,
Who formed me from birth to be his servant,
To bring Jacob again to him,
And that Israel should be gathered unto him:
"It is too light a thing that thou shouldst be my
      servant,
To raise up the tribes of Jacob,
And to restore the dispersed of Israel;
I will also give thee for a light to the Gentiles,
That thou mayest be my salvation to the ends of
      the earth."[36]

REDEMPTION OF THE ANCIENT ENEMIES OF GOD'S PEOPLE

In that day shall five cities in the land of Egypt speak the language of Canaan and swear to the Lord of hosts.

The Lord shall be known to Egypt, and the Egyptians shall know the Lord in that day, and shall worship with sacrifice and oblation; yea, they shall vow a vow to the Lord and perform it.

In that day there shall be a highway out of Egypt to Assyria. And the Assyrian shall come into Egypt, and the Egyptian into Assyria, and the Egyptians shall worship with the Assyrians.

In that day shall Israel be the third part with Egypt and Assyria, even a blessing in the midst of the earth, whom the Lord shall bless, saying,

      "Blessed be Egypt my people,
      And Assyria the work of my hands,
      And Israel mine inheritance."

THE HOME–COMING OF THE NATIONS

It shall yet come to pass that there shall come peoples,
And the inhabitants of many cities;

And the inhabitants of one city shall go to another, saying,
"Let us go speedily to pray before the Lord,
And to seek the Lord of hosts;
I will go also."
Yea, many peoples and strong nations shall come
To seek the Lord of hosts in Jerusalem,
And to pray before the Lord.

In those days it shall come to pass that ten men shall
    take hold
(Out of all languages of the nations),
They shall take hold of the skirt of him who is a Jew,
    saying,
"We will go with you,
For we have heard that God is with you."

THE ALIEN SHALL BE AS THE HOME-BORN

Also the sons of the stranger that join themselves
    to the Lord
To serve him, and to love the name of the Lord,
To be his servants,
Every one that keepeth the sabbath from profan-
    ing it,
And taketh hold of my covenant;
Even them will I bring to my holy mountain,
And make them joyful in my house of prayer;
Their burnt offerings and their sacrifices shall be
    accepted upon mine altar:
For my house shall be called a house of prayer for all
    people.
The Lord God who gathereth the outcasts of Israel
    saith,
"Yet will I gather others to him,
Besides his own that are gathered."

WORLD–WIDE RIGHTEOUSNESS AND PRAISE

I

I will greatly rejoice in the Lord,
My soul shall be joyful in my God;
For he hath clothed me with the garments of
        salvation,
He hath covered me with the robe of righteousness,
As a bridegroom decketh himself with ornaments,
And as a bride adorneth herself with her jewels:
For as the earth bringeth forth her bud,
And as the garden causeth the things that are
        sown in it to spring forth,
So the Lord God will cause righteousness
And praise to spring forth before all the nations.

II

From the uttermost part of the earth have we
        heard songs,
Even glory to the righteous.

III

Look to me, and be ye saved, all the ends of the
        earth;
For I am the Lord, and there is none else:
I have sworn by myself,
The word is gone out of my mouth in righteous-
        ness, and shall not return:
That to me every knee shall bow,
And every tongue shall swear.

THE WISDOM OF OLD AGE
From a painting by Alfred Aghace

THE WORDS OF THE WISE

WISDOM AND ITS TEACHINGS

THE INSTRUCTION OF WISDOM

TO know wisdom and instruction:
To perceive the words of understanding:
To receive the instruction of wisdom, justice, and
      judgment, and equity:
To give prudence to the simple:
To the young man knowledge and discretion:
That the wise may hear and increase in learning:
And that the man of understanding may attain unto
      wise counsels:
To understand a proverb and the interpretation:
The words of the wise and their dark sayings.

THE CALL OF WISDOM

Doth not wisdom cry,
And understanding put forth her voice?
She standeth on the top of high places by the way,
In the places of the paths.
She crieth at the gates at the entrance of the city,
At the coming in of the doors:
"To you, O men, I call;
And my voice is to the sons of men.
O ye simple, understand wisdom:
And ye fools, be of an understanding heart.
Hear, for I will speak of excellent things;
And the opening of my lips shall be right things.
For my mouth shall speak truth:
Wickedness is an abomination to my lips.
All the words of my mouth are in righteousness;
There is nothing froward and perverse in them.

They are all plain to him that understandeth,
And right to them that find knowledge.
Receive my instruction, and not silver;
And knowledge rather than choice gold.
For wisdom is better than rubies;
And all things that may be desired are not to be
      compared to her.

"I, wisdom, dwell with prudence,
And find out knowledge and discretion.
The fear of the Lord is to hate evil.
Pride, and arrogancy, and the evil way, and the
      froward mouth, do I hate.
Counsel is mine, and sound wisdom;
I am understanding; I have strength.

"By me kings reign,
And princes decree justice.
By me princes rule,
And nobles, even all the judges of the earth.
I love them that love me;
And those that seek me early shall find me
Riches and honor are with me;
Yea, durable riches and righteousness.
My fruit is better than gold, yea, than fine gold;
And my revenue than choice silver.
I lead in the way of righteousness,
In the midst of the paths of judgment:
That I may cause those that love me to inherit sub-
      stance,
And that I may fill their treasuries.

"The Lord formed me first of his creation,
Before his works of old.
I was set up from everlasting,

From the beginning of the earth.
When as yet there were no depths, I was brought
　　　forth;
When there were no fountains abounding with water.
Before the mountains were settled,
Before the hills was I brought forth;
While as yet he had not made the earth, nor the
　　　fields,
Nor the beginning of the dust of the world.
When he prepared the heavens, I was there:
When he drew a circle on the face of the deep,[37]
When he established the sky above,
When he strengthened the fountains of the deep,
When he gave to the sea his decree,
That the waters should not pass his commandment,
When he appointed the foundations of the earth;
Then was I by him, as one brought up with him;
And was daily his delight,
Rejoicing always before him,
Rejoicing in his habitable earth;
And my delights were with the sons of men."

IN PRAISE OF WISDOM

Bow down thine ear, and hear the words of the wise,[38]
And apply thy heart to my knowledge.
For it is a pleasant thing if thou keep me within thee;
If they be established together upon thy lips.
That thy trust may be in the Lord,
I have made them known to thee this day, even to
　　　thee.
Have not I written to thee excellent things
Of counsels and knowledge,
To make thee know the certainty of the words of
　　　truth;

That thou mayest answer words of truth to them
    that send thee?

Wisdom is the principal thing;
Therefore get wisdom:
Yea, with all thy getting,
Get understanding.

Exalt her, and she will promote thee;
She will bring thee to honor, when thou dost embrace
    her.
She will give to thy head a chaplet of grace:
A crown of beauty will she deliver to thee.

Through wisdom is a house builded;
And by understanding it is established:
And by knowledge shall the chambers be filled
With all precious and pleasant riches.

My son, eat thou honey, because it is good;
And the honeycomb, which is sweet to thy taste.
So shall the knowledge of wisdom be to thy soul:
When thou hast found it, then there shall be a reward,
And thy expectation shall not be cut off.

Wisdom strengtheneth the wise more than ten mighty
men which are in the city.

My son, attend to my wisdom;
And bow thine ear to my understanding:
That thou mayest regard discretion,
And that thy lips may keep knowledge.

Wisdom is a defense, and money is a defense: but the excellency of knowledge is, that wisdom giveth life to them that have it.

The fear of the Lord is the beginning of wisdom:
And the knowledge of the Holy One is understanding.

How much better is it to get wisdom than gold!
And to get understanding is rather to be chosen than
    silver.

The law of the wise is a fountain of life,
That one may depart from the snares of death.

Wisdom is before the face of him that hath under-
    standing;
But the eyes of a fool are in the ends of the earth.

When the scorner is punished, the simple is made
    wise:
And when the wise is instructed, he receiveth
    knowledge.

The man that wandereth out of the way of under-
    standing
Shall remain in the congregation of the dead.

There is no wisdom nor understanding nor counsel
    against the Lord.

The fear of the Lord is the beginning of knowledge;
But fools despise wisdom and instruction.

Wisdom is good with an inheritance;
And by it there is profit to them that see the sun.

Understanding is a wellspring of life to him that
        hath it;
But the instruction of fools is folly.

By wise counsel thou shalt make thy war:
And in multitude of counselors there is safety.

The eyes of the Lord preserve knowledge:
And he overthroweth the words of the transgressor.

Buy the truth, and sell it not:
Also wisdom, and instruction, and understanding.

WISDOM'S WARNING

Wisdom crieth aloud in the street;
She uttereth her voice in the broad places;
She standeth amid the crossways;
At the entrance of the city gateways she crieth aloud:

"How long, ye simple ones, will ye love simplicity?
And scorners delight them in scorning,
And fools hate knowledge?
Turn you at my reproof:

Behold, I will pour out my spirit unto you;
I will make known my words unto you.

"Because I have called, and ye have refused;
 I have stretched out my hand,
And no man regarded;
But ye have set at nought all my counsel.
And would none of my reproof:
I also will laugh in the day of your calamity;
I will mock when your fear cometh;
When your fear cometh as a storm,
And your destruction cometh on as a whirlwind;
When distress and anguish come upon you.
Then shall they call upon me,
But I will not answer:

"They shall seek me diligently,
But they shall not find me:
Because they hated knowledge,
And did not choose the fear of the Lord:
They would none of my counsel;
They despised all my reproof.
Therefore shall they eat of the fruit of their own way,
And be filled with their own devices.
For the backsliding of the simple shall slay them,
And the prosperity of fools shall destroy them.
But whoso hearkeneth unto me shall dwell securely,
And shall be quiet without fear of evil."

A WISE MAN'S EXPERIMENT WITH LIFE

This philosopher, under the guise of one who experiments with pleasure, action, and wisdom, finds none of them profitable in itself, though wisdom is certainly better than folly. It is best, therefore, he argues, not to seek satisfaction in future hopes, but to be happy in the present and common joys of life. Of course, his viewpoint was imperfect.

Other Hebrew thinkers came to believe that the longings of man are too great for this one world, and saw in immortality the assurance that life is not vanity.

THE DECISION

I Koheleth [a sage] was king
Over Israel in Jerusalem.
And I set my heart to seek and search out wisdom
Concerning all that is done under heaven.

I have taken note of all the works
That are done under the sun;
And, behold, all is vanity
And vexation of spirit [or, a striving after wind].
That which is crooked cannot be made straight;
And that which is wanting cannot be made good.

I had more wisdom than all before me in Jerusalem;
Yea, my mind had great experience of wisdom and
     learning.
But when I gave my heart to learn wisdom,
I learned it was a striving after wind.
For in much wisdom is much worry;
And he that increaseth knowledge increaseth sorrow.

THE EXPERIMENT WITH PLEASURE

I said in my heart,
"Come! I will test thee with mirth;
Therefore enjoy pleasure."
And, behold, this also is vanity.
I said of laughter, "It is mad";
And of pleasure, "What is it worth?"

THE EXPERIMENT WITH ACTION

I made me great works;
I built me mansions;

I planted me vineyards;
I made me gardens and parks,
And planted all sorts of fruit trees;
I made me pools of water,
To water the nursery of young trees.

I got me menservants and maidens,
And slaves were born in my house;
I gathered me also silver and gold,
Fit treasures of kings and of provinces,
I got me men-singers and women-singers,
And the delights of the sons of men.

So I was great,
And was more wealthy than all that were before me in
    Jerusalem.
Whatsoever my eyes desired, I kept not from them;
I withheld not my heart from any pleasure;
And this was my portion from all my labor.

Then I looked on all my hands had wrought,
And on the labor that I had labored to do,
And behold, all was vanity,
And there was no profit under the sun.

So I hated all my labors
Wherein I had labored under the sun;
Because I must leave it unto the man that shall be after
    me,
And who knoweth whether he will be a wise man or a fool?
Yet will he rule over all my labors,
Wherein I have labored and showed wisdom under the
    sun.
So I began to despair of the labor,
Wherein I had labored under the sun.

For if there be a man who hath labored
In wisdom, and knowledge, and skill;
Yet to a man who hath not labored therein he must
      leave it.
This also is vanity, and a great evil.
What then hath a man from all his labor,
And of the striving of his heart,
Wherein he hath labored under the sun?

For his days are but sorrows,
And his occupation grief,
And his heart findeth no rest in the night.
This also is vanity.

There is nothing better for a man than that he should
      eat and drink
And enjoy pleasure for his labor.
This also I saw,
That it was from the hand of God.

The Experiments with Wisdom

I turned myself to behold wisdom,
And madness, and folly.
Then I saw that wisdom excelleth folly,
As far as light excelleth darkness;
For the wise man hath eyes in his head,
But the fool walketh in darkness.

But I myself perceived,
That one fate happened to them all.
Then I said in my heart,
"Since as it happeneth to the fool,
So it happeneth even to me,
What gain hath my wisdom brought me?"
Then I said in my heart, that this also is vanity.

For there is no remembrance of the wise man
More than of the fool forever:
Therefore I hated life;
Because grievous to me was the work
That is wrought under the sun:
For all is vanity and a striving after wind.

The Conclusion

So go thy way,
Eat thy bread with joy,
And drink thy wine with a merry heart.
Let thy garments be always white,
And let thy head lack no ointment.

Live joyfully with the wife whom thou lovest
All the days of the life of thy vanity,
Which he hath given thee under the sun:
For this is thy portion in life,
And in thy labor which thou makest under the sun.

Whatsoever thy hand findeth to do,
Do it with thy might;
For there is no work, nor planning,
Nor knowledge, nor wisdom, in the grave,
Whither thou goest.

SECURITY THE GIFT OF WISDOM

Happy the man that findeth wisdom,
And the man that getteth understanding;
For her gain is better than the gain of silver,
And her increase than fine gold.
She is more precious than rubies;
And all the things thou canst desire cannot compare
        with her.

Length of days is in her right hand;
And in her left hand riches and honor.
Her ways are ways of pleasantness,
And all her paths are peace.
A tree of life is she to them that lay hold on her,
And happy is every one that retaineth her.

The Lord of wisdom hath founded the earth:
By understanding hath he established the heavens.
By his knowledge the deeps were broken open,
And the clouds distil the dew.

My son, let them not depart from thine eyes;
Keep sound wisdom and discretion:
So shall they be life to thy soul,
And grace to thy neck.
Then shalt thou walk in thy way safely.
And thy foot shall not stumble.
When thou liest down, thou shalt not be afraid;
Yes, thou shalt lie down, and sweet shall be thy sleep.
Be not afraid of sudden fear,
Neither of the desolation of the wicked when it cometh;
For the Lord shall be thy confidence;
And he shall keep thy foot from being taken.

WHERE SHALL WISDOM BE FOUND

Surely there is a mine for silver,
And a place for gold where they refine it.
Iron is taken out of the earth,
And copper is molten out of the stone.
Man setteth an end to darkness,
And searcheth out, to the furthest bound,

The stones of obscurity and of the shadow of death.
He breaketh forth a shaft away underground;
They are forgotten of the foot;
They hang afar from men, they swing to and fro.
The earth, out of which cometh bread,
Underneath it is turned up as it were by fire.
The stones thereof are the place of sapphires,
And it hath dust of gold.
That path no bird of prey knoweth,
Neither hath the falcon's eye seen it:
The proud beasts have not trodden it,
Nor hath the fierce lion passed thereby.
He putteth forth his hand upon the rock;
He overturneth the mountains by the roots.
He cutteth out channels among the rocks;
And his eye seeth every precious thing.
He bindeth the floods from overflowing;
And the thing that is hid bringeth he forth to light.

But where shall wisdom be found?
And where is the place of understanding?
Man knoweth not the price thereof;
Neither is it found in the land of the living.
The deep saith, "It is not in me";
And the sea saith, "It is not with me."
It cannot be gotten for gold,
Neither shall silver be weighed for the price thereof.
It cannot be valued with the gold of Ophir,
With the precious onyx, or the sapphire.
Gold and glass cannot equal it,
Neither shall it be exchanged for jewels of fine gold.
No mention shall be made of coral or of crystal:
Yea, the price of wisdom is above rubies.
The topaz of Ethiopia shall not equal it,
Neither shall it be valued with pure gold.

Whence then cometh wisdom?
And where is the place of understanding?
Seeing it is hid from the eyes of all living,
And kept close from the birds of the heavens.
Destruction and Death say,
"We have heard a rumor thereof with our ears."

God understandeth the way thereof,
And he knoweth the place thereof.
For he looketh to the ends of the earth,
And seeth under the whole heaven;
To make a weight for the wind:
Yea, he meteth out the waters by measure.
When he made a decree for the rain,
And a way for the lightning of the thunder;
Then did he see it, and declare it;
He established it, yea, and searched it out.
And unto man he said,
"Behold, the fear of the Lord, that is wisdom;
And to depart from evil is understanding."

LIFE AND ITS COMPENSATIONS

THE INNER SPIRIT OF MAN

KEEP thy heart with all diligence;
For out of it are the issues of life.

The refining pot is for silver,
And the furnace for gold:
But the Lord trieth the hearts.

The heart knoweth its own bitterness:
And a stranger doth not intermeddle with its joy.

The foolishness of man perverteth his way;
And his heart fretteth against the Lord.

The heart of him that hath understanding seeketh knowl-
    edge;
But the mouth of fools feedeth on folly.

Man's goings are of the Lord;
How can a man then understand his own way?

Who can say, "I have made my heart clean,
I am pure from my sin?"

The heart is deceitful above all things,
And desperately wicked.
Who can know it?

Every way of a man is right in his own eyes:
But the Lord pondereth the hearts.

All the ways of a man are clean in his own eyes:
But the Lord weigheth the spirits.

The spirit of man is the candle of the Lord,
Searching all the inward parts.

The spirit of a man will sustain his infirmity;
But a wounded spirit who can bear?

Hope deferred maketh the heart sick:
But when desire cometh, it is a tree of life.

To the wise the way of life goeth upward,
That he may depart from the grave beneath.

The refining pot is for silver,
And the furnace for gold;
And a man is tried by his praise.

THE RIGHTEOUS AND THE WICKED

The eyes of the Lord are in every place,
Beholding the evil and the good.

When wisdom entereth into thy heart,
And knowledge is pleasant to thy soul;
Discretion shall preserve thee,
Understanding shall keep thee:
To deliver thee from the way of the evil man,
From man that speaketh froward things;
Who leave the paths of uprightness,
To walk in the ways of darkness;
Who rejoice to do evil,
And delight in the frowardness of the wicked:
Who are crooked in their ways,
And froward in their paths:
That thou mayest walk in the way of good men,
And keep the paths of the righteous.

"HOPE DEFERRED MAKETH THE HEART SICK"
From a painting by Arthur Faldi

For the upright shall dwell in the land,
And the perfect shall remain in it.
But the wicked shall be cut off from the earth,
And the transgressors shall be rooted out of it.

A good man leaveth an inheritance to his children's chil-
    dren:
And the wealth of the sinner is laid up for the just.

Behold, the righteous shall be recompensed in the earth:
How much more the wicked and the sinner!

When the wicked rise, men hide themselves;
But when they perish, the righteous increase.

The righteous man considereth the house of the wicked,
How the wicked are overthrown to their ruin.

When it goeth well with the righteous, the city rejoiceth:
And when the wicked perish, there is shouting.

A righteous man regardeth the life of his beast;
But the tender mercies of the wicked are cruel.

Even a child is known by his doings,
Whether his work be pure, and whether it be right.

HOPE

From a painting by George F. Watts

HOPE

From a painting by George F. Watts

At first glance one might think that "Despair" is a more appropriate title, for certainly none of the conventional accompaniments of Hope are to be seen on this canvas. The world on which Hope sits is utterly desolate, swept clean by some cosmic destruction. There is nothing left to delight the eye or to call forth expectation of happy days to come. The earth swings through a sky that is starless. The heavens above, usually so thickly strewn with scintillating emblems of hope, are tonight utterly blank. The symbolic figure of Hope sits in a dejected attitude upon the ruins of all that was once dear, and hugs to her bosom a lyre whose strings, all but one, some cruel fate has blasted. Surely there are no more songs in the soul of this harp. But the genius who painted this combination of symbols has by this very device brought out for us the essential quality of Hope, the quality that refuses to be dismayed even in the presence of catastrophe. Hope has bound her eyes that she may not see the destruction about her, has bound one ear that she may shut out the distractions of a distracted world, and now she is concentrating with all her powers of sense and imagination upon the faint vibration of the one remaining string of her lyre. One string at least is left; and though the music be faint, it is yet music. Thus, to her heart of hope the most intangible of all the voices of nature becomes the sure promise of blessing.

The painter of this picture is by temperament a preacher. In the Tate Gallery, London, is a whole room devoted to the allegories of Watts. There one has a chance to realize that, under the strange and sometimes obscure figures that the artist has put upon the canvas, is an earnest purpose to teach some great lesson about life. There, for example, is Mammon, a huge, unlovely creature that sacrifices the life of the rising generation to his lust for gold. There are those other glowing canvases in which Love is represented triumphant over Time and Death. There are pictured life's illusions that man pursues with such fervor, only to find that "the paths of glory lead but to the grave." There is that solemn judgment on the values of life in the somber painting entitled, "Thus Passes the Glory of the World," in which at the foot of a bier are the symbols of all the arts and sciences, the knowledge, the skill, the power that once brought fame but are now worthless in the presence of all-conquering death. The whole series indicates in the most striking way how the beauty and the power of art can be made to serve moral and spiritual ends and may perform the function of the ancient preachers of righteousness. Watts himself says, "All my pictures in the Tate Gallery are symbolical and for all time. My intention has not been so much to paint pictures that will charm the eye as to suggest great thoughts that will appeal to the imagination and the heart, and kindle all that is best and noblest in humanity."

265

The Lord is far from the wicked;
But he heareth the prayer of the righteous.

The way of the wicked is an abomination to the Lord;
But he loveth him that followeth after righteousness.

Thorns and snares are in the way of the froward:
He that doth keep his soul shall be far from them.

Evil men understand not judgment;
But they that seek the Lord understand all things.

The wicked flee when no man pursueth;
But the righteous are bold as a lion.

Oh let the wickedness of the wicked come to an end, but
        establish the just;
For the righteous God trieth the minds and hearts.
My defense is of God,
Who saveth the upright in heart.
God is a righteous judge,
Yea, a God that hath indignation every day.

REWARDS OF THE RIGHTEOUS

The hoary head is a crown of glory,
If it be found in the way of righteousness.[39]

When a man's ways please the Lord,
He maketh even his enemies to be at peace with him.

The path of the just is as the dawning light,
That shineth more and more unto the perfect day.

For God giveth to a man that is good in his sight, wisdom,
and knowledge, and joy; but to the sinner he giveth travail,
to gather and to heap up, that he may give to him that is
good before God.

The fear of the Lord prolongeth days;
But the years of the wicked shall be shortened.

The Lord will not suffer the soul of the righteous to famish;
But he casteth away the substance of the wicked.

In the way of righteousness is life;
And in the pathway thereof there is no death.

The fruit of the righteous is a tree of life;
And he that winneth souls is wise.

The labor of the righteous tendeth to life:
The fruit of the wicked to sin.

The fear of the wicked, it shall come upon him:
But the desire of the righteous shall be granted.

The righteous is delivered out of trouble;
And the wicked cometh in his stead.

Treasures of wickedness profit nothing;
But righteousness delivereth from death.

The wicked worketh a deceitful work:
But to him that soweth righteousness shall be a sure
     reward.

As righteousness tendeth to life,
So he that pursueth evil pursueth it to his own death.

He that diligently seeketh good procureth favor:
But he that seeketh mischief, it shall come to him.

A good man obtaineth favor of the Lord;
But a man of wicked devices will he condemn.

A man shall not be established by wickedness;
But the root of the righteous shall not be moved.

The wicked are overthrown and are not;
But the house of the righteous shall stand.

Evil pursueth sinners;
But to the righteous good shall be repaid.

He that followeth after righteousness and mercy
Findeth life, righteousness, and honor.

The light of the righteous rejoiceth;
But the lamp of the wicked shall be put out.

In the house of the righteous is much treasure;
But in the revenues of the wicked is trouble.

The hope of the righteous shall be gladness;
But the expectation of the wicked shall perish.

As the whirlwind passeth, so is the wicked no more;
But the righteous is an everlasting foundation.

The righteous shall never be moved;
But the wicked shall not inhabit the earth.

The righteousness of the perfect shall direct his way;
But the wicked shall fall by his own wickedness.

The name of the Lord is a strong tower:
The righteous runneth into it and is safe.

The wicked is driven away in his wickedness;
But the righteous hath hope in his death.

Do they not err that devise evil?
But mercy and truth shall be to them that devise good.

Though a sinner do evil a hundred times, and his days be prolonged, yet surely I know that it shall be well with them that fear God.

The blessing of the Lord, it maketh rich,
And he addeth no sorrow with it.

THE LOT OF THE TRANSGRESSOR

There is a way that seemeth right to a man;
But the end thereof are the ways of death.

Be not thou envious against evil men,
Neither desire to be with them:
For their heart studieth oppression,
And their lips talk of mischief.

Fret not thyself because of evil men,
Neither be thou envious at the wicked;
For there shall be no reward to the evil man;
The candle of the wicked shall be put out.

His own iniquities shall take the wicked man himself,
And he shall be held with the cords of his sins.
He shall die without instruction;
And in the greatness of his folly he shall go astray.

The soul of the wicked desireth evil:
His neighbor findeth no favor in his eyes.

Good understanding giveth favor;
But the way of transgressors is hard.

He that soweth iniquity shall reap vanity:
And the rod of his anger shall fail.

The wicked shall be a ransom for the righteous,
And the transgressor for the upright.

When the wicked cometh, then cometh also contempt;
And with ignominy, reproach.

Whoso rewardeth evil for good,
Evil shall not depart from his house.

The evil bow before the good:
And the wicked at the gates of the righteous.

The Lord hath made all things for himself:
Yea, even the wicked for the day of evil.

Be sure your sin will find you out.

Woe unto them that call evil good, and good evil;
That put darkness for light, and light for darkness;
That put bitter for sweet, and sweet for bitter!

TRUST IN THE LORD

Thus saith the Lord:
  "Cursed be the man that trusteth in man,
    And maketh flesh his arm;
    Whose heart departeth from the Lord.
    For he shall be like the heath in the desert,
    And shall not see when good cometh,
    But shall inhabit the parched places in the wilderness,
    In a salt land and not inhabited.

  "Blessed is the man that trusteth in the Lord,
    Whose hope the Lord is.
    For he shall be as a tree planted by the waters,
    That spreadeth out her roots by the river,
    And shall not see when heat cometh,
    But her leaf shall be green;
    And shall not be anxious in the year of drought,
    Neither shall cease from yielding fruit."

  A man's heart deviseth his way:
  But the Lord directeth his steps.

  Say not thou, "I will recompense evil";
  But wait on the Lord, and he will save thee.

  The horse is prepared against the day of battle;
  But safety is of the Lord.

  Commit thy works to the Lord,
  And thy thoughts shall be established.

The ways of man are before the eyes of the Lord,
And he pondereth all his goings.

The fear of man bringeth a snare:
But whoso putteth his trust in the Lord shall be safe.

Every word of God is pure:
He is a shield to them that
     put their trust in him.

In the fear of the Lord is
     strong confidence:
And his children shall have a
     place of refuge.

———

FAITH

From a painting by Sir Edward Burne-Jones

Faith is personified as a beautiful woman in pensive mood. In her right hand she holds a lamp, the flame of which is burning brightly. This is a symbol of the illumination that faith casts upon the pathway of life. Beneath her left hand springs out a branch of olive, symbol of peace, and about it twines a serpent suggestive of wisdom—"Be ye wise as serpents." The artist means to say that peace and wisdom are the accompaniments of faith. At her feet lies the dragon of error, consumed in the flame of truth. This is the consummation toward which faith works. Above on the capitals of the pilasters sit two cherubs playing with strings on which are rows of beads. The children perhaps stand for the childlike attitude of mind and heart which in a sense is the attitude of faith; and the beads suggest those great religions of mankind that have found in prayer-beads an aid to faith as well as to prayer.

GIFTS

"O World-God, give me Wealth!" the Egyptian cried.
His prayer was granted. High as heaven, behold
Palace and Pyramid; the brimming tide
Of lavish Nile washed all his land with gold;
Armies of slaves toiled ant-wise at his feet;
World-circling traffic roared through mart and street.
His priests were gods, his spice-balmed kings enshrined
Set death at naught in rock-ribbed charnels deep.
Seek Pharaoh's race today, and ye shall find
Rust and the moth, silence and dusty sleep.
"O World-God, give me Beauty!" cried the Greek.
His prayer was granted. All the earth became
Plastic and vocal to his sense; each peak,
Each grove, each stream, quick with Promethean flame,
Peopled the world with imaged grace and light.
The lyre was his, and his the breathing might
Of the immortal marble; his the play
Of diamond-pointed thought and golden tongue.
Go seek the sunshine race; ye find today
A broken column and a lute unstrung.
"O World-God, give me Power!" the Roman cried.
His prayer was granted. The vast world was chained
A captive to the chariot of his pride.
The blood of myriad provinces was drained
To feed that fierce, insatiable red heart.
Invulnerably bulwarked every part
With serried legions and with close-meshed code;
Within, the burrowing worm had gnawed its home.
A roofless ruin stands where once abode
The imperial race of everlasting Rome.
"O Godhead, give me Truth!" the Hebrew cried.
His prayer was granted; he became the slave
Of the Idea, a pilgrim far and wide,
Cursed, hated, spurned, and scourged, with none to save.
The Pharaohs knew him, and when Greece beheld,
His wisdom wore the hoary crown of Eld.
Beauty he hath forsworn, and wealth, and power.
Seek him today, and find in every land.
No fire consumes him, neither floods devour;
Immortal through the lamp within his hand.

—*Emma Lazarus*

By permission of The Houghton Mifflin Company

JOB

JOB

THE PROLOGUE

A PIOUS AND PROSPEROUS MAN OF THE EAST

THERE was a man in the land of Uz,[40] whose name was Job; and that man was perfect and upright, and one that feared God, and shunned evil. And there were born to him seven sons and three daughters.

His substance also was seven thousand sheep, and three thousand camels, and five hundred yoke of oxen, and five hundred she-asses, and a very great household; so that this man was the greatest of all the men of the East.

And his sons went and feasted in their houses, every one on his day; and they sent and called for their three sisters to eat and drink with them.

"THUS DID JOB CONTINUALLY"
From a drawing by Blake

And whenever the days of their feasting were come about, Job sent and purified them, and rose up early in the morning, and offered burnt offerings according to the number of them all; for Job said, "It may be that my sons have sinned, and renounced God in their hearts." Thus did Job continually.

SATAN IS PERMITTED TO PUT JOB TO THE TEST

(Now there was a day when the sons of God[41] came to present themselves before the Lord, and Satan[42] came also among them.)

THE LORD

Whence comest thou?

SATAN

From going to and fro in the earth, and from walking up and down in it.

THE LORD

Hast thou considered my servant Job, that there is none like him in the earth, a perfect and an upright man, one that feareth God, and shunneth evil?

SATAN

Doth Job fear God for nought? Hast not thou made a hedge about him, and about his house, and about all that he hath on every side? Thou hast blessed the work of his hands, and his substance is increased in the land. But put forth thy hand now, and touch all that he hath, and he will renounce thee to thy face.

THE LORD

Behold, all that he hath is in thy power; only upon himself put not forth thy hand.

(So Satan went forth from the presence of the Lord.)

The First Test of Job's Faith

(And there was a day when his sons and his daughters were eating and drinking wine in their eldest brother's house: and there came a messenger to Job.)

FIRST MESSENGER

The oxen were plowing,
And the asses feeding beside them:
And the Sabeans fell upon them, and took them away:
Yea, they have slain the servants with the edge of the
     sword:
And I only am escaped alone to tell thee.

(While he was yet speaking, there came also another.)

SECOND MESSENGER

The fire of God is fallen from heaven,
And hath burned up the sheep, and the servants, and
　　　consumed them:
And I only am escaped alone to tell thee.

(While he was yet speaking, there came also another.)

THIRD MESSENGER

The Chaldeans made three bands,
And fell upon the camels, and have carried them away:
Yea, and slain the servants with the edge of the sword:
And I only am escaped alone to tell thee.

(While he was yet speaking, there came also another.)

"AND I ONLY AM ESCAPED ALONE TO TELL THEE"
From a drawing by Blake

FOURTH MESSENGER

Thy sons and thy daughters were eating and drinking wine
    in their eldest brother's house;
And, behold, there came a great wind from the wilderness,
And smote the four corners of the house,
And it fell upon the young men, and they are dead:
And I only am escaped alone to tell thee.

(Then Job rose, and rent his mantle, and shaved his head,
and fell down upon the ground, and worshiped.)

JOB

Naked came I into the world,
And naked must I return out of it.
The Lord gave, and the Lord hath taken away;
Blessed be the name of the Lord.

(In all this Job sinned not, nor charged God foolishly.)

The Second Test of Job's Faith

(Again there was a day when the sons of God came to
present themselves before the Lord, and Satan came also
among them to present himself before the Lord.)

THE LORD

From whence comest thou?

SATAN

From going to and fro in the earth, and from walking
up and down in it.

THE LORD

Hast thou considered my servant Job, that there is none
like him in the earth, a perfect and an upright man, one that

feareth God, and shunneth evil? and still he holdeth fast his integrity, although thou movedst me against him, to destroy him without cause.

SATAN

Skin for skin, yea, all that a man hath will he give for his life. But put forth thy hand now, and touch his bone and his flesh, and he will renounce thee to thy face.

THE LORD

Behold, he is in thy hand; but save his life.

(So Satan went forth from the presence of the Lord, and smote Job with sore boils from the sole of his foot unto his crown. And he took him a potsherd to scrape himself withal; and he sat down among the ashes.)

JOB'S WIFE

Dost thou still retain thine integrity? renounce God, and die.

JOB

Thou speakest as one of the foolish women speaketh. What? shall we receive good at the hand of God, and shall we not receive evil? (In all this did not Job sin with his lips.)

THE COMING OF JOB'S COMFORTERS

Now when Job's three friends heard of all this evil that was come upon him, they came every one from his own place: Eliphaz the Temanite, and Bildad the Shuhite, and Zophar the Naamathite: for they had made an appointment together to come to mourn with him, and to comfort him. And when they lifted up their eyes afar off, and knew him not, they lifted up their voice, and wept; and they rent

"AND WHEN THEY KNEW HIM NOT, THEY WEPT"
From a drawing by Blake

every one his mantle, and sprinkled dust upon their heads
toward heaven. So they sat down with him upon the ground
seven days and seven nights, and none spoke a word to him:
for they saw that his grief was very great.

THE CURSE

JOB

His sufferings are so intense that he curses the day of his birth,
laments that he was ever born, and longs for death.

JOB CURSES THE DAY HE WAS BORN

Let the day perish wherein I was born,
And the night in which it was said, "There
is a man-child conceived."

"LET THE DAY PERISH WHEREIN I WAS BORN"
From a drawing by Blake

Let that day be darkness;
Let not God regard it from above,
Neither let the light shine upon it.
Let darkness and the shadow of death stain it;
Let a cloud dwell upon it;
Let the blackness of the day terrify it.
As for that night, let thick darkness seize
      upon it;
Let it not be joined unto the days of the year;
Let it not come into the number of the
      months.
Lo, let that night be solitary;
Let no joyful voice come therein.

Let them curse it that curse the day,
Who are ready to arouse leviathan.
Let the stars of the twilight thereof be
      dark;
Let it look for light, but have none;
Neither let it see the dawning of the day,
Because it shut not up the doors of birth,
Nor hid sorrow from mine eyes.

Why died I not from birth?
Why did I not give up the ghost when I
      came into the world?
Why on the knees was I welcomed?

THE SHADOWY LIFE BEYOND THE GRAVE

For now should I have lain still and been
      quiet;
I should have slept; then had I been at rest,
With kings and counselors of the earth,
Who built everlasting sepulchers for them-
      selves;
Or with princes that had gold,
Who filled their houses with silver.

There the wicked cease from troubling,
And there the weary are at rest:
There the prisoners rest together;
They hear not the voice of the oppressor.
The small and great are there;
And the servant is free from his master.

JOB CRIES OUT IN MISERY

Wherefore is light given to him that is in
      misery,
And life unto the bitter in soul;

Who long for death, but it cometh not;
And dig for it more than for hid treasures;
Who rejoice exceedingly,
And are glad, when they can find the grave?
Why is light given to a man whose way is hid,
And whom God hath hedged in?
For my sighing cometh before I eat,
And my groans are poured out like the
     waters.
For the thing which I greatly feared is
     come upon me,
And that which I was afraid of is come
     unto me.

I am not in safety, neither have I rest,
Neither am I quiet; but trouble cometh.

THE FIRST CYCLE OF ARGUMENT

ELIPHAZ

A man of age and wisdom, a mystic, a courteous, quiet thinker, the calmest and most considerate of Job's friends, is Eliphaz. He cannot stand silently by when one who has formerly comforted many others in affliction is, by his own pain, plunged into despair. He reminds Job that only the guilty have cause to feel so desolate. A remarkable vision has taught him that no mere human being has any justification for such complaint as Job makes against God. Were he in Job's place, such suffering would drive him to God for correction and discipline, that it might thus result in blessing.

Job's Irreverence Provokes Eliphaz to Reply

If we venture to commune with thee, wilt
     thou be grieved?
But who can withhold himself from speak-
     ing?
Behold, thou hast instructed many,
And hast strengthened the weak hands.

Thy words have upheld him that was fail-
     ing,
And thou hast strengthened the feeble knees.
But now it has come unto thee, and thou
     faintest:
It toucheth thee, and thou art troubled.

Is not this thy fear of God, thy confidence?
And thy hope, the uprightness of thy ways?
Remember, I pray thee, who ever perished,
     being innocent?
Or where were the righteous cut off?

Even as I have seen, they that plow iniquity,
And sow wickedness, reap the same.
By the blast of God they perish,
And by the breath of his nostrils are they
     consumed.

The roaring of the lion, and the voice of
     the fierce lion,
And the teeth of the young lions, are
     broken.
The old lion perisheth for lack of prey,
And the lioness' whelps are scattered
     abroad.

Eliphaz Describes His Vision

Now a thing was secretly brought to me,
And mine ear received a whisper thereof.
In thoughts from the visions of the night,
When deep sleep falleth on men,
Fear came upon me and trembling,
Which made all my bones to shake.
Then a spirit passed before my face:

"THEN A SPIRIT PASSED BEFORE MY FACE"
From a drawing by Blake

The hair of my flesh stood up.
It stood still, but I could not discern the
        form thereof;
An image was before mine eyes.
There was silence, and I heard a voice
        saying:
"Shall mortal man be more just than God?
Shall a man be more pure than his Maker?"
Behold, he putteth no trust in his servants,
And his angels he chargeth with folly:
How much less in them that dwell in houses
        of clay,
Whose foundation is in the dust,
Who are crushed before the moth?
They are destroyed, from morning to eve-
        ning:
They perish forever without any regard-
        ing it.
Is not their tent cord torn up in them?
They die, but not in wisdom.

Only the Foolish Resent God's Dealings

Call now, if there be any that will answer
        thee;
And to which of the angels wilt thou turn?
For wrath killeth the foolish man,
And indignation slayeth the silly one.

I have seen the foolish taking root:
But suddenly his branch became rotten.
His children are far from safety,
And they are crushed in the gate,
Neither is there any to deliver them:
Whose harvest the hungry eateth up,
And taketh it even out of the thorns,

And the thirsty draw from their wells.
For affliction cometh not forth from the dust,
Neither doth trouble spring out of the
   ground;
But man is born to trouble,
As the sparks fly upward.

The Goodness of God Is Shown in His Chastening

Were it I, I would seek unto God,
And unto God would I commit my cause;
Who doeth great things and unsearchable,
Marvelous things without number:
Who giveth rain upon the earth,
And sendeth waters upon the fields:
To set up on high those that be low,
That those who mourn may be exalted to safety.

He frustrateth the devices of the crafty,
So that their hands cannot perform their
   enterprise.
He taketh the wise in their own craftiness:
And the counsel of the cunning is carried
   headlong.
They meet with darkness in the daytime,
And grope at noonday as in the night.
But he saveth from the sword of their mouth,
Even the needy from the hand of the mighty.
So the poor hath hope,
And iniquity stoppeth her mouth.

Behold, happy is the man whom God correcteth:
Therefore despise not thou the chastening of the
   Almighty.
For he maketh sore, and bindeth up;
He woundeth, and his hands make whole.

He will deliver thee in six troubles;
Yea, in seven there shall no evil touch thee.
In famine he shall redeem thee from death;
And in war from the power of the sword.
Thou shalt be hid from the scourge of the tongue;
Neither shalt thou be afraid of destruction when
      it cometh.
At destruction and famine thou shalt laugh;
Neither shalt thou be afraid of the beasts of the
      earth.
For thou shalt be in league with the stones of the
      field;
And the beasts of the field shall be at peace with thee.
And thou shalt know that thy tent is peace;
And thou shalt visit thy fold, and nothing shalt
      thou miss.
Thou shalt know also that thy family shall be
      great,
And thine offspring as the grass of the earth.
Thou shalt come to thy grave in a full age,
Like as a shock of corn cometh in its season.

Lo this, we have searched it, so it is:
Hear it, and know thou it for thy good.

JOB

Job excuses his impatience on account of the intensity of his misery, which his friends do not realize; a misery so great that death would be a welcome relief. He expects kindness from his friends, but he finds them cold and critical. Instead of constructive counsel they offer reproof. In the bitterness of his soul he dares to accuse God of being a tyrannical persecutor, pursuing him with unrelenting severity even unto death.

Job Defends His Impatience

Oh that my vexation were thoroughly weighed,
And my calamity set in the balance against it!

JOB AND HIS THREE FRIENDS
From a painting by R. Leinweber

For now it would be heavier than the sand of the
        sea:
Therefore have my words been rash.
For the arrows of the Almighty are within me,
The poison whereof drinketh up my spirit:
The terrors of God do set themselves in array
        against me.

Doth the wild ass bray when he hath grass?
Or loweth the ox over his fodder?
Can that which is unsavory be eaten without salt?
Or is there any taste in the white of an egg?
The things that my soul refuseth to touch
Are as my loathsome food.

Job Longs for Death

Oh that I might have my request;
And that God would grant me the thing that I
        long for!
Even that it would please God to crush me,
That he would let loose his hand, and cut me off
Then would it still be my consolation,
And I would exult in anguish that spareth not.
For I have not disowned the words of the Holy
        One.

What is my strength, that I should wait?
Or what is mine end, that I should be patient?
Is my strength the strength of stones?
Or is my flesh of brass?
Is it not that my help within me is nought?
And that wisdom is driven quite from me?

His Friends Fail Him

To him that is ready to faint, kindness is due
        from his friend;

Even to him that forsaketh the fear of the Al-
        mighty.
My brethren have dealt deceitfully as a brook,
As the channel of brooks that pass away,
Which are blackish by reason of the ice,
And wherein the snow is hid.
What time they wax warm, they vanish;
When it is hot, they are consumed out of their
        place.
The caravans that bend their course thither
Go up through the waste and perish.
The caravans of Tema looked out for them;
The companies of Sheba kept hoping.
But their confidence brought them to shame;
They came thither and were abashed.

For now ye are nothing;
Ye see a terror and are afraid.
Did I say, "Bring unto me"?
Or, "Give a bribe for me of your substance"?
Or, "Deliver me from the enemy's hand"?
Or, "Redeem me from the hand of the tyrant"?

Job Seeks Instruction Rather than Reproof

Teach me, and I will hold my tongue;
And cause me to understand wherein I have erred.
How forcible are right words!
But your arguing, what doth it reprove?
Do ye think to reprove words,
And the speeches of one that is desperate,
        which are as wind?
Yea, ye would cast lots upon the fatherless,
And make an assault on your friend.
Now therefore, be pleased to look upon me;
For it is evident unto you if I lie.

(The friends turn away in disdain, but with a gesture of appeal Job cries:)

Return, I pray, let there be no injustice:
Turn back, for the right is still mine.
Is there iniquity in my tongue?
Have I lost the sense of wrong?

Job Describes His Suffering

Is there not an appointed time to man upon earth?
Are not his days also like the days of a hireling?
As a servant earnestly desireth the shades of
        evening,
And as a hireling looketh for the reward of his work:
So am I made to possess months of emptiness,
And wearisome nights are appointed to me.
When I lie down, I say, "When shall I rise,
And the night be gone?"
And I am full of tossings to and fro
Unto the dawning of the day.
My skin hardeneth, and then breaketh out afresh.
My days are swifter than a weaver's shuttle,
And are spent without hope.

Oh remember that my life is wind:
Mine eyes shall no more see good.
The eye of him that seeth me shall behold
        me no more;
Thine eyes shall look for me, but I shall be
        gone.
As the cloud is consumed and vanisheth away,
So he that goeth down to the grave shall
        come up no more.
He shall never come back to his house again,
And the place that was his shall know him
        no more.

JOB AND THE FLOCKS
From a painting by Sir John Gilbert

Job Complains to the Almighty

Therefore I will not refrain my mouth;
I will speak in the anguish of my spirit;
I will complain in the bitterness of my soul.

Am I a sea, or a sea monster,
That thou settest a watch over me?
When I say, "My bed shall comfort me,
My couch shall ease my complaint";
Then thou scarest me with dreams,
And terrifiest me through visions:
So that my soul chooseth strangling,
And death rather than these my bones.
I loathe my life; I would not live alway:
Let me alone; for my days are vanity.

What is man, that thou shouldst magnify him,
And that thou shouldst set thy heart upon
    him?
And that thou shouldst visit him every morn-
    ing,
And test him every moment?

Oh, when wilt thou turn thine eyes from me
And leave me though but for a moment?
If I have sinned, what can I do to thee, O
    thou watcher of men?
Why hast thou set me as a target,
So that I am a burden to myself?
And why dost thou not pardon my trans-
    gression,
And take away mine iniquity?
For now shall I sleep in the dust,
And thou shalt seek me diligently, but I
    shall not be.

BILDAD

A man of about middle age, unconsciously arrogant, and full of reverence for the lore of the ancients, Bildad is shocked at Job's complaint
against God. He takes the rôle of defender of the divine justice. He
argues that the justice of God rewards and sustains the righteous, but
punishes the wicked. He appeals to the wisdom of the past for confirma-
tion and encourages Job, if really innocent, which Bildad clearly doubts,
still to hope for prosperity and peace.

Bildad Reproves Job's Indignation

How long wilt thou speak these things?
And how long shall the words of thy mouth
    be like a strong wind?
Doth God pervert justice?
Or doth the Almighty pervert righteousness?
If thy children have sinned against him,

And he have cast them away for their trans-
    gression:
If thou wouldst seek unto God diligently,
And make thy supplication to the Almighty;
If thou wert pure and upright;
Surely now he would awake for thee,
And make the habitation of thy righteous-
    ness prosperous.
And though thy beginning was small,
Yet thy latter end should greatly increase.

BILDAD APPEALS TO THE WISDOM OF THE FATHERS

For inquire, I pray thee, of the former age,
And prepare thyself to that which their
    fathers have searched out:
(For we are but of yesterday, and know
    nothing,
Because our days upon earth are a shadow:)
Shall not they teach thee and tell thee,
And utter words out of their heart?

Can the rush grow up without mire?
Can the flag grow without water?
Whilst it is yet in its greenness, and not cut
    down,
It withereth before any other herb.
So are the paths of all that forget God;
And the hope of the godless man shall perish:
Whose hope shall be cut off,
And whose trust shall be a spider's web.
He shall lean upon his house, but it shall
    not stand:
He shall hold it fast, but it shall not endure.
He is green before the sun,
And his shoots go forth over his garden.

His roots are wrapped about the heap;
He seeth the place of stones.
If one destroy him from his place,
Then it shall deny him, saying, "I have not
      seen thee."
Behold, that is the joy of his way,
And out of the dust another springeth.

Behold, God will not cast away a perfect man,
Neither will he help the evildoers;
He will yet fill thy mouth with laughing,
And thy lips with rejoicing.
They that hate thee shall be clothed with
      shame,
And the dwelling place of the wicked shall
      come to nought.

JOB

Although Job concedes that God judges according to desert, he maintains that man in his weakness stands no chance to prove his merit. Job longs for an unprejudiced umpire who would guarantee him a fair opportunity to maintain his righteousness before his Creator. In his anguish he accuses God of creating him in order to torment him. He begs for a brief respite from pain before death and the grave overtake him.

MAN HAS NO CHANCE AGAINST GOD

I know it is so, of a truth.
But how can a man be just before God?
If he were to desire to contend with him,
He could not answer him one of a thousand.
He is wise in heart, and mighty in strength:
Who hath hardened himself against him,
      and prospered?
Who removeth the mountains, and they
      know it not;
Who overturneth them in his anger;
Who shaketh the earth out of her place,

And the pillars thereof tremble;
Who commandeth the sun, and it riseth not;
And sealeth up the stars;
Who alone spreadeth out the heavens,
And treadeth upon the waves of the sea;
Who maketh the Bear, Orion, and the Pleiades,
And the chambers of the south;
Who doeth great things past finding out,
Yea, and wonders without number.

Lo, he goeth by me, and I see him not;
He passeth on also, but I perceive him not.
Behold, if he seizeth, who can hinder him?
Who dare say unto him, "What doest thou?"

Were I right, I could give him no answer,
But needs must entreat my judge.
If I had called, and he had answered me,
Yet would I not believe that he hearkened
    to my voice.
For he breaketh me with a tempest,
And multiplieth my wounds without cause.
He will not suffer me to take my breath,
But filleth me with bitterness.

If we speak of strength, lo, he is strong!
And if of justice, "Who," [saith he] "will
    appoint me a time?"
Though I were righteous, mine own mouth
    would condemn me:
Though I were perfect, it would prove me
    perverse.

I am perfect; I care not for myself;
I despise my life.

It is all one; therefore I say
He destroyeth the perfect and the wicked.
If the scourge slay suddenly,
He will mock at the calamity of the innocent.
The earth is given into the hand of the wicked;
He covereth the faces of the judges thereof.
If it be not he, who then is it?

Job Cries for Justice

Now my days are swifter than a post:
They flee away, they see no good.
They are passed away as the swift ships:
As the eagle that swoopeth on the prey.

If I say, I will forget my complaint,
I will put off my heaviness, and be of good
      cheer;
I shudder at all my pains,
I know that thou wilt not hold me innocent.
I am to be condemned;
Why then do I labor in vain?
For though I wash me with snow,
And cleanse my hands with lye;
Then wilt thou plunge me in the mire,
So that even mine own clothes shall abhor me.

For he is not a man, as I am, that I should
      answer him,
That we should come together in judgment.
Neither is there any umpire betwixt us,
That might lay his hand upon us both.
Let him take his rod away from me,
And let not his fear terrify me;
Then would I speak, and not fear him.
For not such at heart am I.

JOB

From a painting by Léon Bonnat

My soul is weary of my life.
I will let my complaint take its course;
I will speak in the bitterness of my soul;
I will say unto God: Do not condemn me.
Show me the ground of thy quarrel.
Is it good unto thee that thou shouldst
      oppress?
That thou shouldst despise the work of thy hands?
And shine upon the counsel of the wicked?
Hast thou eyes of flesh?
Or seest thou as man seeth?
Are thy days like the days of mortals,
Or thy years like the days of man,
That thou inquirest after mine iniquity,
And searchest after my sin,
Although thou knowest that I am not wicked,
And there is none that can deliver out of
      thy hand?

THE CREATOR SHOULD BE MERCIFUL

Thy hands have made me
And fashioned me together round about;
Yet thou dost destroy me.
Remember, I beseech thee, that thou hast
      fashioned me as clay;
And wilt thou bring me into dust again?
Hast thou not poured me out as milk
And curdled me like cheese?
Thou hast clothed me with skin and flesh,
And hast hedged me together with bones and sinews.
Thou hast granted me life and favor,
And thy visitation hath preserved my spirit.

Yet these things hast thou hid in thy heart:
I know that this is with thee.

If I sin, then thou markest me,
And thou wilt not acquit me from mine in-
      iquity.
If I were wicked, woe unto me;
And if I were righteous, yet will I not lift up
      my head,
Full of shame and sated with affliction;
For it increaseth.

Thou huntest me as a fierce lion:
And again thou showest thyself marvelous
      upon me.
Thou renewest thy witnesses against me,
And increaseth thine indignation upon me;
Changes and warfare are against me.

Wherefore then hast thou brought me forth
      out of the womb?
Oh that I had given up the ghost, and no eye
      had seen me!
I should have been as though I had not been;
I should have been carried from the womb
      to the grave.

Are not my days few?
Cease then, and let me alone,
That I may take comfort a little,
Before I go whence I shall not return,
Even to the land of darkness and the shadow
      of death;
A land of darkness as darkness itself;
And of the shadow of death, without any
      order,
And where the light is as midnight.

ZOPHAR

Youngest of the three friends of Job, insolent, blunt, and orthodox, Zophar rebukes Job's presumption in criticizing the Omnipotent, and maintains that God is above human comprehension. Implying Job's guilt, he calls him to repentance, describing the joy and peace of the contrite sinner, and comparing it with the hopeless lot of the wicked.

Zophar Condemns Job's Questioning

Should not the multitude of words be answered?
And should a man full of talk be justified?
Should thy lies make men hold their peace?
And when thou mockest, shall no man make thee
    ashamed?
For thou hast said, "My doctrine is pure,
And I am clean in thine eyes."
But oh that God would speak,
And open his lips against thee;
And that he would show thee the secrets of wisdom,
For it is marvelous in effective counsel.
Know therefore that God exacteth of thee
Less than thine iniquity deserveth.

The Divine Wisdom Is Unfathomable

Canst thou by searching find out God?
Canst thou find out the Almighty unto perfection?
It is as high as heaven; what canst thou do?
Deeper than hell; what canst thou know?
The measure thereof is longer than the earth,
And broader than the sea.
If he cut off and shut up,
And summon together to judgment, then who can hin-
    der him?
For he knoweth empty men;
He seeth wickedness also, although he consider it not.

For vain man would be wise,
Though man be born like a wild ass's colt.

Zophar Calls Job to Repentance

If thou prepare thy heart,
And stretch out thy hands toward him;
If iniquity be in thy hand, put it far away,
And let not wickedness dwell in thy tents.
For then shalt thou lift up thy face without spot;
Yea, thou shalt be steadfast, and shalt not fear;
Because thou shalt forget thy misery,
And remember it as waters that pass away:
And thy life shall be clearer than the noonday;
Thou shalt shine forth, thou shalt be as the morning.
And thou shalt be secure,
Because there is hope;
Yea, thou shalt search around thee,
And thou shalt take thy rest in safety.
Also thou shalt lie down,
And none shall make thee afraid.
Yea, many shall make suit unto thee.
But the eyes of the wicked shall fail,
And they shall have no escape;
And their hope shall be the giving up of the ghost.

JOB

After listening to the pious platitudes of his three friends, Job is indignant. He asserts that his knowledge of Omnipotence is as great as theirs, but that close observation shows that Omnipotence frustrates the endeavors of man. Job dares to reason out his case and demands that his sins be pointed out. He affirms that frail humanity requires gentleness rather than ruthlessness from the hand of God. Up to this point Job has no hope of life after death, but believes that death ends all.

Job Ridicules the Arguments of His Friends

No doubt but ye are the people,
And wisdom shall die with you.

But I have understanding as well as you;
I am not inferior to you.
Yea, who knoweth not such things as these?
But ask now the beasts, and they shall teach
          thee;
And the fowls of the air, and they shall tell thee:

Or, speak to the earth, and it shall teach thee;
And the fishes of the sea shall declare unto thee.

Who knoweth not in all these that the hand of
          the Lord hath wrought this?
In whose hand is the soul of every living thing,
And the breath of all mankind.

Doth not the ear try words,
Even as the palate tasteth its food?

"With aged men," ye say, "is wisdom,
And in length of days understanding."
With God is wisdom and strength;
He hath counsel and understanding.
Behold, he breaketh down, and it cannot be built
          again;
He closeth upon a man, and there can be no opening.
Behold, he withholdeth the waters, and they dry
          up;
Again, he sendeth them out, and they overturn
          the earth.

With him is strength and wisdom;
The deceived and the deceiver are his.
He leadeth counselors away stripped,
And maketh the judges fools.
He looseth the bonds of kings,

Auguste Rodin

THE HAND OF GOD

*"Who knoweth not in all these that the hand of the
Lord hath wrought this?
In whose hand is the soul of every living thing,
And the breath of all mankind."*

And girdeth their loins with a girdle.
He leadeth priests away stripped,
And overthroweth the mighty.
He removeth away the speech of the trusty,
And taketh away the understanding of the aged.
He poureth contempt upon princes,
And looseth the girdle of the strong.
He discovereth deep things out of darkness,
And bringeth out to light the shadow of death.
He increaseth the nations, and destroyeth them:
He enlargeth the nations. and he leadeth them
  away.
He taketh away understanding from the chiefs
  of the people of the earth,
And causeth them to wander in a wilderness
  where there is no way.
They grope in the dark without light;
And he maketh them to stagger like a drunken
  man.

Lo, mine eyes have seen all this;
Mine ear hath heard and understood it.
What ye know, the same do I know also:
I am not inferior unto you.

JOB ACCUSES HIS FRIENDS OF PARTIALITY

Surely I would speak to the Almighty,
And I desire to reason with God.
But ye are forgers of lies,
Ye are all physicians of no value.
Oh that ye would altogether hold your peace!
And it should be to your wisdom.

Hear now my reasoning,
And hearken to the pleadings of my lips.

Will ye speak wickedly for God?
And talk deceitfully for him?
Will ye show partiality for him?
Will ye contend for God?
Is it good that he should search you out?
Or as one man deceiveth another, do ye so mock
      him?

He will surely reprove you,
If ye do secretly show partiality.
Shall not his loftiness make you afraid,
And his dread fall upon you?
Your maxims are proverbs of ashes,
Your defenses are defenses of clay.

"THOUGH HE SLAY ME, YET WILL I TRUST IN HIM"
From a drawing by Blake

(They indignantly interrupt, but Job continues:)

Hold your peace!
Let me alone that I may speak,
And let come on me what will!
Why should I take my flesh in my teeth,
And put my life in my hand?
Though he slay me, yet will I trust in him:
Nevertheless I will maintain mine own ways be-
      fore him.
Even that shall be my salvation,
For a hypocrite shall not come before him.
Hear diligently my speech,
And my declaration with your ears.
Behold now, I have ordered my cause:
I know that I am righteous.
Who is he that will plead with me?
For now, if I hold my tongue, I shall give up the
      ghost.

(Job speaks to the Almighty.)

Only do not two things unto me:
Then will I not hide myself from thee.
Withdraw thy hand far from me:
And let not thy dread make me afraid.
Then call thou, and I will answer:
Or let me speak, and answer thou me.
How many are mine iniquities and sins?
Make me to know my transgression and my sin.
Wherefore hidest thou thy face,
And holdest me for thine enemy?
Wilt thou break a leaf driven to and fro?
And wilt thou pursue the dry stubble?
For thou writest bitter things against me,
And makest me to inherit the iniquities of my
      youth.

Thou puttest my feet also in the stocks,
And observest all my paths;
Thou settest a line about the soles of my feet;
Although I am like a rotten thing that consumeth,
Like a garment that is moth-eaten.

Man's Frailty Should Make God Merciful

Man that is born of a woman
Is of few days, and full of trouble.
He cometh forth like a flower, and is cut down;
He fleeth also as a shadow, and continueth not.

And dost thou open thine eyes upon such a one,
And bringest me into judgment with thee?
Who can bring a clean thing out of an unclean?
 Not one.
Seeing his days are determined,
The number of his months are with thee,
Thou hast appointed his bounds that he cannot
 pass;
Turn away from him, that he may rest,
Till he shall accomplish, as a hireling, his day.

For there is hope of a tree, if it be cut down,
That it will sprout again,
And that the tender branch thereof will not cease.
Though the root thereof grow old in the earth,
And the stock thereof die in the ground;
Yet through the scent of water it will bud,
And bring forth boughs like a plant.

But man dieth, and wasteth away;
Yea, man giveth up the ghost, and where is he?
As the waters fail from the sea,
And the flood decayeth and drieth up;

So man lieth down, and riseth not;
Till the heavens be no more, they shall not
    awake,
Nor be raised out of their sleep.

Oh that thou wouldst hide me in the grave,
That thou wouldst keep me secret, until thy
    wrath be past,
That thou wouldst appoint me a set time, and
    remember me!

IS THERE LIFE BEYOND THE GRAVE

If a man die, shall he live again?
All the days of my appointed time will I wait,
Till my change come.
Thou shalt call, and I will answer thee:
Thou wilt have a desire to the work of thy
    hands.
For now thou numberest my steps:
Dost thou not watch over my sin?
My transgression is sealed up in a bag,
And thou sewest up mine iniquity.

And surely the mountain falling, cometh to
    nought,
And the rock is removed out of its place.
The waters wear the stones:
The overflowings thereof wash away the dust of
    the earth;

And thou destroyest the hope of man.
Thou prevailest forever against him, and he
    passeth.
Thou changest his countenance, and sendest him
    away.

His sons come to honor, and he knoweth it not;
And they are brought low, but he perceiveth it
    not of them.
But his flesh upon him shall have pain,
And his soul within him shall mourn.

THE SECOND CYCLE OF ARGUMENT

ELIPHAZ

Eliphaz is deeply hurt by Job's assumption of wisdom superior to
that of his friends. Job's own words, he insists, prove his guilt. He
then vividly describes the conscience-stricken terror and the doom of the
guilty man.

JOB'S DOUBTING HINDERS DEVOTION

Should a wise man utter vain knowledge,
And fill himself with the east wind?
Should he reason with unprofitable talk?
Or with speeches wherewith he can do no good?
Yea, thou castest off fear,
And restrainest meditation before God.
For thy mouth uttereth thine iniquity,
And thou choosest the tongue of the crafty.
Thine own mouth condemneth thee, and not I;
Yea, thine own lips testify against thee.

Art thou the first man that was born?
Or wast thou made before the hills?
Hast thou heard the secret of God?
And dost thou monopolize wisdom to thyself?
What knowest thou, that we know not?
What understandest thou, which is not in us?
With us are both the gray-headed and very aged
    men,
Much older than thy father.

Are the consolations of God small for thee?
The word that dealeth with thee gently?
Why doth thy heart carry thee away?
And what do thine eyes hint at,
That thou turnest thy spirit against God,
And lettest such words go out of thy mouth?
What is man, that he should be clean?
And he that is born of a woman, that he should
      be righteous?
Behold, he putteth no trust in his holy ones;
Yea, the heavens are not clean in his sight.
How much more abominable and corrupt is man,
Who drinketh iniquity like water!

It Is the Wicked that Suffer

I will show thee; hear me;
And that which I have seen I will declare;
Which wise men have told from their fathers,
And have not hid it:
Unto whom alone the earth was given,
And no stranger passed among them.
The wicked man travaileth with pain all his days,
And the number of years is hidden to the oppressor.
A dreadful sound is in his ears;
In prosperity the destroyer shall come upon him.
He believeth not that he shall return out of dark-
      ness,
And he is waited for of the sword.
He wandereth abroad for bread, saying, "Where
      is it?"
He knoweth that the day of darkness is ready
      at his hand.
Trouble and anguish shall make him afraid;
They shall prevail against him, as a king ready
      to the battle.

For he stretcheth out his hand against God,
And strengtheneth himself against the Almighty.
He runneth upon him with a stiff neck,
Upon the thick bosses of his bucklers;
Because he hath covered his face with his fatness,
And maketh collops of fat upon his loins.
And he dwelleth in desolate cities,
In houses which no man inhabited,
Which were ready to become heaps.

He shall not be rich, neither shall his substance
     continue,
Neither shall he prolong the perfection thereof
     upon the earth.
Let not him that is deceived trust in vanity:
For vanity shall be his recompense.

It shall be cut off before its time,
And his branch shall not become green.
He shall shake off his unripe grape as the vine,
And shall cast off his flower as the olive.
For the company of the godless shall be barren,
And fire shall consume the tents of bribery.
They conceive mischief, and bring forth iniquity,
And their heart prepareth deceit.

JOB

His answer is a touching appeal for sympathy, to his friends and to God.

JOB COMPLAINS OF THE TREATMENT HE HAS RECEIVED

I have heard many such things:
Miserable comforters are ye all.
Shall vain words have an end?
Or what emboldeneth thee that thou answerest?

I also could speak as ye do;
If your soul were in my soul's stead,
I could heap up words against you,
And shake my head at you.
But I would strengthen you with my mouth,
    And the moving of my lips would assuage your grief.
Though I speak, my grief is not assuaged;
And though I forbear, what am I eased?
But now he hath made me weary—

(Job complains to God.)

Thou hast made desolate all my company.
And thou hast filled me with wrinkles, which is
        a witness against me,

JOB HEARS BAD TIDINGS
From a painting by James J. Tissot

And my leanness rising up in me beareth witness
    to my face.

(He addresses his friends.)

He teareth me in his wrath who hateth me;
He gnashed upon me with his teeth:
Mine enemy sharpened his eyes upon me.
They have gaped upon me with their mouth;
They have smitten me upon the cheek reproach-
    fully;
They have gathered themselves together against
    me.
God hath delivered me to the ungodly,
And turned me over into the hands of the wicked.

I was at ease, but he hath broken me asunder;
He hath also taken me by my neck, and shaken
    me to pieces,
And set me up for his target.
His archers compass me round about,
He cleaveth my reins asunder, and doth not spare;
He poureth out my gall upon the ground.
He breaketh me with breach upon breach;
He runneth upon me like a giant.
I have sewed sackcloth upon my skin,
And have laid my horn in the dust.
My face is red with weeping,
And on my eyelids is the shadow of death,
Not for any injustice in my hands.
Also my prayer is pure.

Job Hopes for Final Vindication

O earth, cover not thou my blood,
And let my cry have no resting place!
Even now, behold, my witness is in heaven,

And he that voucheth for me is on high.
My friends scorn me;
But mine eye poureth out tears unto God.
Oh that one might plead for a man with God,
As a man pleadeth for his neighbor!

When a few years are come,
Then I shall go the way whence I shall not return.

My spirit is spent, my days are extinct,
The grave is ready for me.
Surely there are mockers with me,
And mine eye dwelleth on their provocation.

(Job speaks to God.)

Give now a pledge, be surety for me with thyself;
Who is he that will strike hands with me?

(Pointing to his friends:)

For thou hast hid their heart from understanding;
Therefore shalt thou not exalt them.
He that informeth against his friends for a prey,
Even the eyes of his children shall fail.

But he hath made me also a byword of the people;
And an object of aversion must I be.
Mine eye also is dim by reason of sorrow,
And all my members are as a shadow.

Upright men shall be astonished at this,
And the innocent shall stir up himself against
     the godless.
Yet shall the righteous hold on his way,
And he that hath clean hands shall wax stronger
     and stronger.

(Job speaks to his friends.)

But as for you all, do ye return and come now,
For I cannot find one wise man among you.

He Despairs of Help in This Life

My days are past, my purposes are broken off,
 Even the thoughts of my heart.
They change the night into day:
The light is short because of darkness.
If I look for the grave as my home,
I have made my bed in the darkness.
I have said to corruption, "Thou art my father,"
To the worm, "Thou art my mother, and my
        sister."
Where then is my hope?
And as for my hope, who shall see it?
It shall go down to the bars of the grave,
When our rest together is in the dust.

BILDAD

By picturing the sure and awful fate of the godless in words suggestive of Job's recent calamities, Bildad conveys the strong hint that Job is
one of these godless ones. This heightens the tragedy of Job's situation
and leads to the climax.

The Fate of the Wicked

How long will ye lay snares for words?
Consider, and afterwards we will speak.
Wherefore are we counted as beasts,
And reputed vile in your sight?
Thou that tearest thyself in thine anger,
Shall the earth be forsaken for thee?
And shall the rock be removed out of his place?

Yea, the light of the wicked shall be put out,
And the spark of his fire shall not shine.

The light shall be dark in his tent,
And his candle shall be put out with him.
The steps of his strength shall be straitened,
And his own counsel shall cast him down.
For he is cast into a net by his own feet,
So that over the network he sprawleth.
A snare shall take him by the heel,
And a trap shall close tightly upon him.
A noose for him is hid in the ground,
And a trap for him in the way.
Terrors shall make him afraid on every side,
And shall chase him at every step.
His strength shall be hunger-bitten,
And calamity shall be ready for his halting.
It shall devour the strength of his skin.
Even the first-born of death shall devour his
     strength.
His confidence shall be rooted out of his tent,
And it shall bring him to the king of terrors.
There shall dwell in his tent that which is none of his:
Brimstone shall be scattered upon his habitation.
His roots shall be dried up beneath,
And above shall his branch be cut off.
His remembrance shall perish from the earth,
And he shall have no name in the street.
He shall be driven from light into darkness,
And chased out of the world.
He shall have neither son nor grandson among
     his people,
Nor any remaining in his dwellings.
They that come after him shall be astonished at
     his day,
As they that went before were affrighted.
Surely such are the dwellings of the wicked,
And this is the place of him that knoweth not God.

JOB

Job protests against the crushing reproaches of his friends. He cries out against the heartlessness of God who has turned friends and kindred against him. He appeals to his friends for pity, but they fail him. He turns to posterity for justification; but this is impracticable. Under the sway of profound emotion he makes his great venture of faith, and asserts his confidence that God will justify him: after death, in one glorious moment, God will appear as a friend on his side to vindicate him, and Job himself will see him.

JOB CRIES OUT AGAINST THE HARSHNESS OF HIS FRIENDS

How long will ye vex my soul,
And break me in pieces with words?
These ten times have ye reproached me:
Ye are not ashamed that ye harden yourselves
    against me.
And if indeed I have erred,
Mine error remaineth with myself.
If indeed ye will magnify yourselves against me,
And plead against me my reproach,
Know now that God hath overthrown me,
And hath encircled me with his net.

GOD SEEMS TO BE HIS ENEMY

Behold, I cry out!
But I am not heard;
I cry for help, but there is no justice.
He hath fenced up my way that I cannot pass,
And he hath set darkness in my paths.
He hath stripped me of my glory,
And taken the crown from my head.
He hath broken me down on every side, and I am
    gone;
And my hope hath he removed like a tree.
He hath also kindled his wrath against me,

And he counteth me unto him as one of his ad-
      versaries.
His troops come on together,
And cast up their way against me,
And encamp round about my tent.

He hath put my brethren far from me,
And mine acquaintance are verily estranged from
      me.
My kinsfolk have failed,
And my familiar friends have forgotten me.
They that dwell in my house, and my maids,
Count me for a stranger:
I am an alien in their sight.
I call unto my servant, and he giveth me no
      answer;
I must entreat him with my mouth.
My breath is strange to my wife,
And I am loathsome to the children of my body.
Even young children despise me:
I would arise, and they speak against me!
All the men of my circle abhor me,
And they whom I loved are turned against me.
My bone cleaveth to my skin and to my flesh,
And I am escaped with the skin of my teeth.

Have pity upon me, have pity upon me, O ye my
      friends,
For the hand of God hath touched me.
Why do ye persecute me as God,
And are not satisfied with my flesh?

Job Has Faith in His Vindicator

Oh that my words were now written!
Oh that they were printed in a book!

That they were graven with iron pen
And lead, in the rock forever!
For I know that my Redeemer[43] liveth,
And that he shall stand up at the last upon the
    earth:
And after my skin hath been thus destroyed,
Yet from my flesh shall I see God,
Whom I shall see for myself,
And mine eyes shall behold,
And not another.

(Job nearly faints with emotion.)

My reins are consumed within me!

(Collecting himself, Job warns his tormentors of the penalty due for unjust accusations.)

If ye say, "How we will persecute him!"
And that the root of the matter [the cause of
    these calamities] is found in me,
Be ye afraid of the sword:
For [God's] wrath bringeth the punishments of
    the sword,
That ye may know there is a judgment.

ZOPHAR

Zophar declares that although the wicked apparently prosper for a time, they perish; their ill-gotten gains are returned; their children suffer want; and even heaven and earth turn against them.

THE TRIUMPH OF THE WICKED IS BRIEF

Therefore do my thoughts cause me to answer;
For this reason I hasten to speak.
I must hear the reproof which putteth me to shame;
But the spirit of my understanding answereth me.

Knowest thou not this of old,
Since man was placed upon earth,

That the triumphing of the wicked is short,
And the joy of the hypocrite but for a moment?
Though his excellency mount up to the heavens,
And his head reach unto the clouds;
Yet he shall perish forever.
They who have seen him shall say, "Where is he?"
He shall fly away as a dream, and shall not be found;
Yea, he shall be chased away as a vision of the night.
The eye also that saw him shall see him no more,
Neither shall his place any more behold him.

His children shall court the favor of the poor,
And his hands shall restore his wealth.
His bones are full of his youth,
But it shall lie down with him in the dust.
Though wickedness be sweet in his mouth,
Though he hide it under his tongue,
Though he spare it, and do not let it go,
But keep it still within his mouth;
Yet his food in his stomach is turned,
It is poison of asps within him.
He hath swallowed down riches,
And he shall vomit them up again;
God will cast them out of his belly.
He shall suck the poison of asps:
The viper's tongue shall slay him.

He shall not see the rivers,
The streams of honey and butter.
That which he labored for shall he restore,
And shall not swallow it down:
According to the gains of his exchange,
He shall not rejoice!
Because he hath oppressed and hath forsaken the
        poor,

Because he hath violently taken away a house
    which he builded not,
Because he knew no quietness within him,
He shall not save of that which he desired.
There shall none of his food be left:
Therefore his prosperity shall not endure.

In the fulness of his sufficiency he shall be in
    straits:
Every hand of the wicked shall come upon him.
God shall cast the fierceness of his wrath upon
    him,
And will rain it upon him as his food.
He shall flee from the iron weapon,
And the bow of brass shall strike him through.
He draweth it forth, and it cometh out of his
    back;
Yea, the glittering sword cometh out of his gall:
Terrors are upon him.
All darkness is laid up for his treasures;
A fire not blown by man shall devour him;
It shall consume that which is left in his tent.

The heavens shall reveal his iniquity;
And the earth shall rise up against him.
The increase of his house shall depart,
And his goods shall flow away, in the day of his
    wrath.
This is the portion of a wicked man from God,
And the heritage appointed unto him by God.

JOB

Job challenges the truth of Zophar's doctrine of the premature destruction of the wicked. Sinners do not receive their due. It is not fair that their punishment should be reserved for their children. The evil man is spared, and dies honored of men.

Why Do the Wicked Prosper?

Hear diligently my speech,
And let this be your consolations.
Suffer me that I may speak,
And after I have spoken, mock on.
As for me, is my complaint to man?
And if so, why should not my spirit be troubled?
Mark me, and be astonished,
And lay your hand upon your mouth.
Even when I remember I am afraid,
And horror taketh hold on my flesh.

Wherefore do the wicked live,
Become old, yea, wax mighty in power?
Their family is established in their sight with them,
And their offspring before their eyes.
Their houses are safe from fear,
Neither is the rod of God upon them.
They send forth their little ones like a flock,
And their children dance.
They sing to the timbrel and harp,
And rejoice at the sound of the pipe.
They spend their days in wealth,
And in a moment they go down to the grave.
Yet they say to God, "Depart from us;
For we desire not the knowledge of thy ways.
What is the Almighty that we should serve him?
And what profit should we have, if we pray unto him?"

Lo, their prosperity is not in their hand.
The counsel of the wicked is far from me.

How often is it that the candle of the wicked is put out?
That their calamity cometh upon them?

That God distributeth sorrows in his anger?
That they are as stubble before the wind,
And as chaff that the storm carrieth away?

Ye say, "God layeth up his iniquity for his chil-
      dren."
Let him recompense it unto himself, that he may know
      it.
Let his own eyes see his destruction,
And let him drink of the wrath of the Almighty.
For what pleasure hath he in his house after him,
When the number of his months is cut off in the midst?

Shall any teach God knowledge,
Seeing he judgeth those that are high?

One dieth in his full strength,
Being wholly at ease and quiet.
His pails are full of milk
And the marrow of his bones is moistened.
And another dieth in bitterness of soul,
And never eateth with pleasure.
They shall lie down alike in the dust,
And the worms shall cover them.

The Wicked Come to a Peaceful End

Behold, I know your thoughts,
And the devices which ye wrongly imagine against
      me.
For ye say, "Where is the house of the prince?
And where are the dwelling places of the wicked?"
Have ye not asked them that go by the way?
And do ye not know their evidences,
That the wicked man is spared in the day of calam-
      ity?

That he is delivered in the day of wrath?
Who shall declare his way to his face?
And who shall repay him what he hath done?
Yet shall he be brought to the grave,
And shall remain in the tomb.
The clods of the valley shall be sweet to him,
And every man shall draw after him,
As there were innumerable before him.
How then comfort ye me in vain,
Seeing in your answers there remaineth nought but
    falsehood?

THE THIRD CYCLE OF ARGUMENT

ELIPHAZ

Job will not acknowledge that he has sinned; yet, according to the view of his friends, no other explanation of his misery is possible. Eliphaz, accordingly, puts aside the method of vague implication and becomes specific. He accuses Job of dishonesty, inhumanity, lack of generosity, and presuming to hide his iniquity from God. He summons Job to repentance and urges him to return to God, promising him joy and peace.

JOB IS DEFINITELY ACCUSED OF SIN

Can a man be profitable to God?
Nay, he that is wise is profitable unto himself.
Is it any pleasure to the Almighty that thou art right-
    eous?
Or is it gain to him that thou makest thy ways perfect?
Will he reprove thee, for fear of thee?
Will he enter with thee into judgment?

Is not thy wickedness great?
And thine iniquities are infinite.

For thou hast taken pledges of thy brother for nought,
And stripped the naked of their clothing.

Thou hast not given water to the weary to drink,
And thou hast withholden bread from the hungry.
But as for the mighty man, he had the earth,
And the eminent man dwelt therein.

Thou hast sent widows away empty,
And the arms of the fatherless have been broken.
Therefore snares are round about thee,
And sudden fear troubleth thee;
Or darkness, that thou canst not see;
And abundance of waters cover thee.

Sin Cannot Be Hidden from God

Is not God in the height of heaven?
And behold the height of the stars, how high they
        are!
And thou sayest, "How doth God know?
Can he judge through the dark cloud?
Thick clouds are a covering to him, that he seeth not;
And he walketh in the circuit of heaven."

Hast thou marked the old way,
Which wicked men have trodden,
Who were cut down out of time,
Whose foundation was overthrown with a flood,
Who said unto God, "Depart from us";
And "What can the Almighty do to us?"
Yet he filled their houses with good things:
But the counsel of the wicked is far from me.

The righteous see it, and are glad;
And the innocent laugh them to scorn,
Saying, "Surely their substance is cut off,
And that which remained to them the fire hath con-
        sumed."

The Sinner Is Urged to Repentance

Acquaint now thyself with him and be at peace:
Thereby shall good come to thee.
Receive, I pray thee, instruction from his mouth,
And lay up his words in thy heart.
If thou return to the Almighty, and humble
    thyself,
If thou put away iniquity far from thy tents;
And lay thou thy treasure in the dust,
And the gold of Ophir among the stones of the
    brooks;
Then the Almighty shall be thy treasure,
And plenty of silver shall be unto thee;
For then shalt thou have thy delight in the Al-
    mighty,
And shalt lift up thy face unto God;
Thou shalt make thy prayer unto him, and he
    shall hear thee,
And thou shalt pay thy vows.
Thou shalt also decree a thing,
And it shall be established unto thee:
And the light shall shine upon thy ways.
And when men cast thee down, thou shalt say,
    "There is lifting up";
And the humble person he shall save.
He shall deliver the innocent:
Yea, thou shalt be delivered through the clean-
    ness of thy hands.

JOB

Job passionately craves access to God, but he cannot find him. Al-though convinced that God knows what he is suffering and that he is testing him through it, yet he is afraid of God. Looking away from himself to the wide world, he sees only evidences of divine indifference to wicked-ness. Sinners perish, but only as do all other men.

Job Longs to Find God

Even today is my complaint defiant:
My stroke is heavier than my groaning.
Oh that I knew where I might find him,
That I might come even to his seat!
I would set out my case before him,
And fill my mouth with arguments.
I would know the words which he would answer me,
And understand what he would say unto me.
Would he contend with me with his great power?
Nay, but he would give heed unto me;
There the righteous might reason with him;
So should I be delivered forever from my judge.

Behold, I go forward,
But he is not there;
And backward,
But I cannot perceive him:
On the left hand, where he doth work,
But I cannot behold him;
He hideth himself on the right hand,
That I cannot see him.
But he knoweth the way that I take:
When he hath tried me, I shall come forth as gold.
My foot hath held to his steps;
His way have I kept, and not turned aside.
Neither have I gone back from the commandment
    of his lips;
I have esteemed the words of his mouth more than
    my necessary food.

Job Fears God's Omnipotence

But he is in one mind, and who can turn him?
And what his soul desireth, even that he doeth.

For he performeth the thing that is appointed for me;
And many such things are with him.
Therefore am I troubled at his presence;
When I consider, I am afraid of him.
For God maketh my heart faint,
And the Almighty troubleth me;
Because I was not cut off before the darkness,
Neither hath he covered the thick darkness from my
    face.

EXAMPLES OF INJUSTICE IN THE WORLD

Why doth God not fix seasons for judgment,
And why do his friends never see his great day?
There are those that remove the landmarks:
They violently take away flocks, and feed thereof.
They drive away the ass of the fatherless;
They take the widow's ox for a pledge.
They turn the needy out of the way:
The poor of the earth hide themselves together.
Behold, as wild asses in the desert,
They go forth to their work, rising early for food;
The wilderness yieldeth food for them and for their
    children.
They reap every one his grain in the field;
And they gather the vintage of the wicked.
They cause the naked to lodge without clothing,
That they have no covering in the cold.
They are wet with the showers of the mountains,
And embrace the rock for want of a shelter.

There are those that pluck the fatherless from the
    breast,
And take a pledge of the poor;
They cause him to go naked without clothing;
And they take away the sheaf from the hungry,

Who make oil within their walls,
And tread their winepresses, and suffer thirst.

Men groan from out of the city,
And the soul of the wounded crieth out:
Yet God regardeth not the folly.
They are of those that rebel against the light;
They know not the ways thereof,
Nor abide in the paths thereof.
The murderer riseth with the light;
He killeth the poor and needy;
And in the night he is as a thief.
The eye also of the adulterer waiteth for the twilight,
Saying, "No eye shall see me";
And he disguiseth his face.
In the dark they dig through houses,
Which they had marked for themselves in the daytime:
They know not the light:
For the morning is to them as the shadow of death:
For they know the terrors of darkness.

"Swiftly," [ye say], "they pass away upon the face of
   the waters;
Their portion is cursed in the earth:
No treader turneth toward their vineyard.
Drought and heat consume the snow waters:
So doth the grave those that have sinned.
The womb shall forget him;
The worm shall feed sweetly on him;
He shall be no more remembered;
And unrighteousness shall be broken as a tree.
He ill-treateth the barren that beareth not,
And doeth not good to the widow."
Yet God preserveth the mighty with his power;
He riseth up that hath no assurance of life.

God giveth him safety, whereon he resteth:
Yet his eyes are upon their ways.
They are exalted for a little while, and they are gone;
Yea, they are brought low, they are taken out of the
        way as all others,
And are cut off as the tops of the ears of grain.
And if it be not so now, who will make me a liar,
And make my speech nothing worth?

BILDAD

Sarcastically Bildad says to Job: "Is God so weak that you can help him, or so ignorant that you can advise him? Indeed he is so powerful that mere man cannot stand vindicated before him. We see his power in nature; yet what we see of it is to its reality as the sound of a whisper is to the noise of thunder."

How hast thou helped him that is without power!
How savest thou the arm that hath no strength!
How hast thou counseled him that hath no wisdom,
And plentifully declared sound knowledge!
To whom hast thou uttered words?
And whose spirit came forth from thee?

Dominion and fear are with him:
He maketh peace in his high places.
Is there any number of his armies?
And upon whom doth not his light arise?
How then can a man be justified with God?
Or how can he be clean, that is born of a woman?
Behold, even the moon hath no brightness;
Yea, the stars are not pure in his sight.
How much less man, that is a worm!
And the son of man, that is a worm!

The shades do tremble,
Whose home is beneath the waters;
Hell is naked before God,

And Abaddon hath no covering.
He stretcheth out the north over empty space,
And hangeth the earth upon nothing.
He bindeth up the waters in his thick clouds,
And the cloud is not rent under them.
He closeth in the face of his throne,
And spreadeth his cloud upon it.
He hath encircled the waters with bounds,
Unto the confines of light and darkness.
The pillars of heaven tremble
And are astonished at his reproof.
He stilleth the sea with his power,
And by his understanding he smiteth through Rahab.
By his spirit he hath beautified the heavens;
His hand pierceth the swift serpent.
Lo, these are but the outskirts of his ways;
And how small a whisper do we hear of him!
But the thunder of his power who can comprehend?

JOB

Job swears that he is right and that his friends are wrong. He will hold fast to the testimony of his own conscience as long as he lives. His intense earnestness and his inner sincerity will permit him to do nothing else.

As God liveth, who hath taken away my right;
And the Almighty, who hath made my soul bitter
(For my breath is yet in me,
And the spirit of God is in my nostrils);
My lips shall not speak wickedness,
Nor my tongue utter deceit.
God forbid that I should justify you:
Till I die I will not remove mine integrity from me.
My righteousness I hold fast, and will not let it go:
My heart shall not reproach me so long as I live.
Ye have all with your own eyes seen it;
Wherefore, then, this idle folly?

ZOPHAR

Zophar reiterates his dogma that the godless are hopeless. God will not hear the wicked man who prays to him in trouble. Not he, but the innocent, will profit from his labors. God and man will hiss him into oblivion.

Let mine enemy be as the wicked,
And let him that riseth up against me
Be as the unrighteous.
For what is the hope of the godless, though he hath
    gained,
When God requireth his soul?
Will God hear his cry
When trouble cometh upon him?
Will he delight himself in the Almighty,
Will he always call upon God?
I will teach you concerning the hand of God;
That which is in the mind of the Almighty will I
    not conceal.

This is the portion of a wicked man with God,
And the heritage of oppressors, which they shall re-
    ceive of the Almighty:
If his children be multiplied, it is for the sword;
And his offspring shall not be satisfied with bread.
Those that remain of him shall be buried in death,
And his widows shall make no lamentation,
Though he heap up silver as the dust,
And prepare raiment as the clay;
He may prepare it, but the just shall put it on,
And the innocent shall divide the silver.

He buildeth his house, as a moth,
And as a booth which the keeper maketh.
He lieth down rich, but he shall not be gathered;

He openeth his eyes, and he is not.
Terrors take hold of him as waters;
A tempest stealeth him away in the night.
The east wind carrieth him away and he departeth:
And it sweepeth him out of his place.
For God hurleth at him, and doth not spare:
He would fain flee out of his hand.
Men shall clap their hands at him
And shall hiss him out of his place.

JOB

Job arouses himself for his final defense. He portrays in words of pathos and beauty a picture of "the good old days" of the past, when he was the honored benefactor of all. Against the quiet beauty of this picture he paints the present with its pain, disgrace, and despair. As a man whose life is in imminent peril, he stretches out eager hands toward men and God.

JOB AND HIS FAMILY
From a painting by James J. Tissot

In vivid detail he describes his deeds of generosity, mercy, and love. Before God he makes his solemn oath of clearance. He closes the long debate with a cry to God for the divine indictment. He would then come before him like a prince, conscience-free and heart-sincere, to clear himself before God.

JOB RECALLS PAST DAYS

Oh that I were as in the months of old,
As in the days when God watched over me,
When his lamp shone upon my head,
And when by his light I walked through darkness;
As I was in the days of my youth,
When the friendship of God was upon my tent;
When the Almighty was yet with me,
When my children were about me;
When my steps were washed in milk,
And the rock poured me rivers of oil.

When I went out to the gate through the city,
When I prepared my seat in the street!
The young men saw me, and hid themselves:
And the aged rose, and stood up.
The princes refrained from talking,
And laid their hand on their mouth.
The nobles held their peace,
And their tongue cleaved to the roof of their mouth.
When the ear heard me, then it blessed me;
And when the eye saw me, it gave witness to me;
Because I delivered the poor that cried,
And the fatherless, and him that had none to help
    him.
The blessing of him that was ready to perish came
    upon me,
And I caused the widow's heart to sing for joy.
I put on righteousness, and it clothed me:
My judgment was as a robe and a diadem.

I was eyes to the blind,
And feet was I to the lame.
I was a father to the poor,
And the cause which I knew not I searched out.
And I brake the jaws of the unrighteous,
And plucked the prey out of his teeth.

Then I said, "I shall die in my nest,
And I shall multiply my days as the sand."
My root was spread out by the waters,
And the dew lay all night upon my branch.
My glory was fresh in me,
And my bow was renewed in my hand.

Unto me men gave ear, and waited,
And kept silence for my counsel.
After my words they spake not again;
And my speech distilled upon them.
And they waited for me as for the rain,
And they opened their mouth wide as for the latter
    rain.
I laughed at them, when they had no confidence;
And the light of my countenance they cast not down.
I chose out their way, and sat as chief,
And dwelt as a king in the army,
As one that comforteth the mourners.

Job Laments His Present Condition

But now they that are younger than I have me in
    derision,
Whose fathers I would have disdained to set with
    the dogs of my flock.
Yea, the strength of their hands,
Whereto should it profit me?
Men in whom firm vigor hath perished.

For want and famine they are gaunt;
Fleeing into the wilderness, in former time desolate
          and waste;
Who cut up mallows by the bushes,
And juniper roots for their meat.
They are driven forth from among men;
A cry is raised after them as after a thief;
They must dwell in the cliffs of the valleys,
In caves of the earth, and in the rocks.
Among the bushes they bray;
Under the nettles they are gathered together.
They are children of fools,
Yea, children of base men;
They were smitten out of the land.

And now I am become their song,
Yea, I am their byword.
They abhor me, they keep their distance from me,
And spare not to spit in my face.
Because he hath loosed my cord and afflicted me;
And they have let loose the bridle before me.
Upon my right hand rise the youth:
They push away my feet,
And they raise up against me the ways of their
          destruction.
They mar my path,
They set forward my calamity,
Even men that have no helper.
As through a wide breach they come,
Rolling on in the midst of the ruin.
Terrors are turned upon me;
They pursue mine honor as the wind;
And my welfare is passed away as a cloud.
And now my soul pours itself out;
The days of affliction have taken hold of me.

My bones are pierced in me in the night season,
And my sinews take no rest.
By the great force of my disease is my raiment dis-
    figured;
It bindeth me about as the collar of my coat.
He hath cast me into the mire;
And I am become like dust and ashes.

I cry unto thee, and thou dost not answer me:
I stand up, and thou gazest at me.
Thou art turned to be cruel to me;
With the might of thy hand thou opposest thyself
    against me.
Thou liftest me up to the wind;
Thou causest me to ride upon it;
And dissolvest me into the storm.
For I know that thou wilt bring me to death,
And to the house appointed for all living.
Howbeit doth not one stretch out the hand in his
    fall?
Or in his calamity will not one cry for help?

Did not I weep for him that was in trouble?
Was not my soul grieved for the poor?
When I looked for good, then evil came:
And when I waited for light, there came darkness.

My heart is troubled, and resteth not;
Days of affliction are come upon me.
I go mourning without the sun:
I stand up in the assembly, crying for help.
I am a brother to jackals,
And a companion to ostriches.
My skin is black and falleth off me,
And my bones are burned with heat.

My harp also is turned to mourning,
And my pipe into the voice of them that weep.

Job Protests His Innocence

I made a covenant with mine eyes;
How then could I even look upon a virgin?
For what is the portion from God above,
And the heritage from the Almighty on high?
Is it not destruction to the unrighteous
And disaster to the workers of iniquity?
Doth he not see my ways,
And number all my steps?

(Job now utters before God his solemn Oath of Clearing.)

If I have walked with vanity,
Or if my foot hath hasted to deceit
(Let me be weighed in an even balance,
That God may know mine integrity);
If my step hath turned out of the way,
And mine heart walked after mine eyes,
And if any spot hath cleaved to my hands:
Then let me sow, and let another eat;
Yea, let the produce of my field be rooted out.

If my heart hath been lured by a woman,
And I have laid wait at my neighbor's door;
Then let my wife grind unto another,
And let others bow down upon her.
For this is a heinous crime;
Yea, it is an iniquity to be punished by the judges:
For it is a fire that consumeth unto destruction,
And would root out all mine increase.

If I did despise the cause of my manservant,
Or of my maidservant, when they contended with me:
What then shall I do when God riseth up?

And when he visiteth, what shall I answer him?
Did not he that made me make him?
And did not one fashion us both?

If I have withheld the poor from their desire,
Or have caused the eyes of the widow to fail;
Or have eaten my morsel alone,
And the fatherless hath not eaten thereof
(For from my youth he was brought up with me as
      with a father,
And I have guided her from my birth);
If I have seen any perish for want of clothing,
Or any poor without covering;
If his loins have not blessed me,
And if he were not warmed with the fleece of my
      sheep;
If I have lifted up my hand against the fatherless,
When I saw my help in the gate:
Then let my shoulder fall from the shoulder blade,
And mine arm be broken from the bone.
For calamity from God was a terror to me,
And by reason of his majesty I could not do so.

If I have made gold my hope,
And have said to the fine gold, "Thou art my con-
      fidence";
If I rejoiced because my wealth was great,
And because my hand had gotten much;

If I beheld the sun when it shone,
Or the moon walking in brightness;
And my heart hath been secretly enticed,
And my mouth hath kissed my hand;
This too were an iniquity to be judged,
For I should have denied the God that is above.

If I rejoiced at the destruction of him that hated
   me,
Or lifted up myself when evil found him
(Yea, I have not suffered my mouth to sin
By wishing a curse to his soul);

If the men of my tent have not said,
"Who can find one that hath not been filled with his
   food?"
The stranger did not lodge in the street;
But I opened my doors to the traveler;

If like Adam I covered my transgression,
By hiding mine iniquity in my bosom,
Because I dreaded the great multitude,
And the contempt of families terrified me,
So that I kept silence, and went not out of the door;

If my land cry out against me,
And the furrows thereof weep together;
If I have eaten the fruits thereof without money,
Or have caused the owners thereof to lose their life:
Let thistle grow instead of wheat,
And cockle instead of barley.

Job Appeals for the Divine Indictment

Oh that I had one to hear me!
(Lo, here is my signature, let the Almighty answer
   me!)
And that I had the indictment which mine adver-
   sary hath written!
Surely I would carry it upon my shoulder;
I would bind it unto me as a crown.
I would declare unto him the number of my steps;
As a prince would I present it unto him.[44]

THE SPEECHES OF ELIHU

So these three men ceased to answer Job, because he was righteous in his own eyes. Then was kindled the wrath of Elihu the son of Barachel the Buzite, of the family of Ram; against Job was his wrath kindled, because he justified himself rather than God. Also against his three friends was his wrath kindled, because they had found no answer, and yet had condemned Job. Now Elihu had waited to speak unto Job, because they were older than he. And when Elihu saw that there was no answer in the mouth of these three men, his wrath was kindled.

ELIHU

Elihu is the critical, self-confident representative of a younger generation. He became angry at Job, "because he justified himself rather

"I AM YOUNG, AND YE ARE VERY OLD"
From a drawing by Blake

than God," and at Job's three friends, "because they had found no answer, and yet had condemned Job." He reproves, recapitulates what
has already been said, and shows that God by affliction disciplines human souls and draws them to himself, giving them "songs in the night."
He acts also as the forecaster of the storm in which God is approaching.

Elihu Decides to Express His Opinion

I am young, and ye are very old;
Wherefore I was afraid, and durst not show you mine
      opinion.
I said, "Days should speak,
And multitude of years should teach wisdom."
But there is a spirit in man,
And the inspiration of the Almighty giveth them un-
      derstanding.
Great men are not always wise,
Neither do the aged understand justice.
Therefore I said, "Hearken to me;
I also will show mine opinion."
Behold, I waited for your words,
I gave ear to your reasons,
Whilst ye searched out what to say.
Yea, I attended unto you;
And, behold, there was none of you that convinced Job,
Or that answered his words.

Beware lest ye say, "We have found wisdom";
God may vanquish him, not man:
For he hath not directed his words against me;
Neither will I answer him with your speeches.

They are amazed. They answer no more.
Words have failed them.
And shall I wait, because they speak not,
Because they stand still, and answer no more?
I also will answer my part,

I also will show mine opinion.
For I am full of words;
The spirit within me constraineth me.
Behold, my breast is as wine which hath no vent;
Like new wine skins it is ready to burst.
I will speak, that I may be refreshed:
I will open my lips and answer.

Elihu Refuses to Flatter Job

Let me not, I pray you, respect any man's person;
Neither will I give flattering titles unto any man.
For I know not to give flattering titles;
Else would my Maker soon take me away.
Howbeit, Job, I pray thee, hear my speech,
And hearken to all my words.
Behold now, I have opened my mouth;
My tongue hath spoken in my mouth.
My words shall be of the uprightness of my heart;
And my lips shall utter knowledge clearly.
The spirit of God hath made me,
And the breath of the Almighty hath given me life.

Elihu Reproves Job's Self-confidence

If thou canst answer me,
Set thy words in order before me; stand up.
Behold, I stand toward God even as thou dost:
I also am formed out of the clay.
Behold, my terror shall not make thee afraid,
Neither shall my hand be heavy upon thee.
Surely thou hast spoken in my hearing,
And I have heard the voice of thy words, saying:
"I am clean, without transgression;
I am innocent, neither is there iniquity in me:
Behold, he findeth occasions against me,
He counteth me for his enemy;

He putteth my feet in the stocks,
He marketh all my paths."
Behold, in this thou art not just:
I will answer thee;
For God is greater than man.

God Speaks to Men in Dreams

Why dost thou strive against him, saying,
"He answereth none of my words"?
For God speaketh once,
Yea twice, yet man perceiveth it not.
In a dream, in a vision of the night,
When deep sleep falleth upon men,
In slumberings upon the bed;
Then he openeth the ears of men,
And sealeth their instruction,
That he may withdraw man from his purpose,
And hide pride from man.
He keepeth back his soul from the pit,
And his life from perishing by the sword.

God Speaks to Men Through Pain

He is chastened also with pain upon his bed,
And with perennial strife in his bones;
So that his life abhorreth bread,
And his soul dainty food.
His flesh is consumed away, that it cannot be seen;
And his bones that were not seen stick out.
Yea, his soul draweth near unto the pit,
And his life to the destroyers.

God Speaks to Men Through Heavenly Messengers

If there be a messenger with him,
An interpreter, one among a thousand,

To show unto man what is right for him;
And if he is gracious unto him, and saith,
"Deliver him from going down to the pit;
I have found a ransom";
His flesh becometh fresher than a child's;
He shall return to the days of his youth.
He shall pray unto God, and he will be favorable unto
        him:
And he shall see his face with joy:
For he will restore unto man his righteousness.
He looketh upon men, and if any say,
"I have sinned, and perverted that which was right,
And it profited me not":
He will deliver his soul from going into the pit,
And his life shall see the light.
Lo, all these things worketh God,
Twice, yea thrice, with a man,
To bring back his soul from the pit,
To be enlightened with the light of the living.
Mark well, O Job, hearken unto me;
Hold thy peace, and I will speak.
If thou hast anything to say, answer me:
Speak, for I desire to justify thee.
If not, hearken thou unto me:
Hold thy peace, and I will teach thee wisdom.

Elihu Censures Job for His Irreverence

Hear my words, ye wise men;
And give ear unto me, ye that have knowledge.
For the ear testeth words,
As the palate tasteth food.
Let us choose for us that which is right:
Let us know among ourselves what is good.
For Job hath said, "I am righteous,
And God hath taken away my right:

Notwithstanding my right I am in pain;
My wound is incurable, though I am without trans-
          gression."
What man is like Job,
Who drinketh up scoffing like water,
Who goeth in company with the workers of iniquity,
And walketh with wicked men?
For he hath said, "It profiteth a man nothing
That he should delight himself with God."

Elihu Vindicates the Justice of God

Therefore hearken unto me, ye men of understanding:
Far be it from God, that he should do wickedness,
And from the Almighty, that he should commit iniquity.
For the work of a man will he render unto him,
And cause every man to find according to his ways.
Yea, surely, God will not do wickedly;
Neither will the Almighty pervert justice.
Who hath given him a charge over the earth?
Or who hath disposed the whole world?
If he should recall his spirit,
And gather his breath to himself,
All flesh would perish together,
And man would return unto dust.

Elihu Emphasizes the Sovereignty of God

If now thou hast understanding, hear this:
Hearken to the voice of my words.
Shall even one that hateth justice govern?
And wilt thou pronounce him wicked that is righteous
          and mighty?
Him that saith to a king, "Thou scoundrel!"
Or to nobles, "Ye wicked!"
Who respecteth not the persons of princes,
Nor regardeth the rich more than the poor;

For they all are the work of his hands.
In a moment shall they die, even at midnight;
The rich are smitten and pass away,
And the mighty are taken away without hand.
For his eyes are upon the ways of a man,
And he seeth all his goings.
There is no darkness, nor shadow of death,
Where the workers of iniquity may hide themselves.
No time doth he set for man,
That he should go before God in judgment.

He breaketh in pieces mighty men without investiga-
        tion,
And setteth others in their stead.
Therefore he taketh knowledge of their works;
And he overturneth them in the night, so that they are
        destroyed.
He striketh them as wicked men
In the open sight of others;
Because they turned aside from following him,
And would not have heed to any of his ways:
So that they cause the cry of the poor to come unto
        him,
And he heard the cry of the afflicted.

When he giveth quietness, who then can condemn?
And when he hideth his face, who then can behold him?
Alike whether it be done against a nation, or against
        a man:
That the godless man reign not,
That there be none to ensnare the people.

Elihu Accuses Job of Rebellion Against God

For hath any said unto God, "I have borne chastise-
        ment;

I will not offend any more:
That which I see not teach thou me:
If I have done iniquity, I will do it no more"?
Shall his recompense be as thou wilt, that thou refus-
     est it?
For thou must choose, and not I:
Therefore speak what thou knowest.

Men of understanding will say unto me,
Yea, every wise man that heareth me:
"Job speaketh without knowledge,
And his words are without wisdom.
Would that Job were tried unto the end,
Because of his answering like wicked men."
For he addeth rebellion unto his sin;
He clappeth his hands among us,
And multiplieth his words against God.

Elihu Accuses Job of Presumption

Thinkest thou this to be just,
Or sayest thou, "My righteousness is more than
     God's,"
That thou sayest, "What advantage is mine?
Wherein am I better off than if I had sinned?"
I will answer thee,
And thy companions with thee.
Look unto the heavens, and see;
And behold the clouds, which are higher than thou.
If thou hast sinned, what effectest thou against him?
And if thy transgressions be multiplied, what doest
     thou unto him?
If thou be righteous, what givest thou him?
Or what receiveth he of thy hand?
Thy wickedness may hurt a man as thou art;
And thy righteousness may profit a son of man.

By reason of the multitude of oppressions men cry out;
They cry for help by reason of the arm of the mighty.
But none saith, "Where is God my Maker,
Who giveth songs in the night,
Who teacheth us more than the beasts of the earth,
And maketh us wiser than the birds of the heavens?"
Then they cry, but none giveth answer,
Because of their impious pride.
Surely God will not hear an empty cry;
Neither will the Almighty regard it.
How much less when thou sayest thou beholdest him
　　　not,
That the cause is before him, and thou waitest for him!
But now, because he hath not visited in his anger,
Thou sayest, "He careth not much about transgres-
　　　sion";
Therefore Job doth open his mouth in vanity;
He multiplieth words without knowledge.

Elihu Speaks on Behalf of God

Suffer me a little, and I will show thee;
For I have yet words to say on God's behalf.
I will fetch my knowledge from afar,
And will ascribe righteousness to my Maker.
For truly my words are not false:
One that is perfect in knowledge is with thee.

Behold, God is mighty, and despiseth not any:
He is mighty in strength and wisdom.
He preserveth not the life of the wicked,
But giveth to the afflicted their right.
He withdraweth not his eyes from the righteous:
And with kings upon the throne
He setteth them forever, and they are exalted.
And if they be bound in fetters,

And be caught in the cords of affliction;
Then he showeth them their work,
And their transgressions, that they behave themselves
        proudly.
He openeth also their ear to instruction,
And commandeth that they return from iniquity.
If they hearken and serve him,
They spend their days in prosperity,
And their years in pleasures.
But if they hearken not, they perish by the sword,
And they die without knowledge.
But they that are godless in heart heap up anger:
They cry not for help when he bindeth them.
They die in youth,
And their life perisheth among the unclean.
He delivereth the afflicted by their affliction,
And openeth their ears by distress.

Job's Rebelliousness Is Condemned

But thou hast been lured by thy freedom
Into a broad place, where there is no straitness;
And by that which is set on thy table which was full
        of fatness.
Thou hast fulfilled the judgment of the wicked:
Judgment and justice take hold on thee.

For let not wrath stir thee up into mockery;
Neither let the greatness of the ransom turn thee aside.
Will thy riches avail, without distress,
Or all the exertions of thy strength?
Long not for the night,
When peoples are cut off in their place.
Take heed, regard not iniquity;
For this hast thou chosen rather than affliction.
Behold, God doeth loftily in his power:

Who is a teacher like to him?
Who hath enjoined him his way?
Or who can say, "Thou hast wrought iniquity"?

God Is Recognized in the Approaching Storm

Remember that thou magnify his work,
Whereof men sing.
All men have looked thereon:
Man beholdeth it afar off.
Behold, God is great, and we know him not:
The number of his years is unsearchable.
For he gathereth up the drops of water,
Which distil in rain from his vapor,
Which the skies pour down
And distil upon man abundantly.

Also can any understand the spreadings of the clouds,
The thunderings of his pavilion?
Behold, he spreadeth his light upon it,
And he covereth the bottom of the sea.
For by these he nourisheth the peoples:
He giveth food in abundance.
He covereth his hands with the lightning,
And commandeth it that it strike the mark.
The noise thereof telleth concerning him,
The cattle also concerning the storm that cometh up.

At this also my heart trembleth,
And is moved out of its place.
Hearken attentively to the noise of his voice,
And the sound that goeth out of his mouth.
He directeth it under the whole heaven,
And his lightning unto the ends of the earth.
After it a voice roareth:
He thundereth with the voice of his excellency:

And he will not stay them when his voice is heard.
God thundereth marvelously with his voice:
Great things doeth he,
Which we cannot comprehend.

God Has Control over Nature

For he saith to the snow,
"Be thou on the earth";
Likewise to the small shower,
And to the great rain of his strength.
He sealeth up the hand of every man,
That all men may know his work.
Then the beasts go into dens,
And remain in their places.

Out of the south cometh the whirlwind,
And cold out of the north.
By the breath of God frost is given;
And the breadth of the waters is frozen.
Also he ladeth the thick cloud with moisture;
He scattereth the cloud of his lightning:
And it is turned round about by his counsels,
That they may do whatsoever he commandeth them
Upon the face of the world in the earth.
He causeth it to come, whether for correction,
Or for his land, or for mercy.

Hearken to this, O Job;
Stand still, and consider the wondrous works of God.
Dost thou know how God disposed them,
And causeth the lightning of his cloud to shine?
Dost thou know the balancings of the clouds,
The wondrous works of him who is perfect in knowledge?
How thy garments are warm,
When he quieteth the earth by the south wind?

Hast thou with him spread out the sky,
Which is strong, and as a molten looking-glass?
Teach us what we shall say unto him;
For we cannot set our speech in order by reason of
    darkness.
Should it be told him that I would speak?
Or should a man wish that he be swallowed up?

(As the rain and darkness pass, Elihu notes a mighty wind that is driving the clouds before it, and a strange, golden splendor descending from the north.)

And now men see not the light, though it is bright in
    the clouds;
But a wind passeth, and cleanseth them.
Out of the north cometh golden splendor:
God hath upon him terrible majesty.

Touching the Almighty, we cannot find him out:
He is excellent in power,
And in judgment and in plenteous justice: he will not
    afflict.
Men do therefore fear him:
He regardeth not any that are wise of heart.

THE ANSWER OF GOD

"Then God answered Job out of the whirlwind." The bewildered sufferer had asked that the Lord should prove himself as just, as open, as friendly as a human being; and now, through the wonders of creation, Job is shown that God himself is greater than man's greatest need. In the majesty, the evident order, and the joyousness of his works he reveals his own nature.

THE VOICE OF THE ALMIGHTY

Who is this that darkeneth counsel
By words without knowledge?
Gird up now thy loins like a man;
For I will demand of thee, and answer thou me.

Where wast thou when I laid the foundations of the
      earth?
Declare, if thou hast understanding.
Who laid the measures thereof, if thou knowest?
Or who hath stretched the line upon it?
Whereupon are the foundations thereof fastened?
Or who laid the corner stone thereof,
When the morning stars sang together,
And all the sons of God shouted for joy?

Who shut up the sea with doors,
When it broke forth at birth?
When I made the cloud the garment thereof,
And thick darkness a swaddling band for it,

"THEN GOD ANSWERED JOB OUT OF THE WHIRLWIND"
From a drawing by Blake

And broke up for it my decreed places,
And set bars and doors,
And said, "Hitherto shalt thou come, but no further;
And here shall thy proud waves be stayed"?

Hast thou commanded the morning since thy days,
And caused the dayspring to know its place;
That it might take hold of the skirts of the earth,
And the wicked be shaken out of it?
It changeth like clay under the seal,
And is dyed like a garment.

Hast thou come into the springs of the ocean?
Or hast thou walked in the depths of the sea?
Have the gates of death been opened unto thee?
Or hast thou seen the doors of the shadow of death?
Hast thou perceived the breadth of the earth?
Declare it, if thou knowest it all.

Where is the way where light dwelleth?
And as for darkness, where is the place thereof,
That thou shouldst take it to the bound thereof,
And that thou shouldst know the paths to the house
          thereof?
Knowest thou it, because thou wast then born,
Or because the number of thy days is great?

Hast thou entered into the treasuries of the snow?
Or hast thou seen the treasuries of the hail,
Which I have reserved against the time of trouble,
Against the day of battle and war?
By what way is the light parted,
And the east wind scattered upon the earth?
Who hath divided a channel for the rain flood,
Or a way for the lightning of thunder;

"WHEN THE MORNING STARS SANG TOGETHER"

From a drawing by Blake

To cause it to rain on the earth where no man is;
On the wilderness, wherein there is no man;
To satisfy the desolate and waste ground,
And to cause the bud of the tender herb to spring
    forth?
Hath the rain a father?
Or who hath begotten the drops of dew?

Who was mother of the ice?
And the hoary frost of heaven, who hath given birth
    to it?
The waters are become like stone,
And the face of the deep is frozen.

Canst thou fasten the cluster of the Pleiades,
Or loose the bonds of Orion?
Canst thou bring forth the Mazzaroth in their season?
Or canst thou lead the Bear with her sons?
Knowest thou the ordinances of heaven?
Canst thou set the dominion thereof in the earth?
Canst thou lift up thy voice to the clouds,
That abundance of waters may cover thee?
Canst thou send forth lightnings, that they may go,
And say unto thee, "Here we are"?
Who hath set in the fleecy clouds wisdom,
Or given to the meteor insight?
Who numbereth the clouds by wisdom?
Or who poureth out the bottles of heaven,
When the dust groweth into hardness,
And the clods cleave fast together?

Wilt thou hunt the prey for the lioness,
Or fill the appetite of the young lions,
When they couch in their dens,
And abide in the covert to lie in wait?

Who provideth for the raven his food,
When his young ones cry unto God,
And wander for lack of food?
Who hath sent out the wild ass free?
Or who hath loosed the bonds of the wild ass,
Whose home I have made the wilderness,
And the barren land his dwelling place?
He scorneth the multitudes of the city;
Neither regardeth he the shoutings of the driver.
The range of the mountains is his pasture,
And he searcheth after every green thing.

Will the wild ox be willing to serve thee,
Or abide by thy crib?
Canst thou bind the wild ox with his band in the fur-
        row?
Or will he harrow the valleys after thee?
Wilt thou trust him, because his strength is great?
Or wilt thou leave thy labor to him?
Wilt thou believe in him, that he will bring home thy
        seed,
And gather it into thy barn?
The wing of the ostrich beats joyously,
But her pinions and feathers are cruel,
Which leaveth her eggs in the earth,
And warmeth them in the dust,
And forgetteth that the foot may crush them,
Or that the wild beast may break them.
She dealeth harshly with her young ones, as though
        they were not hers:
Her labor is in vain, she is without fear,
Because God hath deprived her of wisdom;
Neither hath he imparted to her understanding.
When she raiseth up herself on high,
She scorneth the horse and his rider.

Hast thou given the horse might?
Hast thou clothed his neck with thunder?
Hast thou made him to leap as a grasshopper?
The glory of his nostrils is terrible.
He paweth in the valley, and rejoiceth in his strength:
He goeth on to meet the armed men:
He mocketh at fear, and is not affrighted;
Neither turneth he back from the sword.
The quiver rattleth against him,
The glittering spear and the shield.
He swalloweth the ground with fierceness and rage;
Neither standeth he still at the sound of the trumpet.
He saith among the trumpets, "Aha!"
And he scenteth the battle afar off,
The thunder of the captains, and the shouting.

Doth the hawk fly by thy wisdom,
And stretch her wings toward the south?
Doth the eagle mount up at thy command,
And make her nest on high?
She dwelleth and abideth on the rock,
Upon the crag of the rock, and the strong place,
From thence she seeketh the prey;
And her eyes behold afar off.
Her young ones also suck up the blood:
And where the slain are, there is she.

Shall he that cavileth contend with the Almighty?
He that reproveth God, let him answer it.

JOB

Behold, I am too small: what can I answer thee?
I will lay my hand upon my mouth.
Once have I spoken, but I will not do so again;
Yea, twice, but I will proceed no further.

THE VOICE OF THE ALMIGHTY

Gird up thy loins now like a man:
I will demand of thee, and declare thou unto me.
Wilt thou even make void my judgment?
Wilt thou condemn me, that thou mayest be justified?
Or hast thou an arm like God?
And canst thou thunder with a voice like him?
Deck thyself now with majesty and excellency;
And array thyself with glory and beauty.
Pour out the overflowings of thine anger;
And look upon every one that is proud, and abase him.
Look on every one that is proud, and bring him low;
And tread down the wicked where they stand.
Hide them in the dust together;
Bind up their faces in the hidden world.
Then will I also confess to thee
That thine own right hand can save thee.

Behold now behemoth, which I made with thee:
He eateth grass as an ox.
Lo now, his strength is in his loins,
And his force is in the muscles of his belly.
He moveth his tail like a cedar:
The sinews of his thighs are knit together.
His bones are as strong tubes of brass;
His ribs are like bars of iron.
He is the chief work of God:
He only that made him can bring near his sword.
Surely the mountains bring him forth food,
Where all the beasts of the field do play.
He lieth under the lotus trees,
In the covert of the reed, and the fens.
The lotus trees cover him with their shadow;
The willows of the brook encircle him about.

Behold, if a river overflow he trembleth not:
He trusteth that he can draw up Jordan into his mouth.
Can any take him when he is on the watch,
Or pierce through his nose with a snare?

Canst thou draw out leviathan[45] with a hook?
Or press down his tongue with a cord?
Canst thou put a cord into his nose?
Or bore his jaw through with a hook?
Will he make many supplications unto thee?
Will he speak soft words to thee?
Will he make a covenant with thee?
Wilt thou take him for a servant forever?
Wilt thou play with him as with a bird,
Or wilt thou bind him for thy maidens?
Will bands of fishermen bargain over him?
Shall they part him among the merchants?
Canst thou fill his skin with barbed irons,
Or his head with fish spears?

Lay thy hand upon him!
Of battle thou shalt think no more!
Behold, the hope of him is in vain:
Shall not one be cast down even at the sight of him?
None is so fierce that he dare stir him up!
Who then is able to stand before me?
Who hath ever confronted him and prospered?
Whatsoever is under the whole heavens, such a one is
        not!

I will not keep silence concerning his limbs,
Nor his power, nor his comely proportion.
Who can strip off his outer garment?
Who can enter within his double coat-of-mail?
Who can open the doors of his face?

His teeth are terrible round about,
His scales are his pride,
Shut up together as with a close seal.
One is so near to another
That no air can come between them.
They are joined one to another,
They stick together, so that they cannot be sundered.
By his sneezings a light doth shine,
And his eyes are like the eyelids of the morning.
Out of his mouth go burning torches,
And sparks of fire leap out.
Out of his nostrils goeth smoke,
As out of a seething pot or caldron.
His breath kindleth coals,
And a flame goeth forth from his mouth.

In his neck abideth strength,
And dismay danceth before him.
The flakes of his flesh are joined together:
They are firm upon him, they cannot be moved.
His heart is firm as a stone;
Yea, as hard as a piece of the nether millstone.
When he raiseth himself up the mighty are afraid:
By reason of consternation they are beside themselves.
If one assail him with the sword, it cannot hold;
Not the spear, nor the dart, nor the pointed shaft.
He esteemeth iron as straw,
And brass as rotten wood.
The arrow cannot make him flee;
Sling stones are turned with him into stubble;
Darts are counted as stubble:
He laugheth at the shaking of a spear.

His underparts are like sharp potsherds:
He spreadeth as it were a threshing-drag upon the mire.

He maketh the deep to boil like a pot:
He maketh the sea like a pot of ointment.
He maketh a path to shine after him:
One would think the deep to be hoary.
Upon earth there is not his like,
Who is made without fear.
He beholdeth all high things;
He is king over all the children of pride.

JOB

The Almighty has at last drawn near. Job's bold confidence changes
to awed humility. His physical suffering is still as great as ever; but
the reality and nearness of God makes it tolerable. He does not repent
of sin, for he still believes his life is blameless; but a new and vivid sense
of the divine greatness and nearness makes him repent of the defiant
attitude he had taken toward God.

"I HAD HEARD OF THEE, BUT NOW MINE EYE SEETH"
From a drawing by Blake

"AND MY SERVANT JOB SHALL PRAY FOR YOU"

From a drawing by Blake

I know that thou canst do everything,
And that no purpose of thine can be cut off.[46]

"Who is he that hideth counsel without knowledge?"

I have uttered that which I understood not;
Things too wonderful for me, which I knew not.
Hear, I beseech thee, and I will speak;
I will demand of thee, and declare thou unto me.

I had heard of thee by the hearing of the ear,
But now mine eye seeth thee:
Therefore I loathe my words
And repent in dust and ashes.

"EVERY MAN ALSO GAVE HIM A PIECE OF MONEY"
From a drawing by Blake

THE EPILOGUE

The Lord Condemns Job's Friends

And it was so, that after the Lord had spoken these words unto Job, the Lord said to Eliphaz the Temanite: "My wrath is kindled against thee, and against thy two friends; for ye have not spoken of me the thing that is right, as my servant Job hath. Therefore, take to you now seven bullocks and seven rams, and go to my servant Job, and offer up for yourselves a burnt offering; and my servant Job shall pray for you: for him will I accept, lest I deal with you after your folly, in that ye have not spoken of me the thing which is right, like my servant Job."[47]

"SO THE LORD BLESSED THE LATTER END OF JOB"
From a drawing by Blake

"THE DAUGHTERS OF JOB"
From a drawing by Blake

So Eliphaz the Temanite and Bildad the Shuhite and Zophar the Naamathite went, and did according as the Lord commanded them. The Lord also accepted Job.

Job's Prosperity Is Restored

And the Lord turned the captivity of Job, when he prayed for his friends: also the Lord gave Job twice as much as he had before.

Then came there to him all his brethren, and all his sisters, and all they that had been of his acquaintance before, and did eat bread with him in his house; and they bemoaned him, and comforted him over all the evil that the Lord had brought upon him: every man also gave him a piece of money, and every one an earring of gold.

So the Lord blessed the latter end of Job more than his beginning: for he had fourteen thousand sheep, and six thousand camels, and a thousand yoke of oxen, and a thousand she-asses. He had also seven sons and three daughters. And he called the name of the first, Jemimah [Dove]; and the name of the second, Keziah [Fragrant as Cinnamon]; and the name of the third, Keren-happuch [Beautifier]. And in all the land there were no women found so fair as the daughters of Job: and their father gave them inheritance among their brethren.

After this lived Job a hundred and forty years, and saw his sons, and his sons' sons, even four generations. So Job died, being old and full of days.

EXPLANATORY NOTES

THE LIVING WISDOM

THE SCROLL is the venerable symbol of wisdom, the ancient book, the record of a revelation from the prophet, from the gods, from God himself. It had to be unrolled to be read. The reading of it was a progressive revelation of the truth it contained. At every moment of the reading the future was hidden, the past rolled up, done with: only that portion in the process of being read was evident to the eye. The scroll, then, was like life itself—the past obscured, the future unknown, only the present in immediate possession. The scroll is thus a peculiarly appropriate symbol of THE LIVING WISDOM—the enduring wisdom, past, present, and future.

THE DELPHIC SIBYL

From a fresco by Michelangelo

This is one of the loveliest and most inspired of all those multitudinous creations of the great Florentine that adorn the Sistine Chapel in Rome.   The Delphic Sibyl, with five or six others, is placed along the cornice of the room alternating with the Biblical prophets. They are given this position of honor because throughout the Middle Ages the Church placed the authority of these creatures of classic mythology almost on a par with that of the Hebrew prophet.   They represent the spirit of prophecy; and each is given a name suggestive of some place in the ancient world where the divine oracles were wont to be consulted.   The Delphic Sibyl of course stands for Delphi, the most famous oracle of antiquity.

The goddess is here seated upon a marble throne, unrolling the scroll of the future. Having lighted upon a significant passage, she raises her eyes and gazes into the distance, quite lost in the contemplation of some vast pageant of future history that unrolls before her imagination.

THE GREAT MESSAGES OF THE PROPHETS

1. THE DEVELOPMENT OF THE PROPHETS. In the very early time the idea of prophecy was such as prevails among all primitive peoples. Prophecy was considered a kind of magic power to see the future, to predict success or failure in war, to find lost articles, and the like. This was the idea of Saul's servant when he suggested that Samuel might help them find the lost asses. It was the idea which produced the bands of prophets who excited themselves by music and other means so that they might speak while in a state of ecstasy. This low conception of prophetic powers still exists; and there is yet ignorance enough to support whole droves of fortune-tellers, clairvoyants, and magic healers. But even in Samuel's day there was also a better conception, which was mostly due to him; for people came to know him as one who knew God and was therefore wiser than those who knew him not. The lower grade of prophets developed afterwards into the professional class, the court prophets, who were always ready to give the king a message from the supernatural, and to give such a message as they thought he would like. But there were others, like Elijah and Micaiah, who had a real moral insight and purpose, and told the kings and the people, as they believed, the very truth revealed to them by God.

The great prophets of the eighth and seventh centuries were of this nobler class. They were men who had great convictions of truth and duty, which they held as the direct word of the Lord; and they not only spoke their message, but, fortunately for the world, they wrote their prophecies, in order that the truth of them might be tested by future events.

2. BETHEL was in the days of Amos a royal sanctuary of great wealth and splendor, where Jehovah was worshiped under the patronage of the kings of Israel. The first Jeroboam had set up here a golden calf, and later kings, especially the reigning monarch, Jeroboam II, had enriched the place with the spoils of victory. The people revered Bethel as the scene of Jacob's vision in patriarchal times. For the rustic Amos thus to interrupt this lordly and popular worship required courage of the highest order.

3. THE HOME OF HOSEA, traditionally, was at Belemon, near Dothan, at the edge of the Plain of Esdraelon. In any case, Hosea, because of his many references to the beauty of nature, seems to have been a native of the country, rather than of the city. "His sacraments are the open air, the mountain breeze, the vine, the lilies, the pines."

4. THE CALL OF ISAIAH. "The scene was the threshold of the temple, where Isaiah had gone to worship. In front of him stood the door leading to the inner shrine, with the Ark as the visible witness to the Divine, and near it the altar of sacrifice and the brazen serpent, the

emblem of heavenly help and healing. The choirs pealed forth their choruses, and the smoke of the sacrifice ascended to heaven, when, lo! as Isaiah prayed, the outward symbolism vanished, and the eternal realities themselves were unveiled before his spiritual imagination. Through the open door he now saw Jehovah in person seated upon a throne, 'high and lifted up,' beyond all contact with human imperfection and sin. The skirts of his flowing robe filled the temple, carrying the touch of his influence into every niche and corner of the building, while round the throne were shining companies of seraphim floating before God's presence and singing in responsive chorus."—ALEXANDER R. GORDON

5.   LIVE COAL. The prophet here uses a symbol drawn from common life. In the cooking of food, stones were made red hot at the central hearth, and these were then applied to the various articles of food or the receptacles containing them. The image, thus, naturally suggests the conveyance of spiritual fire from the altar to Isaiah. Fire burns, and so purifies: when the young man's lips were touched, his sin was not merely forgiven, but burned out of him; and he stood before God pure.

6.   MORESHETH OF GATH, the home of the prophet Micah, was situated upon a terrace of the low hills which lie between the hill country of Judah and the Philistine plain. It is twenty-two miles from the sea. "The olive groves are fine. There is herbage for cattle. Bees murmur everywhere, larks are singing, and you are seldom beyond sound of the human voice—shepherds and plowmen calling to each other across the glens."

7.   THE NEW COVENANT. This remarkable passage is not merely of deep personal value to the devout reader of Scripture; it also marks a transition point in the Hebrew religion. Under the judges and the kings, the religion of Israel was national: the individual householder served the Lord with his king and the rest of the nation, and shared God's favor or his displeasure, as manifested in the peace or the distress of the land. But in Jeremiah's day, with the Israelites beginning to be scattered into many lands, this old theory of a national covenant religion could no longer be held. Religion, to be preserved at all, must be individual, a matter between each man and his God. In this great passage the prophet makes this clear.

8.   EZEKIEL'S HOME was in Babylonia, in the great alluvial plain of the lower Euphrates, through which ran many irrigating canals. One of these, the Chebar, or "grand canal," ran east of the old city of Nippur; and on its bank lived this pastor prophet of the Jewish colony.

9.   THE MATERIAL OF EZEKIEL'S VISION. George Adam Smith thinks Ezekiel's vision of the appearance of God was suggested by a thunderstorm in Mesopotamia. "The languor of the flat country, the stagnancy and sultriness of the air, is suddenly invaded by southerly winds

of tremendous force, laden with clouds of fine sand, which render the air so dense as to be suffocating, and 'produce a lurid red haze intolerable to the eyes.' Thunderstorms are frequent, but the winds are the most tremendous. In such an atmosphere we may perhaps discover the original shapes and sounds of Ezekiel's turbulent visions,—the fiery wheels; the great cloud with a fire enfolding itself; the color of amber, with sapphire, or lapis lazuli, breaking through; the sound of a great rushing."

10. FULL OF EYES. It is characteristic of the Oriental mode of description that the figures described cannot be visioned in literal fashion. The details of the description are symbolic, like those of a so-called "futuristic" painting. Each one is a symbol, suggesting an idea rather than portraying a fact. We cannot see the marvelous objects thus described, but we can feel the effect intended. This touch, "full of eyes," means simply that the rolling objects were full of alertness and vision.

11. DIGGING THROUGH. Unbaked brick, "adobe," being the universal building material in Babylonia, it was easy to dig through a thick wall, and equally easy to build up the hole again.

12. THE KING'S FATE. By this curious object lesson or dramatization, Ezekiel presented to his fellow-exiles the tragic close of the kingdom of Judah. When Jerusalem could no longer be defended, Zedekiah, the last king, escaped by night with his retainers; he was captured and brought before Nebuchadnezzar; he saw his sons slain; and he then was blinded and carried as a captive to Babylon.

13. SONS OF ZADOK, that is, the true and lawful inheritors of the priestly office. In David's day, Abiathar was the high priest; but he afterwards proved disloyal to Solomon, and Zadok was made priest in his stead. Thus Zadok, whose descent was traced back to Levi, became ancestor of the priestly line at Jerusalem. In the Maccabean times the priestly party, opponents of the Pharisees, called themselves the Sons of Zadok, or the Zadokites, which became in Greek the Sadducees.

14. CLEAN AND UNCLEAN. Here we see Ezekiel laying emphasis on the old Hebrew form of "taboo," so common to all primitive peoples, by which some things are made "clean," approachable or edible, and others "unclean," or prohibited. In exile the Jews might easily have lost this, had not the old Mosaic lessons been thus renewed, to be later reinforced in the work of Nehemiah and Ezra. To this day the careful Jews feel as did Ezra. A Jew thus remonstrated with a clergyman, "Why do you, at a funeral, bring the body into the church? You ought not to do so. A church is a clean place, and a dead body is unclean." In that remonstrance more than thirty centuries of inherited instinct found expression.

15. THE CRIME OF ACQUIESCENCE. Obadiah's stern rebuke of these Edomites, not for any overt attack on hapless Israel but simply for looking

with satisfaction on the Jews' misfortune, recalls the ethical judgment pronounced by Hawthorne on Miriam in *The Marble Faun*. By one glance of exultation, as her obnoxious enemy is hurled to his death, she becomes a partner in the crime and must share the penalty.

16. SYMBOLISM OF NUMBERS. Orientals are less exact and more imaginative than those of Western lands. Where we use round numbers for convenience, they frequently use symbolic numbers to convey an association. Thus, seven is associated with God and holiness, ten with heathen domination, twelve with God's people Israel, forty with a full generation or a long reign. Seventy years, therefore, suggests to the prophet God's time of chastisement for Jerusalem by the hand of the Gentile conquerors.

17. LOCUSTS. These names of insects probably refer to the locust in its several stages of development—first as a grub, then as a young locust able to march by hops in the mighty locust army, and finally as the full-grown locust with wings. The voracity of these insects is terrible, as is the resistless might of their advancing host. They first devour grass and leaves, fruit and foliage,—everything that is green and juicy. They then attack the tender twigs and young branches of trees, and then the hard bark of the trunks. George Adam Smith, after witnessing a locust invasion in Palestine, said: "For eighty or ninety miles they devoured every green herb and every blade of grass. The gardens outside Jaffa are now completely stripped, and look like a birch tree forest in winter." Of their onset Dr. W. M. Thomson says: "When the head of the mighty column came in contact with the palace of the Emeer, they did not take the trouble to wheel round the corners, but climbed the wall like men of war, and marched over the top of it. So, when they reached the house of Dr. Van Dyck, in spite of all his efforts to prevent it, a living stream rolled right over the roof." He asserts that every touch in Joel's picture is true to the life.

SOCIAL IDEALS OF THE HEBREWS

18. DRUNKENNESS A SIN OF LUXURY. In the Bible, drunkenness is condemned as a sin of luxury, wealth, and power. Its effect on rulers, and so on the safety of the state, is often referred to. Warnings are given, by the teachers of wisdom, against over-indulgence in wine and strong drink. But no such general concern is shown for public temperance as we should expect any moral leader to show today. The reason for this is that wine and "strong drink," or fermented fruit juice, when strong enough to intoxicate easily, were so expensive as to be out of reach of the common people. Only the rich, therefore, were likely ever to drink to excess. It was the invention, in the Middle Ages, of the process of distillation that made strong liquor cheap, and so gave the world its modern temperance problem.

19. "THE FAT VALLEY." The reference is to a broad and fertile valley extending northwestward from Shechem, between the mountains of Ebal and Gerizim, to the seacoast plain. Within this valley, on an isolated hill, stood the now rich and luxurious city of Samaria, the "crown of pride" of the dissolute rulers of the kingdom of Israel.

20. THE QUEEN OF HEAVEN was Ishtar, or Astarte (in Hebrew, Ashtoreth), whose symbol in the heavens was the moon. The Jewish women inclined to idolatry carried this worship with them when they fled to Egypt after the fall of Jerusalem.

21. TAMMUZ, the god for whom the Jewish women wept in the days of Ezekiel, was in Babylonian mythology the husband or son of Ishtar, or Ashtoreth, the goddess of fertility. After the summer vegetation decays, Tammuz, according to legend, retires to the underworld, whither he is followed by the disconsolate Ishtar, who would bring him back to the world that he has left desolate. It is one of the numerous myths or old folk stories relating to the sun. The weeping for Tammuz, which was common throughout the north-Semitic world, occurred in September. This myth was carried to Greece and Rome; Tammuz becoming Adonis, and Ishtar, Venus. Shakespeare retells the story in his *Venus and Adonis*, and Milton refers to it as follows:

> "Thammuz came next behind,
> Whose annual wound in Lebanon allured
> The Syrian damsels to lament his fate
> In amorous ditties all a summer's day,
> While smooth Adonis from his native rock
> Ran purple to the sea, supposed with blood
> Of Thammuz yearly wounded."

22. "THE CALF OF SAMARIA," set up as a representative of Jehovah at the ancient shrine of Bethel by Jeroboam I, first king of the kingdom of Israel which revolted from Rehoboam.

23. THE INVIOLABILITY OF ZION. After the remarkable deliverance of Jerusalem from Sennacherib in Hezekiah's day, a few years after the tragic siege and capture of Samaria, the doctrine seems to have gained currency in Jerusalem that the Lord had promised that the holy city should never be taken. In later years this grew to be so fixed a belief that the rulers laughed at the prophets' warnings, and went on with their sinning. It is against this false hope that Jeremiah delivers this prophecy.

24. PREPARING THE WAY. Roads in Palestine are usually no more than stony trails, rough, and in many places dangerous. In recent years some good carriage roads have been built; but from ancient days until now it has been the rule that when a king or eminent visitor is to make a journey, the command goes forth to prepare his way. The population then turns out to repair and rebuild the road on which he is to travel.

25. THE MESSIANIC IDEA. The term "Messiah," or "Anointed," was primarily applied to any one anointed with the holy oil. He was then "the Lord's Anointed." In this sense David spoke of King Saul as the Lord's Messiah, whom therefore he must not kill. Aaron, as high priest, was called the Lord's Messiah; and in Leviticus the same designation refers to any future high priest. Cyrus, who released exiled Israel from captivity and gave them leave to return to their own land, is referred to as the Lord's Messiah. After the establishment of David's line as kings of Judah, the title became in a special sense the designation of David and those who should follow him as inheritors of his throne and of God's promises to him. Like the other ideals of a perfect state, the Messianic ideal of the prophets and the New Testament was developed.

26. THE DAY OF THE LORD. When the prophets foresaw Israel's future glory, they conceived of some crisis or juncture that should intervene between that and their present misery. Gradually there grew up the belief that Jehovah would come to judge the hostile nations, and also his own people, before that happy era could arrive. So the phrase, "the Day of the Lord," came to mean not merely a day, but a whole period of judgment and readjustment before the glorious future should be ushered in.

PATRIOTIC POETRY

27. THE TRIBAL BLESSINGS, which may have been used as popular folk songs, are interesting in themselves as shrewd portrayals of individual human traits. Dan is the serpent that lies in wait; Benjamin, the ravening wolf; Naphtali, the freedom-loving hind; Issachar, the stolid, contented ass; Judah, the kingly lion. Reuben is "unstable as water"; Zebulun at Acre, "the haven of the sea," "rejoices in his going out" for adventure and commerce; but Issachar abides "in his tents."

28. HADADRIMMON, names of two Syrian gods. The reference seems to be to a religious custom involving a mourning rite, like the weeping for Tammuz referred to by Ezekiel.

29. DRAGONS. The word translated "dragon" in the Bible, where it refers to a real animal, has reference to the jackal, or, occasionally, the wolf. The word signifies "a howler." Metaphorically it refers to a mythical sea monster. There have been beliefs in such a creature in all lands. Apollo slew the Python, and the Babylonians told of the contest between Marduk, the creator, and Tiamat, the chaos monster.

30. LUCIFER, "son of the morning," was the day star, either the sun or the planet Venus. The phrase, "fallen from heaven," suggests the imagery of a meteor. In the Middle Ages Lucifer was identified with Satan, and this identification was accepted by Milton in his *Paradise Lost;* but it has no support in the Book of Isaiah. The reference is to the king of

Babylon, who had exalted himself to the sky, but who was to be plunged like a falling star to destruction.

Milton mentions also another angel who fell, Mulciber, the Roman Vulcan. The beautiful lines are famous:

> "Sheer o'er the crystal battlements, from morn
> To noon he fell, from noon to dewy eve,
> A summer's day; and with the setting sun
> Dropped from the zenith, like a falling star,
> On Lemnos."

31. "THE KING OF TYRE," whose doom is announced by Ezekiel, is Ethbaal (Ithobaal II). The first Ethbaal, a priest of Astarte, was a usurper who took the throne about 880 B.C., and had a long and successful reign. He was the father of Jezebel. The Ethbaal of whom Ezekiel speaks in this beautiful but obscure description seems to be regarded as typical of the haughty pride of his people. He is described satirically as "the anointed cherub that covereth," and was "set upon the holy mountain of God," whose arrogance is to bring him and his people "to ashes." He was contemporary with King Jehoiakim, and lost his independence at the hands of Nebuchadnezzar, about 600 B.C.

32. THE TYRIANS were the greatest sea traders of antiquity, and were excelled in enterprise and daring only by the discoverers of America. They had harbors all along both shores of the Mediterranean, some of them extending as far as Spain. They had rounded the Cape of Good Hope "in ships no larger than a herring boat"; "their trade tapped river basins as far apart as those of the Indus, the Euphrates, probably the Zambesi, the Nile, the Rhone, and the Guadalquivir." They sailed from the coasts of Britain to those of northwest India. Matthew Arnold described them thus:

> "As some grave Tyrian trader from the sea . . .
> . . . snatch'd his rudder, and shook out more sail,
> And day and night held on indignantly
> O'er the blue Midland waters with the gale,
> Betwixt the Syrtes and soft Sicily,
> To where the Atlantic raves
> Outside the western straits; and unbent sails
> There, where down cloudy cliffs, through sheets of foam,
> Shy traffickers, the dark Iberians come;
> And on the beach undid his corded bales."

Tyre, because of its location on an island and its commercial grandeur, resembled ancient Venice, and Isaiah's description of Tyre would have applied to the Venice of the Doges:

> "The giver of crowns,
> **The maker of kings,**

> Whose merchants are princes,
> And her traffickers are the honorable of the earth."

Unlike the Venetians, the Tyrians were not creators or artists; they were merely traders. "There is not throughout history a more perfect incarnation of the mercenary spirit than the Phœnician nation." They left no mighty works; and if it be true that they invented or disseminated the alphabet, they made no profitable use of it. Their ruin was complete, and Tyre today is only a stagnant Turkish village, too unimportant even to be a stop for coasting vessels.

33. BEULAH. The word means "married," and is used in prophecy to foretell that desolate, widowed Israel shall be again as happy as a wife in her own home. Bunyan made a beautiful use of the idea in his *The Pilgrim's Progress*, when he makes Beulah Land the place "where the Shining Ones commonly walked, because it was upon the borders of heaven." "In this country the sun shineth night and day; wherefore this was beyond the reach of the Valley of the Shadow of Death, and also out of the reach of Giant Despair; neither could they from this place so much as see Doubting Castle. Here they were in sight of the city they were going to."

34. DIFFICULTY OF RESTORING THE HOLY LAND TO THE JEWS. One of the difficulties faced by the modern state of Palestine is the fact that only a small percentage of the present population is Jewish. Thus, in the 9,000 square miles included in that part of Palestine west of the Jordan, there were in 1919, according to "The Statesman's Yearbook," 515,000 Moslems, 65,300 Jews, 62,600 Christians, 150 Samaritans, and 4,900 others. "The feeling between Moslem, Christian, and Jew is perhaps more intense," adds Dr. Albert T. Clay, "than in any other land."

35. WORLD INFLUENCE OF THE JEW. Says Rabbi Solomon Schechter: "The selection of Israel, the indestructibility of God's Covenant, the immortality of Israel as a nation, and the final restoration of Israel to Palestine, where the nation will live a holy life, on holy ground, with all the wide-reaching consequences of the conversion of humanity, and the establishment of the Kingdom of God on earth—all these are the common ideals and the common ideas that permeate the whole of Jewish literature extending over nearly four thousand years."

36. AMERICA THE REFUGE OF THE NATIONS. It seems as if this prophecy had been at last fulfilled. Every immigrant who enters the port of New York looks first with eager eyes for the Statue of Liberty, which casts the light from its uplifted torch far across the harbor. To the Jews particularly, America has been a land of refuge. New York City is the largest Jewish city in the world, and more Jews live there than in the whole of Palestine. Of America's welcome that eloquent Jewish poet, Emma Lazarus, wrote these lines, now engraved upon the Liberty statue:

"Keep, ancient lands, your storied pomp!" cries she
With silent lips. "Give me your tired, your poor,
Your huddled masses yearning to breathe free,
The wretched refuse of your teeming shore.
Send these, the homeless, tempest-tossed, to me;
I lift my lamp beside the golden door!"

THE WORDS OF THE WISE

37. THE HEBREW WORLD. Here, and in the first of the two accounts of the creation, we see how the Hebrews regarded the world. The earth was a flat expanse, bordered by the sea and covered by the arching firmament. Above the firmament were waters, from which dropped the rain; and below the earth was the "great deep" of water, whose fountains were opened to make the deluge. Somewhere below the earth, also, was Sheol, or Hell, the abode of the dead. The sun, moon, and stars moved in the firmament, above the clouds. These conceptions are not taught in the Bible: they were merely inherited from earlier ages and shared by the peoples of Semitic origin. In the early Babylonian literature these ideas are elaborated in fantastic detail.

38. THE WISE. In Doughty's *Arabia Deserta* there is a description of a session of "wise men" in a modern Palestine home. "In the shadow at the rear the young men who had been admitted sat in silence. The old men, elders of the village community, sat in a row on stone benches right and left of the door. The elders sat silently leaning on their staves, except now and then, when one of them would slowly rise and expatiate on something the sheik had said, beginning his interruption almost literally in the words of Job's friends: 'Hearken unto me, I also will show my opinion.' So has it been in Palestine since time out of mind."

The difference between the Greek way of approaching knowledge and the Hebrew way was that the Greek was a philosopher, the Hebrew an observer. The Greek used his reason to solve the enigmas of human life; the Hebrew began with belief in the Divine, and then started to interpret life as tokens of his working. "Unless he began with the 'God who is,' he could see no clue to the 'things that are.'"

39. OLD PEOPLE IN THE BIBLE. Nothing is more beautiful in Oriental life than the respect that is shown for old age, regardless of any accompaniment of wealth, office or personal accomplishment. "Thou shalt rise up before the hoary head," was the Mosaic national law. One of the loveliest stanzas in the *Wisdom of Ben Sirach* is this appreciation of age:

"As the clear light is upon the holy candlestick,
So is the beauty of the face in ripe age;
As the golden pillars are upon the sockets of silver,
So are the fair feet with a constant heart."

JOB HEARING OF HIS RUIN
From a drawing by Gustave Doré

Old age was believed to be wise. Other young men in the East beside Elihu in the Book of Job have acknowledged that

"Days should speak,
And multitude of years should teach wisdom."

This wisdom gave the old an almost official authority, so that all listened when the old men of the village uttered their thoughts. The result was that there was a deep affection for the aged. The happiest dream of the ideal state was:

"There shall yet old men and old women dwell in the streets
of Jerusalem,
And every man with his staff in his hand for very age."

JOB

40. Uz, the home of Job, has been identified as having been in the North Arabian Desert about two hundred miles east of Petra. It has been located in the oasis of Jauf, and possibly at the village of Owsit, which at least suggests Uz. It is described as "a broad, deep valley, everywhere studded with tufts of palm groves and clustering fruit trees in dark green patches, with flat house-roofs half buried amid the garden foliage, the whole plunged in a perpendicular flood of light and heat." Its fertility is great, and is aided by irrigation, so that its dates and other fruits are famous throughout Arabia.

41. THE SONS OF GOD were the hosts of angels, who were thought of as members of God's heavenly court, or soldiers of his celestial army. The Lord God of "hosts" meant the God of the angels. When spoken of as "watchers," they are thought of as listening to God's counsels in his court. As his "ministers," or servants, they make use of the forces of nature, but they are not identified with them. They are thought of as intermediary between God and men; and in one of the narratives in Genesis they are spoken of as having come down to earth, intermarrying with the daughters of men, and having become the parents of "the mighty men of old, men of renown."

When "the Angel of his Presence" is spoken of, the thought seems to be that God himself condescends to the form of a messenger, and the word that is given has the authority of God himself.

The Jews in later times placed the angels in varying ranks, regarding four as the archangels. These four were Gabriel, the interpreter of dreams, whose field of service was the earth, whose assistants were the cherubs, and who was the guardian of Paradise; Michael, whose field of service was heaven, and who was the special guardian of Israel; Uriel, whose charge were the sun and moon; and Raphael, whose care was the spirits of men. In the Book of Tobit the angels are reckoned as seven, of whom Raphael is one.

42. SATAN IN THE BOOK OF JOB, or more properly "the Satan," or "the Adversary," is portrayed as that one among the Sons of God who form his heavenly council whose field of service is this earth. He goes up and down in it and makes stated reports of his territory, as do the other Sons. His function has been stated to have been that of "a celestial prosecuting attorney." He tries men, to find out whether they deserve approval. He is not pictured as evil or malicious; but his experience has no doubt made him cynical, and the step from testing men to tempting them is, of course, a short one.

There is no authority in Job for the supposition that this Satan was a fallen or a rebellious angel, or for those magnificent portraits in Dante and in Milton of "that emperor who sways the realm of sorrow"; or of the archangel, whose face

> "Deep scars of thunder had intrenched, and care
> Sat on his faded cheek, but under brows
> Of dauntless courage, and considerate pride
> · Waiting revenge."

The Satan of Milton, possibly partly because of the poet's known sympathy for fallen royalty, is so magnificent that he has been called "the hero of *Paradise Lost*." But, in the later Scriptures, especially in the Book of Revelation, the attitude is rather that of contempt for one who has become an ignoble, because no longer a non-partisan, Adversary.

43. REDEEMER. This word in Jewish criminal law was applied to "the avenger of blood," who was the next of kin, authorized to secure blood-revenge for homicide or murder. In the Book of Job and in two other cases, the word refers to the "advocate," whose business it is to defend the innocent and helpless from all wrong and dishonor. Job, seeking to reach the ear of the Almighty, rises to the lofty faith that God is not only a fair judge but his own personal defender. The following translation brings the thought out even more clearly:

> "I know that my Advocate is alive,
> And afterward on the dust he shall stand up;
> And after they destroy even this, my skin,
> Without my flesh shall I see God,
> Whom I shall behold *for me*,
> And mine eyes shall behold, no more a Stranger."

44. THE SELF-RESPECT OF JOB. "The real grandeur of Job was his impatience. His humility before God is but the more beautiful side of his anger with his friends, and his self-abasement before his Maker is the crowning dignity of a self-respect which is one of the epics of the world. The only proof he had of his righteousness was himself."

—GERALD STANLEY LEE

45. LEVIATHAN, in one or two Biblical references, seems to be the mythical sea monster, in whom all ancient people believed. In the Book

of Job he is clearly the crocodile, although so glorified in the description as to suggest traces of the primeval monster.

46. JOB AND SOPHOCLES. "An interesting analogy to Job's solution of the problem," says Alexander R. Gordon, "may be found in Sophocles' ripest dramas. Sophocles views suffering in the light of the eternal harmony of things. Thus, the grievous sorrows Philoctetes had to bear are conceived to have been laid upon him 'by the care of one of the gods,' that he might be held in reserve, and braced in character for his appointed task in the overthrow of Troy. The tragedy of Œdipus ends in the same atmosphere of peace. The sorely afflicted hero finds himself now reconciled to Heaven, surrounded by the love of devoted children, and honored by the friendship of Athens and its chivalrous king, and gently yields his life to the touch of the gods, his destiny thus finding 'a perfect end.' In both these dramas, Sophocles views the problem of human suffering with the eye of faith; and in proportion as he sets before him an ideal of an all-powerful divinity, who is merciful, loving, and gracious, so does it become easy for him to bear patiently with the evil and suffering in the world, in the serene belief that, were man's vision wide enough, he would see joy and sorrow to be parts of one harmonious whole."

47. THE LARGER FAITH OF JOB. "He was too spiritual to have a Land-of-Uz God, or a Job's God, or a Jews' God. With their tiny, compacted, Land-of-Uz faith, his friends gathered around him, and accused him of blasphemy because God was so much more of a God to him than to them; because he gave him room and gave him time—the prerogatives of a God."   —GERALD STANLEY LEE

BIBLE REFERENCE INDEX

This index shows the Biblical passages used on any particular page of this volume. The figures in heavy type indicate chapters and the figures in light face type indicate the verses.